By Raymond Sokolov

COOKERY

Great Recipes from *The New York Times*

The Saucier's Apprentice

FICTION

Native Intelligence

BIOGRAPHY

Wayward Reporter: *The Life of A. J. Liebling*

TRANSLATION

Imperialism in the Seventies *by Pierre Jalée*

Fading Feast

A

COMPENDIUM OF

DISAPPEARING

AMERICAN

REGIONAL

FOODS

BY

Raymond Sokolov

Farrar · Straus · Giroux

NEW YORK

Fading

Feast

Library of Congress Cataloging in Publication Data
Sokolov, Raymond A. / Fading feast.
Includes index. / 1. Cookery, American. / I. Title.
TX715.S67812   641.5973   81-12564
AACR2

For Johanna

Acknowledgments

Alan Ternes, editor of *Natural History* and a fellow Michigander, sent me on the road and turned me into a subversive patriot. He paid the bills and never interfered except with creative mockery. Also at *Natural History*, Carol Breslin, Tom Page, Kay Zakariasen, Florence Edelstein, Rita Campon, and Ernestine Weindorf all helped immeasurably.

Adelaide de Menil's beautiful photographs speak for themselves, but they do not convey her extracameral talents as boon companion in blizzards, on dungheaps, and in a hundred deserted villages across rural America.

Covering agriculture is impossible without the assistance of the incredibly well-informed county agents and other local representatives of the U.S. Department of Agriculture. They know where the hams are hidden and where the persimmons dangle.

For their help with research, I thank the staffs of the New York Public Library and the library of the New York Botanical Garden.

Far and away the most indispensable people to this book were the regional American cooks, gardeners, and farmers who talked to me, showed me their crops and animals, and fed me wonderful food. They are all named in the appropriate places. With gratitude, I celebrate them here collectively for their steadfast contribution to the preservation of the national character.

My wife and sons came along and helped with the work on some of the trips, endured my absences on others, and always supported and sustained me.

CONTENTS

Introduction / 3

THE MIDWEST

The Independence Fair / 13

The Hoosier Secret: Native Persimmons / 23

The Taming of the Grain: Minnesota Wild Rice / 36

Morel Victory: Wild Mushrooms in Michigan / 45

Geese on the Run / 55

Tasty Pasty: Michigan's Finnish-Cornish Meat Pie / 64

THE SOUTH

A Squirrel in Every Pot: Brunswick Stew and Burgoo / 75

The Lime That Failed / 83

White Lightning / 92

Living High Off the Hog: Smithfield Ham / 101

Planter's Lunch / 109

Hot Cajun Sausage / 125

THE EAST

An Original Old-Fashioned Yankee Clambake / 137

Blueberry Blues / 147

Moses and Manhasset: The Kosher Kitchen / 158

Jupiter's Walnut in the New World / 173

Stalking the Cultivated Gooseberry / 180

THE WEST

Fleece Afoot: Colorado Lamb / 189

Chili con Blarney / 203

Tillamook Cheddar / 215

The Giant Snail of La Jolla: Diving for Abalone / 222

Breakfast at Shungopavi: Hopi Cooking / 230

Olympia Oysters / 242

Pacific Salmon / 250

INDEX / 261

Fading Feast

INTRODUCTION

When most of us talk about "this country," we mean the whole of America. Television watchers, interstate-highway motorists, plane passengers—we achieve the national perspective as easily and naturally as we breathe the air of the cities and suburbs where we live. But in this era of bicoastalism, of fore-shortened horizons and rampant social homogenization, it is still possible to find some Americans with an almost purely local outlook. When certain farmers I know say "this country," they have nothing more grandiose in mind than the land around them.

"I grew up in this country," an Iowa hog breeder told me once, "and I've never gone farther from it than Chicago." "In this country." It is an old usage with an antique flavor to it, persisting from a day not so long ago when farm families lived in isolation and could not imbibe dizzying draughts of slick citification simply by tuning in Johnny Carson. It was in such times and such solitary places that regional American foods and food customs sprang up and flourished.

Because early settlers on the Oregon coast couldn't ship whole milk from their ideal pasture country, dairymen around the town of Tillamook turned to cheese with its long "shelf life." New England Pilgrims, thrown in among Indians and with few manufactured utensils brought from home, adopted Indian methods of cooking and dug ovens on the beach for clambakes. Midwestern yeomen foraged in the woods for the abundant, delicious, and easily identifiable morel mushrooms they found by fallen elms. Hoosiers in log-cabin times supplemented their diet with a slew of new recipes for the tiny, wild, local persimmon. At the same time, they concocted a botanically erroneous persimmon folklore which still misleads their descendants today.

Such regional quiddities have endured down to the present time, even after the various regions themselves have lost most of their original character, even after they no longer enjoy the isolation that made them regions in the first place. For the most part, however, the survival of regional foods and food customs in the United States is a token survival. I am not, of course, referring to that handful of wildly successful regional foods, such as Southern fried chicken, which have overflowed their original boundaries and become, for better or worse, national foods. Most regional foods never left home and are rarely served even there except in distorted, modernized versions warmed over for tourists in "historic" restaurants or on special occasions sponsored by chambers of commerce and other groups dedicated to the promotion of local pride.

In New England, almost all clambakes are cooked in metal washtubs, and they are usually jazzed up with lobster. Tillamook cheese is produced in a chrome-clad factory, and the heavy demand for this Pacific cheddar discourages its manufacturer from aging it long enough to give it the complex tang that once made Tillamook unique. As more land in the Midwest has been cleared, fewer morels have a chance to grow. The native persimmon lost any chance it ever had to be widely cultivated when the larger, less interesting, but vigorously marketed oriental persimmon came to our shores. And even on its own turf, the American persimmon falls increasingly to the ground, unnoticed except by squirrels. The Indiana homesteaders who used to gather these luscious fruits and process them at home for winter pleasure have mostly moved to town.

This exodus of farmers away from their farms has totally changed American life in only two generations. Farm population has fallen to a fifth of what it was in 1920. At that time, well within the memory of many people still alive, every third American lived on a farm. By 1950, farm folk were a mere 15 percent of the total population. Today, fewer than 5 percent of us live the agricultural life and less than 2 percent actually work at farming.

The causes for this monumental shift are obvious and well known. Machines have replaced people. Big landholders with the capital to buy the machines have bought out inefficient subsistence farmers, who have sought employment and a life of greater plenty and more varied amusement in an urban setting.

This is precisely the scenario which I once argued would solve the "farm problem." At the time, I did not believe it would happen. It was simply a convenient line to take if you were a high school debater in 1957, when the topic set for that year's debating season by the National Forensic League forced you to think strategically about farm surpluses and what to do about them. As I recall it, the conventional choice was between price supports, which rewarded farmers for growing more, and the so-called Soil Bank, which rewarded them for growing less. It was difficult to win a debate by supporting supports, with their long history of failure, but as debaters we had to be ready to defend this wobbly system whenever we drew the "affirmative" side. At my school we hedged our position ingeniously by blaming the small farmer and proposing his elimination. In brief, we argued that price supports should be continued, while a battery of other social and economic programs would lure smallholders to the cities and another set of federally financed programs would distribute surpluses to hungry mouths abroad. Once the inefficient farmers had all come to work at, say, the Ford assembly plant (we lived in Detroit and had seen thousands of Southern sharecroppers make this move with fair success) or at other urban jobs, the remaining farm community would be strong enough to fend for itself in a free, unsupported market. Then price supports could be eliminated, and market forces would, in turn, cut back agricultural production to match real demand.

When our coach, a resonant debater for Wayne State University named Chuck McAndrews, came up with this crafty plan, we recognized it as a winning tactic, both appealingly humane and a stunning surprise for other teams, but we never thought it would actually come to pass. Or that the decline of the country's rural populace would bring with it such terrible consequences: social disruption on a vast and ghastly scale as well as an unspeakable degradation of food quality. Small farmers may have been inefficient, but they provided fresh and varied produce close to everyone's retail market. Efficient agribusinessmen have concentrated on a small number of cost-effective crops that can be shipped easily, and they have brought us the bounceable tomato.

Every city dweller knows this. Swollen welfare rolls and sterile supermarkets are the ugly results of the McAndrews plan. But if cities have suffered from the influx of the rural poor and from the depredations of a megalithic agriculture, rural America has become a desert, stripped bare of the people who once, not very long ago, grew and ate the foods of our multifarious regional cuisines.

Without flourishing rural communities, there can be no authentic regional cooking. And, as a nation, we have the lowest proportion of our population employed in agriculture of any important country in the world, today or ever in human history. Japan has more than five times as many farm workers as we do, with 12 percent of its people in agricultural employment. France has 9 percent. West Germany has 7 percent. The United Kingdom has 3 percent. Our smidgeonlike 1.5 percent is extraordinarily productive, but, as a cultural group, farmers are a tiny minority spread very, very thinly across the land.

For farmers themselves, this state of affairs is a social disaster. They are a lost splinter group which doesn't fit into mainstream American life any more. Their way of life is a quaint survival when they practice it as their parents did. And they know it. An elderly farmwife sitting in the living room of the white clapboard house on rich Ohio Valley bottomland that her family had owned for more than a century said to me during a commercial break in the Merv Griffin show: "We must seem like freaks to you."

That woman continued to set a traditional farm table, with fresh-killed meat from the family barn, a kaleidoscope of vegetables pulled from her kitchen garden, home-canned preserves, and apple pies put together expertly with apples from an ancient backyard tree.

In two years of back-road travel through rural America, from Eastport, Maine, to San Diego, California, from Puget Sound to Key West, I searched out such survivors. As the roving food columnist for *Natural History* magazine, I talked with these last, authentic exponents of regional foods, learning their recipes and recording the food wisdom of our past before it fades completely from view except at pumped-up special events.

In the twenty-four columns reprinted in this book, I have tried to show the specific reasons why regional foods are in trouble in our country. Looking closely at the problems of the Maine blueberry industry or California abalone divers, of Cajun sausagemakers and Texas chili "heads," or of mutton burgoo in Kentucky, I have found that each case is different but that every one of these gastronomic invalids is a victim of a food-delivery system that is highly regulated and built to serve faceless millions in the most convenient, efficient way. This way leads inevitably to a radical loss of diversity. Only those with the capacity to grow their own food and the wish to follow their parents' antiquated type of home economy can effectively combat the juggernaut of modern agribusiness. With luck I have managed to locate some of these rugged individuals.

These last practitioners of regional cuisine almost all cook for themselves, not for public consumption in restaurants. Only one market in southwest Louisiana's Cajun country still sells the spicy blood pudding called *boudin rouge*, because regulations for livestock-slaughter inspection make the collection of blood difficult and unprofitable. Key West natives with their own backyard trees still make real Key lime pies, but there are no commercial groves left in south Florida; so storebought pies are almost invariably made from conventional lime juice.

The Key lime could not hold its own against leatherskinned, easy-to-ship, hardier, seedless, larger but far less delicious Persian limes. The story is the same with dozens of traditional crops that could not compete with less interesting but more practical foods. Maine lowbush blueberries have to be harvested by hand and don't travel as well as Michigan's insipid highbush berries. Black walnuts are extremely difficult to shell. Tiny Olympia oysters grow more slowly than giant Pacific oysters transplanted from Japan.

Other traditional American foods and food preparations have been legislated out of existence or regulated to the point where they are not attractive business propositions. Because hunters cannot legally sell their game, Virginia restaurants cannot legally sell true Brunswick stew made with squirrel. Home-cured Virginia hams cannot be sold in interstate commerce. Gooseberries are illegal in many states because they host a disease that spreads to trees valuable for timber. Open-range sheep compete with campers and coyotes for public range land. Geese are prohibitively expensive because of strict federal plucking regulations designed for chickens. White lightning, the folkloric American liquor, is a felony as well as a distinctive beverage.

Still other foods are perishing as the people who cook them assimilate into the hamburger culture. Only a small fraction of American Jews maintain kosher kitchens or prepare food in strict observance of the orthodox dietary laws. Only the conservative "traditionalist" faction of the Hopi tribe preserves the desert cuisine of time immemorial. Northwest Coast Indians long ago abandoned their pretechnological, salmon-centered economy and have kept up only a few of the old-time methods of salmon preservation and cookery.

Meanwhile, in the cities, consumers whose tastes have been massaged and manipulated by advertisements vote for an ever narrower range of basic foodstuffs when they load their shopping carts with junk foods, overpackaged novelty items, and low-grade, chemically preserved, or genetically doctored outrages against the palate. The end result of this negative form of consumer pressure on farm producers is to constrict further the variety in our markets. Food retailers stock what will sell, and what sells is bland, gaudily packaged, and sweet.

For all these reasons, documented in detail in this book, the larder vanishes. And with it vanishes the traditional quality and style of American life as millions knew it, in their own local way, until a few decades ago.

The process is largely irreversible. Barring the advent of a totalitarian government on the order of the Khmer Rouge, we are not going to see significant numbers of people returning to the land. People who have abandoned traditional forms of life are not likely to return to them in great numbers. No one is seeding new beds of Olympia oysters or pressing for the legalization of moonshine. History has taken its inexorable toll.

Still, traces remain of the way things were. Anyone who cares can go to Maine in August for the blueberries. It remains possible to buy Olympias in Washington State or find morels in the Michigan woods. A few Virginians will sell you year-old hams if you drop in on them. A consortium of investors reportedly intends to plant Key limes in Key West. Overfishing has not completely eliminated Northwest salmon, and scuba divers can still pry loose abalones that have not yet been made extinct.

The opportunity is there to sample the taste of an older America in all its rich variety. As a fieldworker on an unusual expedition for the American Museum of Natural History, I have collected recipes from authentic sources still in contact with their regional heritage. And the zealous reader of these essays will find in them much practical information on where to go to find real regional food. As the Michelin guide to regional French restaurants says, when it recommends a particularly good provincial place to eat, *"Vaut le voyage."* It's worth the trip. Especially so in this country, because time is running out.

The Midwest

THE INDEPENDENCE

FAIR

"As American as apple pie," we say, meaning that this apparently simple dessert is a symbol of the nation. But there is nothing at all simple about either the country or the pie. Needless to say, America has changed radically since early settlers brought their recipes for apple pie with them from Europe. And like all immigrants to these shores, apple pie took on a new nature in the New World. It became our preeminent national dish because in the isolated, primitive farmhouses of colonial America, apple pie was much more than a dessert. Ideally suited to the rugged climate and the low technology of the farms where most settlers lived, the apple pie was a basic means of survival: appetizer, entree, and dessert at winter meal after winter meal in the dawn of the Republic.

On the Ulster County, New York, farm he worked after the Revolution, Michel Guillaume Jean de Crèvecoeur harvested

100 apple trees for his own use, something he would not have done in his native France, and felt obliged to explain when he wrote about his life in a series of letters aimed at an urban European audience:

Perhaps you may want to know what it is we want to do with so many apples . . . In the fall of the year we dry great quantities, and this is one of the rural occupations which most amply reward us. Our method is this: we gather the best kind. The neighboring women are invited to spend the evening at our house. A basket of apples is given to each of them, which they peel, quarter, and core . . . The quantity I have thus peeled is commonly twenty bushels, which gives me about three of dried ones.

Next day a great stage is erected either in our grass plots or anywhere else where cattle can't come. Strong crotches are planted in the ground. Poles are horizontally fixed on these, and boards laid close together . . . When the scaffold is thus erected, the apples are thinly spread over it. They are soon covered with all the bees and wasps and sucking flies of the neighborhood. This accelerates the operation of drying. Now and then they are turned. At night they are covered with blankets. If it is likely to rain, they are gathered and brought into the house. This is repeated until they are perfectly dry.

Processed in this way, Crèvecoeur's apples would last through the winter—a staple food source that required only an overnight soaking in warm water to be ready for the oven. Apples were at the very center of this pioneer farmer's diet. He wrote: "My wife's and my supper half of the year consists of apple-pie and milk."

Today, two centuries later in our history, no farmer sustains his family on apple-pie suppers all winter long. And even if he did, a farmer is no longer typical of American life, for there are too few of them. But farmers are still the guardians of symbolic values and practices sacred to the nation's sense of itself. They are uniquely equipped to continue and preserve our traditions, particularly our food customs, in pristine form because almost without exception, American food customs arose in farmhouses as adaptations to rural conditions. And so, to check on the health of our edible traditions, one goes to the heartland. Since Crèvecoeur's day, the geographical center of American farm life has moved westward, and the best place to observe the ritual of apple pie at its zenith is at a Midwestern county fair with a serious apple-pie contest.

Practically the first thing I saw after arriving at the Buchanan County Fair in eastern Iowa was a black bull galloping free as you please in a rampaging circle that ran from the cattle stalls to the livestock judging arena, around to the midway, past the 4-H exhibit hall, and then back to the pickup that had brought him, not fully broken, from the farm. He made several snorting circuits, once or twice dragging a man who grabbed his trailing halter, but causing no harm to him or anyone else except to the Band Boosters, who had to repitch one corner of their tent, which the bull had grazed, before they could resume selling bandburgers (sloppy Joes) and homemade apple pie and ice cream to raise money for the Independence High School band.

Independence, Iowa, is the seat of Buchanan County and the site of its annual fair, a showpiece of old-fashioned agricultural vigor held in the baking heat of late July when the hay is mostly in and the corn and soybeans are not yet ready to harvest. Similar fairs are staged all over the country during this relatively slow time for farmers, each one an individual expression of the quality of rural life in a single county.

The Buchanan fair is no more typical of the status quo of American agricultural life than any other. Indeed, the town of

Independence, although small, with fewer than 6,000 inhabitants, has a definite urban feel to it, stemming partly from its proximity to industrial Waterloo, twenty-three miles to the west, and partly from its past as a milling center and the Midwest's harness-racing capital. Today, however, the beautiful brick Wapsipinicon Mill stands empty, a casualty of gigantism in the grain trade, and all that remains of the Rush Park racetrack is the show barn, restored and converted into a restaurant. Yet from my room at the Rush Park Motel, which is still within the city limits, I could see fields and smell the unmistakable smell of hogs.

Independence is, above all else, the center of a region that, while practicing modern agriculture with its overwhelming emphasis on machines, has managed to hold on to at least some of its human, cultural traditions. People still have the upper hand in Buchanan County. You can see it at the fairgrounds, which gives space to the collection of the county historical society—antique farm tools, an old-time kitchen, and an early blacksmith shop—but does not, as so many fairs do, have displays of hulking tractors and other modern machinery hauled in by salesmen from John Deere and Massey-Ferguson.

During fair week at Independence, you can learn something about traditional farm life—and the vanishing species of farm families who still live it—by driving just a short way out of town on the perfectly perpendicular network of crushed-limestone roads that link the spacious fields of corn and soybeans springing up in some of the world's richest topsoil. In this immense grid of unparalleled fecundity, a road that cuts across the others on a diagonal is a landmark. And it is shortly after you have turned off at such an oblique intersection that you arrive at the Priebe family's farm.

Meeting the Priebes takes a minute or two, since the whole clan, assembled for dinner, includes Clifford and Wilma

Priebe; their married daughter Bonnie; her husband, Mike O'Brien; and their little daughter, Marie; twenty-one-year-old Stan Priebe, who will some day take over the farm's several hundred acres; teenage live wire Cindy; and two children of grade-school age, Celia and Dale.

When the assembled Priebes sit down to dinner (they would call it supper; "dinner" means lunch in the Corn Belt), they eat almost no food they do not produce themselves. The day I visited, the extremely tasty pork roast came from one of their many hogs; this one had been butchered at a local abattoir called a "locker." The sweet corn on the cob was picked fresh, and although it was not quite ripe enough to satisfy the Priebes' refined expectations, it still surpassed most corn that finds its way to Manhattan retailers. The cabbage for Wilma Priebe's tart slaw came from her large kitchen garden. And there were mashed potatoes and fruit jello and a pitcher of creamy raw milk coaxed by hand from the family milch cow. Dessert was, of course, apple pie, with a crust flaky from lard and a tart filling of early Harvester apples picked from a nearby tree and made elegant with cream (see recipe below). As a menu, the meal was mundane, except for the sheer number of vegetable side dishes. But the freshness of the ingredients and the skill of the cook raised it to a high level. At the Priebes' table, one finds mainline American cookery at its best, the food of the farmhouse, splendid there, close to the soil. But when exported in cans or in the recipe files of Midwestern dietitians to institutional dining rooms or to the pages of women's magazines, this perilously simple cuisine almost invariably becomes second-rate and insipid.

No doubt Wilma Priebe could make a first-class apple pie from supermarket apples in a city apartment kitchen, but the right context can be important for a cook; and it goes a long way toward enhancing the taste of food. Certainly it would be hard to imagine a better context for appreciating pork roast and apple pie with a lard crust than a farmhouse where hogs get loose during supper and little Dale runs out to shoo them back to their pen.

The Priebes, without intending it, are big on context. Unlike many successful Midwestern farmers, they have not eliminated livestock and confined their operation to profitable, relatively undemanding grains. Pork and beef and broiler chickens all prosper on their land. There is a bull called Delbert, a pet mule, and a goat whose milk is used to feed the pet raccoon.

The pet raccoon is not as tame as Cindy Priebe would like it to be, but she hasn't had the time to work with it properly because, she says, she's been too busy with 4-H work. Her club has been emphasizing sewing. The club also puts her in touch with neighbor girls she might not otherwise see too often since she attends a parochial high school in town. Through 4-H camp counseling and other statewide events, she has acquired contacts throughout Iowa, while her brother Stan visited a big farm in Mount Upton, New York, on a 4-H exchange.

On a national scale, 4-H (for head, heart, hands, health) has five million schoolchildren as members; only 25 percent of them, however, live on working farms. Administered under the Department of Agriculture's Cooperative Extension program, 4-H is no longer a supplementary education service reserved for farm kids. There is even a 4-H program in New York County, New York (Manhattan). With the dramatic exodus from farms after World War II, 4-H has moved into nonrural areas because that is where the children are. But in a rural county such as Buchanan, 4-H still functions in the old way and reaches its culmination at the annual fair.

All the livestock shown at the Buchanan County fair is exhibited by 4-H members. Parents may help with the elaborate grooming of the animals, but their children have spent hours and hours working with the cattle and sheep and hogs, feeding them to produce a prize shape and training them to behave properly for the judges.

A 4-H sponsored garden contest was won in 1980 by Sandy Oliphant, who managed to cultivate staked tomatoes, purple beans (they turn green when cooked, but their purple color makes them easy to locate for picking), Concord grapes, black raspberries, zucchini, purple kohlrabi, cabbage, broccoli, cauliflower, acorn squash, pumpkin, bell peppers, cucumbers, and a patch of carrots left unthinned to show children with thumbs less green why thinning is necessary for producing big carrots.

There are 4-H sponsored competitions in almost every imaginable area, from house plants to geology to photography, including a "self-determined" class for the recognition of un-classified achievement. The 1980 self-determined winner was a scrapbook compiled over several years by Rachelle Reid, who adopted wild burros from the federal government and recorded the experience in progressively more sophisticated essays writ-ten as she and the burros grew older.

In the area of prepared foods, the Buchanan County 4-H conducted judgings in seventeen categories of canned fruit, eleven categories of pickles and relishes, and thirty-three cate-gories of baked goods, ranging from white bread to rhubarb cake. Indeed, the only food event at the fair not sponsored by 4-H is the pie contest, which is run by the Buchanan County Porkettes. Wives of pork producers, the Porkettes volunteer their time to promote the use of pork products. They give food demonstrations with pork in supermarkets. They work with pigskin. And at the fair, under the aegis of Lady Loinette, the nattily skirted and jacketed sow that is their symbol, they superintended the baking of thirty-nine pies. According to offi-cial contest rules, every crust had to contain lard, and the con-

test was judged with meticulous expertise by two home econo-
mists and crowned by an auction in the fair's livestock show
ring. Local bankers and seed merchants bid hot and heavy,
spending $60 and more to get a pie and some good PR in the
bargain.

Virtue was rewarded. Wilma Priebe won the blue ribbon in
the adult division. Her daughter Cindy took the junior division
championship. Their crusts flaked; their fillings fulfilled every
criterion of excellence. In one county in Iowa, at least, people
are keeping the American heritage in apple-pie order.

☞ WILMA PRIEBE'S GRAND CHAMPION APPLE PIE

(Buchanan County Fair, Independence, Iowa, 1980)

CRUST

3 cups flour
1 teaspoon salt
1 cup (8 ounces) lard
1 tablespoon vinegar

5 tablespoons water (or milk
   for golden crust)
1 egg

(1) Mix flour, salt, and lard together in a bowl, cutting in
the lard with a pastry blender until you produce a crumbly texture like that of uncooked oatmeal.

(2) In another bowl, mix vinegar, water (or milk), and egg with a rotary beater. Then blend into the flour-lard mixture a little at a time. Blend well.

(3) Divide dough into four equal pieces, enough for two double-crusted, 9-inch pies. This dough rolls easily and will take a lot of handling and still make a flaky crust. Refrigerate or freeze until needed.

FILLING

3½ cups peeled, cored, and sliced tart cooking apples	2 tablespoons flour
1 cup sugar	1 teaspoon vanilla
	⅔ cup half-and-half

(1) Combine all ingredients in a bowl and mix together thoroughly. This is enough filling for one 9-inch pie.

FINAL ASSEMBLY AND BAKING

(1) Preheat oven to 450 degrees.

(2) Roll out one of the balls of dough into a circle about one-eighth inch thick. Dust the work surface lightly with flour before you start. Use more flour as necessary to prevent sticking. When you have a circle of dough large enough to fill and slightly overlap the edge of a 9-inch pie pan, transfer the crust to the ungreased pie pan. Trim off excess. Crimp along the edge with tines of a fork or your finger, pressing dough to the flange of the pan.

(3) Place apple filling in the pie pan, spreading it evenly over the dough.

(4) Roll out another ball of dough as above. Moisten the edge of the bottom crust with a small amount of water. Place the top crust over the pie. Press around the edges. Slash through the crust in a few places or make a small hole in the center.

(5) Bake 10 minutes. Then reduce oven temperature to

350 degrees and bake another 30 to 40 minutes, until crust is nicely browned and the apples feel tender when probed with a trussing needle through the top crust. Cool on a rack.

Y I E L D: One 9-inch double-crusted pie, plus dough for a second double-crusted pie.

THE HOOSIER SECRET:

NATIVE PERSIMMONS

The only reason anyone without a flat tire stops in Gnaw Bone, Indiana, is to visit the Brown County Sorghum Mill. It isn't really a mill, just a big farm stand on a highway in southern Indiana. It opens for business only during the fall harvest season and sells the typical crops of Brown County's rolling, picturesque farm country: pumpkins, apples, twists of bitter-sweet, sorghum molasses, apple butter. The mill did not have any of the big goose-necked gourds or the strawberry popcorn, grown on tiny dark red ears, that I had bought at another stand just north of Nashville, a tourist center and artist's colony that makes a big business out of Indiana's log-cabin era, with one hokey olde-time shoppe after another flogging folksy crafts and souvenirs. Gnaw Bone has its own specialties.

At the Brown County Sorghum Mill, only three miles or so from Nashville, Nancy Roberts preserves Midwestern homestead tradition without cuteness or hoopla. She makes fudge and candy and a cakelike "pudding" from the fruit of the native persimmon tree. Well, some days she does. But Mrs. Roberts also drives the Gnaw Bone school bus, and she has trouble getting persimmons, which are a tiny and tastier cousin of the Asian variety sold in supermarkets. Her usual supplier, busy with a new job in Indianapolis, hadn't delivered any pulp last fall when I happened by.

"Pulp?" I asked, inwardly cursing Jane and Michael Stern, whose excellent guide to American highway restaurants, *Roadfood*, had led me to this remote hamlet with visions of native persimmons dancing in my head. Instead, there was nary a piece of fudge, just talk of a pulp scarcity.

"She used to process the fruit from her orchard, get rid of the skins and seeds, and sell me the pulp," Mrs. Roberts said. But the supplier wasn't home. Mrs. Roberts didn't know where or on which back road she lived. At any rate, if I came back the next day, Mrs. Roberts would have a batch of persimmon fudge she was going to cook that night from some of last year's pulp still left in her freezer.

I took another tack. I checked the main supermarket in Nashville. No persimmons, at the height of the season. Next, I dropped in at the local office of the U.S. Department of Agriculture's Cooperative Extension Service. The woman behind the counter said there were no proper persimmon orchards in the county. Nobody cultivated persimmons. They just grew wild: in open places, clearings, abandoned fields. You waited until after the first frost and then picked them up off the ground where they fell. Fruit still on the tree was too astringent to eat. The fall had been so mild that the persimmons might not be ready yet. She told me to go look at a tree in her mother-in-law's yard at the edge of town.

An understandably suspicious older woman greeted me

and pointed out her tree—slender, fifty feet high, with dark bark deeply divided into squarish sections. Up in the leafless branches I saw tiny orange fruits. The woman's relatives had gathered all the fallen fruit the day before, and the ground under the tree was bare.

At the post office, I got directions to the house of Mrs. Roberts's supplier, the woman with the "orchard." An hour later, after losing my way in a delightful labyrinth of tree-lined lanes, I pulled up to a desolate mobile home set behind a half-built house in the early stages of dilapidation. Stepping out of the car, I was attacked by a small mongrel, a dingy beige bitch who took a bite of my left ankle and would have taken a second helping if another, larger but better-behaved cur had not chased her away. Expecting the report of a shotgun, I waited a minute or two by the car. But no Jukes or Kallikak emerged from the battered trailer, so I limped across the field toward a scraggly stand of trees. A few feet from them, I slipped on what felt like a spot of mud. It was red orange and had three large black seeds. In the branches overhead, hundreds of similar persimmons dangled. And in the brown grass, strewn in every direction, were squishy-squashy ripe persimmons waiting to be saved from their natural predators: squirrels, opossums, skunks, quails, raccoons, and deer.

Having liberated as many fruits as I could gather in my shirt, I retired to the safety of my vehicle. They were definitely the fruit of *Diospyros virginiana,* the American persimmon. Small, about the size of walnuts or cherry tomatoes, they resembled the much larger, heart-shaped oriental persimmon (*Diospyros kaki*) only in color and in the gooey texture of their inner flesh. In flavor, these American persimmons far surpass their imported cousins. They are powerfully fragrant, sweet and luscious, and taste like dates. Indeed, one of their vernacular names is date plum. They are wonderful fruits.

Early settlers realized this almost immediately upon their arrival in America. De Soto wrote the first description of the persimmon in 1539 in Florida. The name itself apparently derives from the Algonquin *putchamin* or *pasiminan,* meaning "dried fruit." Well into the colonial era (and perhaps still), dried persimmons were stored and eaten like figs. Colonists must also have learned from Indians that the little fruit lent itself to baking in breads, cakes, and puddings. And we can be sure the Pilgrims had the good sense to consume persimmons out of hand, knowing from bitter experience that they had to wait for this treat until the natural ripening process had masked the fruit's tannin and made it sweet. As Captain John Smith put it: "If it not be ripe, it will drawe a man's mouth awrie with much torment; but when it is ripe, it is as delicious as an Apricock."

Easily grown from seed, the persimmon was established in English gardens before 1629 and was introduced into Europe in the early eighteenth century, where it can still be found, but sun-starved American persimmons in the Old World rarely reach a height of more than thirty feet. On native ground, persimmons do much better, normally topping out at something under fifty feet.

D. virginiana is a member of the Ebenaceae family, but unlike almost all the other ebonies, it is not tropical. Its range extends across the United States from Florida and Texas into New England. Particularly valued for its timber, this hardwood has been characteristically employed for shoe lasts, weaver's shuttles, and golf club heads. The dark heartwood takes a century to develop, but then it surpasses in hardness any native wood except ironwood and dogwood.

Small flowers bloom in early June and typically evolve into ripe fruit by October. Contrary to persistent folklore, frost has nothing to do with the ripening process. Indeed, the notion that a hard frost was required before the fruit would lose its tannic, mouth-puckering astringency has probably kept the native persimmon from achieving popularity as a commercial fruit. Everyone I met in Indiana told me that frost was essential and that I should only attempt to eat fruit that had fallen on the ground. Unimpeachable botanical authority asserts that this is false, that fruit with a good, dark orange color should be picked while still solid (cut rather than pulled from the stem) and that it can be ripened fully, until it is very soft, off the tree. I tested this proposition with several firm fruits, and it is so. Furthermore, ripening can be hastened along by bagging persimmons together with an apple.

In other words, there is no reason to wait until persimmons have fallen to the ground from their own heaviness and gone smash. A commercial grower could easily harvest a crop while it was still firm enough to travel and get it to market in good shape. Off-tree ripening, by the evidence of my own experiment, produces just as flavorful a fruit as the benign neglect preached by tradition.

Other factors besides the frost legend have also worked against popular acceptance of the persimmon. The fruit is small. Most varieties have several seeds. Indeed, the seeds are such a prominent feature of the fruit that a woman in Bloomington, Indiana, told me there was a local tradition of using them to divine the severity of the approaching winter.

Seeds, tannin, and frost legend notwithstanding, it has been obvious to everyone who ever tried a ripe persimmon that it is a fruit of enormous appeal and sophistication worth commercial exploitation. At the end of the nineteenth century and the beginning of the twentieth, nurserymen developed various cultivated varieties: some early blooming, one virtually seedless. But a market never materialized. City people didn't want native persimmons. But the cultivars are still available.

Those interested in planting a persimmon tree should write Gerardi Nursery, Route 1, O'Fallon, Illinois 62269 or California Nursery Company, Box 2278, Fremont, California 94336 or Waynesboro Nurseries, Waynesboro, Virginia 22980. Do not try to transplant a wild tree without professional assistance, as the extremely deep taproot makes this a very dicey project. I met a man in Brown County who had failed on several tries. He at least had several other trees that bore fruit almost at his doorstep. And almost no one was competing with him for their bounty.

Only the initiated seem to bother with wild persimmons, which are either out of reach, overly tannic, or lying squashed or unappealingly flaccid on the ground. I was able to glean another shirtful at the edge of a recreational-vehicle parking lot in Brown County State Park. Vacationers sitting on vinyl folding chairs eyed me with disdain as I gathered persimmons from a nearby grassy knoll littered with fruit and the paper debris of human tourism.

Some of those same rusticating urbanites must have driven home and found bigger but not nearly as interesting heart-shaped oriental persimmons in their markets for fifty cents apiece. In recent years, *Diospyros kaki* has established a foothold in U.S. groceries as a specialty fruit. After a long history as a cultivated plant in Asia (especially in Japan, where it amounts to the national fruit), the *kaki* persimmon has been astutely marketed in this country.

Meanwhile, the native fruit, clearly superior, remains misunderstood and neglected. Country people who value it gather it in the same spirit of woodland foraging that they approach wild mushrooms. And they have preserved the dozens of recipes developed for *D. virginiana* in earlier times. Bear Wallow Books (P.O. Box 579, Nashville, Indiana 47448) publishes a cookbook completely devoted to the various persimmon cakes, puddings, breads, cookies, pies, salads, ice creams, and candies that Hoosiers have traditionally prepared.

Early settlers in Pennsylvania made persimmon wine. In Virginia and Maryland, they distilled persimmon brandy. As a girl in Freetown, Virginia, Edna Lewis helped to make persimmon beer. In *The Taste of Country Cooking*, she recalls:

We would pick over all that we had gathered and then stir them into a medium-soft batter made from the bran of white cornmeal mixed with spring water. After it was all well mixed, we would spoon the batter into a large bread pan and bake it in the oven. After it had baked and cooled, the cake was placed in a stone crock or a wooden keg with twice as much spring water, then covered and left to ferment until Grandfather decided it was ready for drinking—usually in late winter.

"Simmon" beer will never replace Schlitz. And the American persimmon will probably never supplant the oriental persimmon in American markets. *D. kaki* has an even bigger head start over its native rival than Honda has over Chrysler's K cars. But Hirohito himself would probably agree that our persimmon is better than his. This isn't chauvinism, but fact. Anyone who needs further convincing can just head for Gnaw Bone in the fall. If Mrs. Roberts doesn't have any fudge (which is delicious and worth waiting a day for), just find a tree and start eating.

☞ BEAR WALLOW PERSIMMON PUDDING

1 egg, lightly beaten

2 cups persimmon pulp (made by pushing ripe fruit through a colander)

¾ cup sugar

3 cups milk

2 cups sifted flour

½ teaspoon baking soda

1 tablespoon butter, cut in small slivers

¼ teaspoon salt

½ teaspoon vanilla

(1) Preheat the oven to 350 degrees.

(2) Stir the egg into the pulp. Then stir in the sugar, salt, and vanilla.

(3) Next, stir in the milk and flour, alternating between the two, adding a half cup or so at a time. Beat well.

(4) Dissolve the baking soda in a teaspoon of hot water and beat it into the persimmon mixture. Then beat in butter.

(5) Pour into a greased 9 by 13 baking pan. Bake for 1 to 1½ hours, or until dark in color. Four or five times during baking, stir mixture so that it will not harden at edges of pan. (Remove pudding from oven each time so as not to lose oven heat during stirring.)

YIELD: 8 to 10 servings.

☞ JEFFREY STEINGARTEN'S

PERSIMMON ICE CREAM

1 cup milk
¾ cup sugar
Juice of 1 large lemon
1¼ to 1½ cups persimmon pulp

2 cups heavy cream (avoid ultra-pasteurized cream if at all possible)

(1) Scald milk. Stir in sugar until dissolved. Cool to room temperature.

(2) Stir lemon juice and pulp into milk mixture. Then stir in cream. Correct taste if necessary by adding more lemon juice.

(3) Chill 8 to 10 hours or overnight, if possible.

(4) Freeze in an ice cream freezer.

YIELD: 5 to 6 cups.

☞ BROWN COUNTY PERSIMMON FUDGE

1 cup persimmon pulp
6 cups sugar
2½ cups milk

½ cup light corn syrup
½ cup butter or margarine
1 cup chopped nuts

(1) Combine pulp, sugar, milk, and syrup in large saucepan.

(2) Cook slowly 1½ to 2 hours until mixture reaches soft ball stage (or 230 degrees). Cool to lukewarm. Stir often. Add butter. Beat well.

(3) When mixture begins to thicken, stir in 1 cup chopped nuts. Spread in buttered 8½ by 12 pan.

YIELD: 8 to 10 servings.

☞ PERSIMMON BISCUITS

½ cup persimmon pulp	½ cup scalded milk
¼ cup sugar	¼ cake yeast dissolved in
1 teaspoon salt	¼ cup lukewarm water
¼ teaspoon mace	2½ cups flour
4 tablespoons butter	

(1) Add pulp, sugar, salt, mace, and butter to milk. Cool to lukewarm and add dissolved yeast cake, then add flour. Cover and put in warm place to rise overnight.

(2) Preheat oven to 375 degrees.

(3) Shape into biscuits and place on greased pan. Let rise again. Bake until golden brown on top.

YIELD: 8 to 10 servings.

☞ PERSIMMON TEA LOAF

1 cup sugar	½ teaspoon salt
2 eggs, beaten	½ teaspoon baking soda
1 cup persimmon pulp	½ cup vegetable oil
2 cups flour	¾ cup chopped nuts
3 teaspoons baking powder	1 cup raisins

(1) Preheat oven to 350 degrees.

(2) Beat together sugar, eggs, and pulp. Sift together flour, baking powder, salt, and soda.

(3) Combine pulp mixture and dry ingredients, then stir in oil. Mix well. Add nuts and raisins. Pour batter into greased loaf pan and bake 45 to 50 minutes.

YIELD: 6 to 8 servings.

☞ SPICY PERSIMMON BREAD

3 cups flour	1 teaspoon cloves
1 teaspoon salt	2 cups sugar
2 teaspoons baking powder	2 eggs
2 teaspoons baking soda	2 cups persimmon pulp
1 teaspoon cinnamon	½ cup chopped nuts
1 teaspoon nutmeg	½ cup raisins

(1) Preheat oven to 350 degrees.

(2) Sift dry ingredients into bowl. Beat eggs, add to pulp, then add liquids. Mix dry ingredients into pulp mixture; add raisins and nuts. Pour batter into two well-greased loaf pans. Bake 1 hour.

YIELD: 6 to 8 servings.

☞ PERSIMMON YEAST BREAD

½ cup butter	1 cup scalded milk
⅔ cup sugar	½ cake yeast dissolved in
1 cup persimmon pulp	½ cup lukewarm water
1 teaspoon salt	5 cups flour

(1) Blend butter and sugar, combine with pulp, salt, and milk. When mixture is lukewarm, add dissolved yeast. Then stir in flour. Cover and let rise overnight.

(2) Preheat oven to 375 degrees.

(3) In the morning shape into large loaf and bake for 20 minutes. Reduce heat to 350 degrees and bake 40 more minutes.

YIELD: 6 to 8 servings.

☞ SPICY, RICH PERSIMMON PUDDING

2 cups persimmon pulp	1½ cups flour
1 cup sugar	1 teaspoon baking soda
1 teaspoon baking powder	½ cup melted butter
½ teaspoon salt	2 teaspoons cinnamon
1 cup milk	1 teaspoon ginger or allspice
1 cup half-and-half	1 teaspoon ground cloves
½ teaspoon nutmeg	(optional)
2 eggs	

(1) Preheat oven to 350 degrees.

(2) Mix together pulp, sugar, melted butter, and milk. Mix dry ingredients separately. Then combine both mixtures. Stir well. Pour into greased 9 by 13 pan and bake for 1 hour. Stir several times while pudding is baking.

YIELD: 6 to 8 servings.

☞ CHRISTMAS PERSIMMON-DATE PUDDING

2 cups persimmon pulp	½ teaspoon cinnamon
1 cup sweet milk	¼ teaspoon ginger
2 tablespoons melted butter	¼ teaspoon ground cloves
2 tablespoons vanilla	¼ teaspoon nutmeg
2 cups flour	2 cups chopped walnuts
2 cups sugar	1 cup chopped dates
4 teaspoons baking soda	1 cup raisins
1 tablespoon baking powder	1 teaspoon grated orange peel

(1) Preheat oven to 350 degrees.

(2) Combine pulp, milk, butter, and vanilla. Stir in flour, sugar, soda, baking powder, spices, and rest of ingredients. Mix

well. Spoon the thick mixture into a well-greased and floured 9 by 13 baking dish.

(3) Bake for 1 hour or until inserted silver knife blade comes out clean. Serve with whipped cream, ice cream, or hard sauce.

Y I E L D: 6 to 8 servings.

THE TAMING OF THE GRAIN: MINNESOTA WILD RICE

Unmolested worked the women,
Made their sugar from the maple,
Gathered wild rice in the meadows
—Longfellow, *The Song of Hiawatha*

Sitting in Cambridge, Massachusetts, in the big Brattle Street house his father-in-law had given him, Longfellow presumed to write an epic of Indian tribal life in northern Minnesota. How true a general picture of Native American civilization by the shores of Gitche Gumee he may have managed to draw I cannot say. But it is certain that the real Minnehahas, when they harvested wild rice for their Hiawathas, did not do the job on any meadow.

Wild rice, the only native North American grain, grows in the lakes and rivers of Minnesota, upper Michigan, Wisconsin, and adjoining parts of Canada. Wild rice is an aquatic grass, appropriately labeled *Zizania aquatica* in scientific nomenclature. At least the second half of the botanical name is appropriate. *Zizania*, picked as wild rice's genus name for no reason I can fathom, comes from a Greek word for a weed, probably the darnel, that grows among wheat. The vernacular name is even more misleading, since wild rice is not some uncultivated version of domesticated rice, *Oryza*, but closer in nature to wheat. The early French explorers of its native range did not help dispel the general confusion when they dubbed it *folle avoine*, or "crazy oat."

With so much misinformation surrounding wild rice, perhaps Longfellow should be pardoned for his relatively trivial error. It is a shame, though, that he did not know about the exceedingly poetic, traditional Ojibway technique for harvesting wild rice, which would have made a splendid episode in *Hiawatha*.

Instead of striking out over dry land, the Indian women, two to a canoe, collected the rice while entirely waterborne. An observer, writing in 1820, described harvesting on Big Sandy Lake:

It is now gathered by two of the women passing around in a canoe, one sitting in the stern and pushing it along, while the other, with two small pointed sticks about three feet long, collects it in by running one of the sticks into the rice, and bending it into the canoe, while with the other she threshes out the grain. This she does on both sides of the canoe alternately, and while it is moving.

On a good day the women went home with a canoe full of grain. And that is still the way wild, so-called lake rice is harvested in Minnesota. State law regulates every aspect of the rice harvest, setting an opening day for the season, protecting

Indian rights over waters on their reservations, and forbidding the use of any harvesting tools other than Indian-style sticks. Such rules were intended not only to perpetuate a charming technique but, principally, to safeguard the interests of Indians and other individuals against competition from an extremely efficient harvesting machine perfected in 1923 and then quickly outlawed after a public outcry went up against it.

As a result, the rice harvest on Minnesota lakes, which normally begins in late August, is what you might call a grass-roots phenomenon involving all manner of folk—Indians and white hobbyists alike. The total crop of lake rice is not immense, averaging about 500,000 pounds a year in the seventies. But the local, atomized nature of the harvest lends it an appealing, communal quality. On the other hand, the scarcity of the grain and its prestige among gourmets have made wild rice an expensive item outside the state, one that is too valuable for many poor Indians to keep for their own use. That, at any rate, is what some Native American radicals charge, yearning perhaps for the return of precolonial days when wild rice played a crucial role in the survival of the 50,000 Ojibways who lived in the forests of the Upper Great Lakes.

Even today it is still possible to observe Ojibways processing wild rice in the unbelievably laborious traditional manner. First, the green rice has to be cured so that it will not spoil in storage and so that the hull can be removed. Originally, this was done with the heat of the sun or over smoky fires. But when white settlers introduced metal pots, Ojibways quickly switched over to them, toasting the rice in caldrons set over wood fires and stirring the grains with a canoe paddle. At this point, men take over the process. They dig a shallow hole in the ground, line it with skin, and pour in cured rice. Wearing moccasins and leather gaiters to keep rice from working its way inside the moccasins, they literally dance on the rice to loosen the hulls.

To gain more leverage and better balance while they "jig," they steady themselves by holding on to poles placed outside the hole. Finally, the rice is poured over a blanket, so that the wind can blow away the chaff as the heavier grains fall to earth.

Few Indians do this anymore. Commercial processors with mechanical parchers, threshers, and winnowers can do the job much faster. But the old ways have not completely died. At Cass Lake, Minnesota, I was able to purchase a small quantity of jigged rice so meticulously produced that it lacked all but the faintest light-brown trace of hull.

The majority of Ojibways prefer to sell their rice as a cash crop to commercial processors. The ultimate product is hard to fault and would probably have been approved by the Ojibways of yesteryear. At Northern Lakes Wild Rice Company in Cass Lake, for example, Ernie and Cindy Anderson do custom processing on a small scale. They live in the midst of Indians, and in the title of the cookbook they have published, *Minnesota Mahnomen Recipes*, they show their respect for Indian ways by perpetuating the Ojibway word for wild rice (*mahnomen* is also the source of the name of a neighboring tribe, the Menominees).

Strictly speaking, one could argue that the Andersons are paying lip service to a tradition they are also exploiting for personal profit. But it is hard to work up much animus against their cottage industry after you have visited the holdings of a new company that has as its aim the cultivation of *Zizania aquatica* on hundreds of acres of paddies.

The very idea of domesticating America's most folkloric wild plant may strike you as an abomination, a final blow struck against the aboriginal order by the same kinds of free-wheeling entrepreneurs who raped the country's forests and pillaged Appalachia's hills. But I was reserving judgment as I flew over the neat paddies in the amphibious plane of one of the company's investors. After all, the original stands of wild rice on the lakes are as safe as a strict environmental code can make them. Meanwhile, below me, an agronomic drama of the first order was in full swing.

It was as if I was on hand for the domestication of corn and wheat from their original wild grasses in prehistoric times. But in twentieth-century Minnesota, a band of green-thumbed businessmen and inventive farmers are accomplishing in a decade the same job that occupied ancient agriculturists for generations.

Modern science and machinery help a great deal. Laser-guided land planes can smooth a paddy on a slight slope so that water drains in and out of an ingenious system of dikes and ditches. Old-time American ingenuity has improvised flotation wheels for a Rotavator that tills the paddies' peat soil without churning it excessively as a plow would. Combines to harvest ordinary rice, built on halftracks and full tracks suitable for soft peat, have been rigged with extra-large headers that match the height of the wild rice plants.

These mechanized marvels were the easy part. They just cost money, lots of money. The hard part was, and to a certain extent still is, finding a strain of *Zizania aquatica* that can be sown and reaped like any other cultivated grain. Over the years many Minnesotans tried to tame wild rice, but they all failed. The plant's basic biology foiled them because the mature seeds —the part we harvest and eat—shatter at maturity and fall off the stem. Worse, seeds of the same plant mature at different times, starting with the topmost and progressing downward along a spikelike cluster. For this reason, traditional lake harvesting has to be done in several stages, with canoes passing through the same stand at intervals of several days, until all the seeds have matured and been knocked off their stems.

The paddy rice farmers can only harvest once, since the

combine chews off the plants' entire spikes in one pass. For paddy production, then, the ideal wild rice plant would have seeds that did not shatter, that remained on the plant until the whole spike was ripe.

Pioneers in the paddy business like Harold Kosbau scoured lake crops looking for naturally occurring, nonshattering strains. Eventually, they found them, planted them in paddies, and by 1972, they were in business. Last year, paddy production had expanded to 2.2 million pounds, roughly 80 percent of Minnesota's overall crop. And in that same period, after a sophisticated marketing effort by the paddy growers and by wild rice retailers, United States consumption tripled. Meanwhile, the retail price, especially outside Minnesota, zoomed to a level at least as high as $17 a pound. The wild rice market is wilder than the plant. Mail-order sources charge widely divergent amounts, ranging from a low of $5 per pound to $14.50 for ten ounces.

To be sure, there are different grades of wild rice, from fancy long grain to broken debris, but these are unofficial ratings, rarely mentioned and affecting price only erratically. Questions of price apart, in the new, two-tiered wild rice market, there is the further question, the most fundamental of all, Is paddy rice as good as lake rice?

Naturally, the paddy growers' stock response is, "They're genetically the same. There's no difference." This claim is obviously false. By definition, a nonshattering strain of rice is a genetically different variety from the majority of naturally occurring plants. And the state of Minnesota is full of diehards like Ron Libertus, an Ojibway art historian and special services director for the Minnesota Department of Natural Resources, who will tell you that paddy rice is "a different product," cured longer to soften the harder seed, darker in color, ultimately quite different in taste. Paddy people deny this.

To test the claims of both sides, I collected six samples of lake and paddy rice. All the paddy rice had been industrially processed, except for one package parched and jigged in an exhibition of Indian techniques. The lake rice came from three different sources; one sample had been prepared by hand (foot?). I attempted to cook them all until they just began to split so that they would be chewy, or what Italians would call *al dente*.

At one extreme, the jigged paddy rice turned to mush in minutes without passing through an intermediate, chewy stage that I could detect. At the other extreme, the very light and delicate, Indian home-processed rice was so light, subtle, and fluffy that it approached true rice in appearance and flavor. Frankly, I preferred the four intermediate varieties, which all had the gutsier, chewier, smokier conventional taste of wild rice, whether they came from lakes or paddies. No doubt, the lake varieties had a gentler feel on the tongue, a higher color, and perhaps a greater complexity of taste. But the distinction seemed to me a very thin one. From lakes or paddies, all four samples tasted very good with roast duck.

Ultimately, as paddy cultivation improves its genetic base and expands still further, it may reduce lake harvesting to the status of a colorful hobby. At the moment, however, illogical prices notwithstanding, the market is absorbing lake and paddy production almost indiscriminately. Nevertheless, the advent of paddy rice has already had one clear result. More than a century too late, Longfellow has been vindicated. Minnesotans are finally harvesting wild rice on dry land.

☞ BASIC PREPARATION OF WILD RICE

1 cup wild rice   1 teaspoon salt

(1) Put rice and 1 teaspoon salt in a saucepan with 3 cups water.

(2) Bring to a boil, lower heat, and simmer, covered, for about 30 minutes. It is impossible to give a precise cooking time. Some small-grained, highly polished varieties will cook quickly. Others will take longer, up to 50 minutes. But wild rice is not nearly so sensitive as ordinary rice. By all means uncover the pan and taste as often as you like. If cooked too long, wild rice turns to mush and loses much of its taste and nutritional value. But if you catch it just as the grains begin to split, it will have an appealingly crunchy texture and a nutty flavor.

(3) Drain and serve. Leftover rice will keep for several days under refrigeration. Or it can be frozen. It will also stand up to reheating very nicely, especially if it has not been overcooked the first time around.

YIELD: About 4 cups or 6 servings.

☞ WILD RICE MUFFINS

(Adapted from Wild Rice for All Seasons Cookbook, *by Beth Anderson,*
$6.95 postpaid from Minnehaha Publishing, Suite 406, 625 Second Avenue,
Minneapolis, Minnesota 55402)

1 cup cooked wild rice	1¼ cups flour
2 eggs, lightly beaten	1 tablespoon baking powder
5 tablespoons oil	½ teaspoon salt
1 cup milk	3 tablespoons sugar

(1) Preheat oven to 425 degrees. Grease a 12-muffin tin.

(2) Stir the wild rice together with the eggs, oil, and milk in a mixing bowl.

(3) Combine the flour, baking powder, salt, and sugar in another bowl. Stir together until well mixed.

(4) Stir the dry ingredients into the liquid ingredients, gradually and thoroughly, until blended.

(5) Spoon the batter into the muffin cups. Bake 15 to 18 minutes, until lightly browned.

Y I E L D: 1 dozen muffins.

MOREL VICTORY:

WILD MUSHROOMS IN

MICHIGAN

When Gerald Ford was President, certain Washington wags predicted that he would fire the White House chef and bring in someone from his hometown of Grand Rapids who knew how to cook the cuisine of Michigan. Not particularly a fan of Ford, I was nonetheless stung to hear the food of my natal region so scurrilously dismissed as a gastronomic nullity. True, Michigan could boast no local dishes worth matching against Louisiana gumbos or Key lime pie, but we had raw materials second to none: Lake Superior whitefish and Traverse City cherries. Come to think of it, Michigan was also the best place in the country to find a delicacy that even the White House chef, a Frenchman whom Mr. Ford wisely did not dismiss, would have been delighted to present to the most discriminating international guests. Morels.

    Morels are generally conceded to be the most delicious of

all mushrooms. But they are hard to find in most areas and they fruit for only a few short days in the spring, usually in May. Also, no one has ever succeeded in cultivating morels.

The true gourmet will never pass up an opportunity to eat their distinctively pitted, furrowed caps. On my most recent trip to France, which took place providentially in May, the giant asparagus was in season, but I needed no special encouragement to opt, at the legendary Restaurant de la Pyramide in Vienne, for a first course of morels and cream in puff pastry. The *patronne* must have employed a small army of people to scour the woods for all the morels she served that Sunday. Morels camouflage themselves brilliantly in leaves and underbrush. Stands of oak, tulip poplar, and old elms, abandoned apple orchards, and burned-over fields are all likely places to look, but no set of conditions is guaranteed to produce morels, and they often pop up singly rather than in bevies. At least they do seem to grow in the same places year after year.

Once, taken to proven morel sites in Rockland County, New York, I came away with four pounds, a gift from the forest worth, to me, its weight in caviar. And so I felt confident that I could hold my own with the mycophiles who assemble each May at Boyne City, Michigan, for the National Mushroom Hunting Championship.

That the woods around Boyne City were full of morels was obvious even to the casual motorist driving north from Detroit. At the Sugar Bowl Restaurant in Gaylord, the jumping-off place for the northern Lower Peninsula, morels were a "special" on the menu. We were only a few miles from Boyne City now, and farmers' mailboxes had mushroom signs on them to show they had morels for sale. At other times of the year, residents of this hilly, wooded region might vaunt its ski slopes or its lakes or remind you that Ernest Hemingway came here as a boy on vacation from Oak Park, Illinois, and later wrote about the area in his Nick Adams stories. But in mid-May, the morel is king in the Boyne Valley.

In Boyne City itself, on the morning of the first day of the two-day championship, a banner over the main street welcomed contestants. The marquee of the Boyne River Inn said: "Have a Mushroom Burger." Nearly every store window had been painted over with mushroom scenes, and children had worked botanically accurate morels into brightly colored cartoons featuring Big Bird, the Cookie Monster, and Snoopy. One precocious youngster had executed a faintly risqué window painting and captioned it: "Boyne City has Wild-n-Crazy Morals."

The hoopla didn't stop there. At the registration area manned by the Boyne Valley Lions and the Chamber of Commerce, there were mushroom T-shirts and stationery for sale. A small carnival midway was opening as contestants from all over the country lined up at 7 a.m. to get their official numbers and paper collecting bags. Then there was a motor parade of contestants through the town and on out to the secret hunting grounds.

Some 200 cars snaked their way to a remote road that ran past farms up to the edge of a woods. Here, we all piled out and waited for the starting signal. Most of the contestants were outsiders. Only about twenty-five people were local, and they had to compete in a separate division because they knew the territory too well. Dana Shaler, a young millwright from nearby Advance, had won twice before in the local division. The rest of us were mainly first-timers.

"I would say 90 percent of the people come to say they've been in a national event," said Bud Bates, one of the organizers of the contest. He was quick to point out that participants have come from as far as Hawaii and Alaska. But, he added, most come from Ohio and Michigan. And when you stop to talk to the contestants, it is clear that they have more on their minds than the tinny luster of winning a hokey national contest.

Homer Syfert, 77, who worked in the Detroit Post Office for thirty years before retiring, has been coming to the Boyne hunt for the past ten years. He has made it to the finals nearly every year but has never won. His interest in mushrooms goes back to his boyhood on a farm south of Decatur, Illinois. "I once picked eleven bushels," he said. "My father told me which ones to pick. You have to look on hills facing south. In Illinois, there were more woods then. All our neighbors ate mushrooms."

Paul Whipple also grew up on a farm—in Michigan—and learned how easy and safe it was to pick morels. Today, he works as a painting contractor in Muskegon, Michigan, but during the season he drives north more than a hundred miles and spends three days foraging for mushrooms that he will parcook, freeze, and eat for the rest of the year. For Whipple, and many other entrants in the National Mushroom Championship, the contest is in large part just an excuse to relive their youthful involvement with mushrooms. Poised and ready to charge into the Michigan woods, they are hoping to win some public acclaim for a vestigial skill learned during their agricultural, postfrontier Midwestern childhood.

To the outsider, who had always thought of morels as part of a sophisticated European culinary world, it was a surprise to discover that this American heartland tradition of mushrooming centered almost exclusively on the elusive members of the morel genus, *Morchella*. But as with most folk traditions, this one has a pragmatic logic behind it.

Midwestern woods, like all woods, teem with hundreds of mushroom varieties, many of which are toxic or inedible. Morels, however, are delicious and safe, virtually foolproof. Because they fruit so early in the season, there are almost no other mushrooms around to confuse them with. And morels don't even look like classic mushrooms. They have neither gills nor pores. Their cone-shaped caps are pitted or ridged. Once you have seen one, or even a picture of one, you can never mix them up with anything else, except possibly the false morels, which have wrinkles, not pits or ridges. Also, the cap of the true morel is attached directly to the stalk, whereas the head of the false morel is attached only at the top and hangs down over the stalk like a skirt. It is the case that one true morel, *Morchella semilibera,* is only partially attached, but the exterior of its cap is ridged in the same way as other true morels. In any event, a look at the photographs in a mushroom field manual will make positive and safe identifications a simple matter, as simple as they were for farm folk in Michigan and Illinois earlier in the century.

When Homer Syfert was growing up, his family and their neighbors were too cautious to attempt foraging for other kinds of mushrooms that required more sophisticated knowledge. They had the sense to know the limits of their mycological information, so that what they didn't know didn't hurt them. They were certain, however, that *Morchella* looked different from "ordinary" mushrooms even if they didn't realize that it belonged to a special class of fungi, called ascomycetes, whose spores are produced in a microscopic saclike cell called an ascus. (Most of the mushrooms in the woods are basidiomycetes, fungi whose spores are found on spinelike projections, or basidia, on the outside of a club-shaped cell.)

The Syferts and the Whipples did know, however, that true morels are hollow and should be sliced in half lengthwise, examined for insect infestation, and then thoroughly rinsed to remove sand or dirt. They did not have to be reminded not to use plastic collecting bags—plastic causes morels to wilt almost immediately—because there weren't any in those days. But they did master the simple technology of morel preservation.

Drying is probably still the best way, and you can do it most easily in a fruit and vegetable dehydrator. Barring that, spread the morels out in an oven set at the lowest temperature, with the door open, and leave them there until they are crisp. Store in jars in a cool dark place. Reconstitute by soaking one cup of mushrooms in two cups of hot water for thirty minutes. You can also sauté morels in butter until all moisture has boiled away and then freeze them with decent results.

This kind of morel lore was easy to come by as one waited for the contest to begin. Morel hunters are basically generous with information. But once the actual competition began, once we had all run uphill into the woods, it was every man and woman for himself and herself.

Ninety minutes later, breathless from the chase, I returned to the starting line with a slim but still precious bag of fifteen morels. Others had hundreds. I didn't survive the cut and had to sit out the finals the next day, when Paul Whipple won the outsiders' title with 309 mushrooms and Dana Shaler copped the local division championship with 445.

That is a lot of morels, but contest veterans were quick to remind us that the highest total in previous years was well over 900 and that the largest single mushroom ever found in the state—10½ inches tall and weighing 14 ounces—would have dwarfed any mushroom picked that day.

Even so I was impressed with the superior skills of the winners, impressed until I stopped on the way south at a farm with a roadside mushroom sign. A little girl led me into a garage filled with bushels of morels. She had collected them after school and on weekends, just as generations of Midwest-erners had done before her. "I know where to look," she explained nonchalantly. For her and a few other farm children in the Boyne Valley, the National Mushroom Festival was irrelevant. In their world, what matters is that the woods are still able to produce their bounty—and their parents have shown them where to look for it.

☞ MOREL SOUFFLÉ

(Adapted from Morel Mushroom Cookbook, *by Betty Ivanovich, R-B Food Products, 7626 Auburn Road, Utica, Michigan 48087)*

½ pound morels, chopped	Pepper
4 tablespoons butter, approximately	4 egg yolks
	5 egg whites, beaten until
Heavy cream	stiff but not dry
3 tablespoons flour	Bread crumbs
Salt	

(1) Sauté the chopped morels in 3 tablespoons of the butter for 5 minutes. Meanwhile, butter the inside of a soufflé dish and set aside. Preheat oven to 375 degrees.

(2) Remove mushrooms from pan with a slotted spoon, draining juice thoroughly back into pan. Reserve mushrooms.

(3) Measure the cooking liquid in the sauté pan. Add enough heavy cream to make ¼ cup liquid. Pour this mixture back into the pan. Add the flour. Heat, stirring constantly, until the mixture reaches the boil. It should be smooth and thick.

(4) Remove flour mixture from heat. Stir in salt and pepper to taste and continue stirring until cool.

(5) Add mushrooms to cooled mixture. Stir in egg yolks, one at a time, mixing until well incorporated.

(6) Fold in egg whites and pour soufflé batter into buttered soufflé dish. Sprinkle lightly with bread crumbs. Dot with butter. Bake for 30 to 35 minutes, or until the top springs back when touched lightly.

Y I E L D: 3 to 4 servings.

☞ MOREL FONDUE

1 cup morels, chopped	¼ cup sherry
2 tablespoons butter	1 cup cheese (Colby mild is best)

(1) Sauté morels in butter until the juice is absorbed.

(2) Blend sautéed morels in a blender at high speed until pureed.

(3) Pour morel puree into a fondue pot, add sherry, and heat until bubbly. Add cheese and stir until melted. Serve with cubes of French or Italian bread.

Y I E L D: 2 servings.

☞ PICKLED MORELS

2 cups vinegar	2 tablespoons oil
1 tablespoon salt	¾ pound morels
6 peppercorns	

(1) Mix all ingredients, except morels, and boil for approximately 2 to 3 minutes. Add morels, making sure that the liquid covers the morels.

(2) Boil 15 to 20 minutes, pour into sterilized jars, and seal. It is best to wait about 2 weeks, to allow the vinegar to penetrate the morels, before using them.

Two recipes adapted from *Wild Mushroom Recipes*, by the Puget Sound Mycological Society, Pacific Search, 715 Harrison Street, Seattle, Washington 98109:

☞ MOREL-BEEF, ORIENTAL STYLE

1½ pounds flank steak	2 cups sautéed mushrooms
Oil	Salt
3 slices fresh ginger, peeled and slivered	¼ cup dry white wine

(1) Slice flank steak diagonally in thin strips.

(2) Heat oil in pan on high heat. Add flank steak and stir. Add slivered ginger and stir. Add sautéed mushrooms and stir. Add salt. Add wine. Cook only until pink color in meat is gone.

YIELD: 6 servings.

☞ CHINESE GREENS WITH PORK AND MORELS

Oil	4 cups sautéed mushrooms
2 pork steaks, cut diagonally in thin strips	2 cups chicken stock
8 cups greens, cut diagonally (broccoli and bok choy)	Cornstarch
	Salt

(1) Heat oil in a skillet. Add pork strips, stir, and cook, covered, for 5 minutes on medium heat.

(2) Add broccoli first and cook, covered, 1 minute. Add

bok choy and mushrooms. Add stock, bring to a boil, and thicken slightly with a small amount of cornstarch dissolved in water. Add salt.

(3) Remove pan from heat immediately. Vegetables must be crisp. Serve with hot rice.

Y I E L D: 2 to 3 servings.

GEESE ON THE RUN

By mid-December, all serious Americans are asking themselves the question, What shall I serve for Christmas dinner? Some iconoclasts I know have opted for Chateaubriand or even lobster. Italian-Americans of a traditional sort prepare capon, elaborately stuffed. But for most people, the mainstream, colonial, Anglo-Saxon tradition dictates a big bird. And almost invariably, these days this means a turkey.

Turkeys are cheap, as cheap as any meat source. They are widely available, and the militant seeker after quality can find them freshly killed without waging a campaign at the butcher's. Connoisseurs, on the other hand, serve goose, which is equally traditional for Christmas. But goose is expensive, not universally marketed, and almost never sold unfrozen. Goose, a tastier fowl than turkey, takes a distant second to the gobbler in modern American Christmas celebrations.

This is exactly the reverse of the way things used to be. Goose was the preeminent Christmas bird in early America and in England, where the tradition of yuletide goose pies and roast goose began. To be more precise, in England goose was the customary bird and turkey was a special luxury. Tiny Tim and the other poor Cratchits made do, happily enough, with a goose in Dickens's *A Christmas Carol:*

There never was such a goose. Bob said he didn't believe there ever was such a goose cooked. Its tenderness and flavour, size and cheapness were the themes of universal admiration. Eked out by apple-sauce and mashed potatoes, it was a sufficient dinner for the whole family; indeed, as Mrs. Cratchit said with great delight (surveying one small atom of a bone upon the dish) they hadn't ate it all at last! Yet every one had had enough, and the youngest Cratchits in particular were steeped in sage and onion to the eyebrows!

Enough is as good as a feast, of course, but when Uncle Scrooge awakens from his threefold nightmare, brimming over with Christmas spirit, the first thing he does is buy the Cratchits a huge turkey. ("He never could have stood upon his legs, that bird. He would have snapped 'em short off in a minute, like sticks of sealing-wax.")

The lesson this teaches is that in Dickens's England, goose was cheap and turkey was dear. A similar state of affairs obtained in prerevolutionary China when Chiang Jung-feng was growing up on a farm outside Chengdu in the heart of Sichuan. "Geese and their eggs were usually cheaper than chickens because they were bigger," she told Ellen Schrecker when they were preparing *Mrs. Chiang's Szechwan Cookbook.*

In other places and times, geese have also been an ordinary feature of barnyard life, waddling reservoirs of fat, down, and estimable flesh. Since they can feed themselves almost entirely by grazing on inferior pastureland, they are simple and cheap to raise. They can be taught to herd sheep, and they also make good watchdogs. Geese will fiercely "goose" an intruder with their beaks or honk loudly in alarm when one approaches.

The ancient Egyptians kept geese. And the early Romans revered them from time immemorial, especially after the invasion of the Gauls in the fourth century B.C., when, Livy recounts, a nocturnal raiding party of barbarians eluded Rome's sentries and watchdogs but did not succeed in overrunning the Capitoline because their stealth "did not deceive the geese that were kept there as sacred birds of Juno and never eaten even when food was most scarce."

In Christian Europe, geese also have a religious significance, being associated with Saint Michael's Day, or Michaelmas, September 29, one of the so-called quarter-days when tenants traditionally paid a fourth of their annual rent. They also presented a goose to their landlords at the same time. As a result, Michaelmas is also known as Goose Day, and there are various old customs revolving around the consumption of the Michaelmas goose. Germans believed they could foretell the weather by close examination of its breastbone. In Ireland, not only was the Michaelmas goose said to ward off disease, but a goose pie was baked with a golden ring inside and whoever found the ring would marry well and early.

Goose Day came to the United States roughly 200 years ago, when a Pennsylvania Dutch farmer, Andrew Pontius, settled in Snyder County in the center of the state and hired a young British deserter from the king's navy as a tenant farmer. The tenant, one Archibald Hunter, arranged for his accounts to be settled on Michaelmas, and when the day rolled around, he surprised Pontius by arriving with a goose under his arm.

So, according to this supposedly true story, began central Pennsylvania's Goose Day, a celebration that still thrives. In most other places, however, geese are rarely seen, even on working farms, although some people in exurbia keep geese as semipets. There were a few geese roaming a meadow in northern Maine where I stayed this August at a rural homestead that also accommodated a few horses and chickens picturesquely by the banks of a tidal river. It was hard to tell if the farmer lady was going to eat her backyard geese for Christmas, and I didn't have the heart to ask.

Geese are good at making themselves part of the family. They will come when called, untie your shoes, or take the valve cap off automobile tires. And, as ethologist Konrad Lorenz discovered, geese will attach themselves to a human being and make that person their "parent" if he or she is the first living thing they see upon hatching. When a graylag gosling (*Anser anser*) did this to Lorenz, the bird insisted on spending every waking moment with the scientist, making his life hectic for several months but also giving him a special chance to "relate" to a bird and subsequently to write a famous study of goose behavior.

Lorenz did little more than establish in a rigorous way what myriad goose girls and boys had learned over generations of "interaction" with their geese. In this country, as in Europe, until this century geese were raised by hand, a few at a time, for the family, on small farms. But as America's small farmers fled the land in droves and their farms were swallowed up by agribusiness and suburbia, barnyard geese disappeared from the land along with the yeomen who had bred them for their Christmas tables.

Mechanized agriculture did not step into the breach. In all of America, there are not enough geese in commercial production to make it worthwhile for the U.S. Department of Agriculture to publish figures for them in its annual compendium *Agricultural Statistics.* The same book counts almost 300 million American chickens and about 135 million turkeys. An unofficial but educated estimate of the size of the national goose slaughter runs to a mere 600,000.

The primary problem with geese in modern America is not that people traditionally have eaten them only at Christmas. Thirty years ago, the turkey was also a specialty bird, but Swift and Company and other major producers invested heavily in turkeys, learned to raise them in confinement as if they were hothouse tomatoes, and brought the price per pound down to a level so low it changed national eating habits, turning Scrooge's delicacy into every delicatessen's favorite bargain.

With geese, biology imposed a different destiny. "We tried confinement," says Wilbur Ramble, who runs the hatchery at Pietrus Foods, a large goose production company in Sleepy Eye, Minnesota. "The goose is a grazing bird. In confinement, the geese went down on their legs. Their feet had swelled up with infection from walking on wooden slats. They pecked so bad, they had to be debeaked so they wouldn't kill each other."

Geese need twice the space that turkeys do, as much space as a hog. Goslings are still put out to pasture, in huge, billowing flocks that sometimes number as many as 10,000. And they do well on nothing but grass and a modest grain supplement. But that is not enough to make them competitive with chickens as protein machines. A hen will lay more than 200 eggs in a season, while a good goose will not do better than 40. Moreover, 90 to 95 percent of chicken eggs hatch into chicks. Wilbur Ramble estimates that only 78 percent of his goose eggs hatch successfully.

Worst of all is the problem of pinfeathers. Geese get "pinny" three times during their maturation period, at roughly nine, sixteen, and twenty-two weeks of age. When the new feathers are just coming in, apparently as part of some vestigial genetic process preparing the plumage for a seasonal migration, the geese are virtually impossible to pluck. At least, they cannot be plucked cleanly enough to satisfy stringent Department of Agriculture inspection standards.

In most other countries, geese simply have the main feathers removed. In the United States, despite the objections of producers, geese have to be depinned and this, allegedly, runs the cost of processing up to uncompetitive levels, to $4 a bird in 1978 and as high as $6 in 1979, which helps explain why geese run well over $2 a pound in supermarkets for Christmas.

To get those pins out, slaughtered birds with the main feathers already removed are dipped in wax and then in cold water. Teams of women pull off the wax and if all goes well, the pinfeathers come out with it. Otherwise, spot-checking USDA inspectors shut the line down. On a good day, Pietrus processes 3,000 geese. A comparable chicken-processing facility can handle 80,000 birds in the same space of time.

These figures do not make goose producers happy, but they and the rest of the anachronistic factors in goose breeding may have something to do with the delicious, nonindustrial taste of geese. At any rate, good geese do appear in our markets in the late fall. Vigorous publicity by the National Goose Council has even caused a slight rise in annual sales. This has recently encouraged modest gains in production. And that means that more of us can join the happy Americans who enjoy a traditional American Christmas dinner. Few, however, will dine on Mr. Bordley's Christmas Pie, as described in the Lloyd Papers at the Maryland Historical Society (reprinted in *Maryland's Way: The Hammond-Harwood House Cook Book*):

In Glasse's Book [*Art of Cookery Made Plain and Easy*, by Hannah Glasse, first published in England in 1747, and frequently reissued in America as well as England] is a Yorkshire Christmas Pie which seems to be much like what used to be in my Family: but the Cooke is dead who made them, so that the method she used is lost.

A *fat* Swan, however old, is fine; as is the whole Pie, when it has been frozen and thawed several Times, and is of sound standing. Our Materials were, a Swan, a Turkey or two, a Goose, 2 or 4 Pullets, 2 or 4 Ducks, sometimes Beef Steaks, etc. It is fortunate to have a cold Winter for freezing the Pie often, by which the old Swan, the Crust etc. are improved and made tender—the Crust short.

Mr. Bordley's recipe is obviously uncookable as written but may serve as a rough example of how traditional British cuisine was transplanted to America. A more practical old Maryland goose recipe, adapted from *Maryland's Way,* follows.

☞ ROAST GOOSE WITH POTATO

AND SAUSAGE STUFFING

1 10-pound goose	4 cups potatoes, parboiled
Salt	5 minutes, peeled, and diced
Marjoram	½ pound sausage meat
3 tablespoons chopped onion	Pepper
3 tablespoons butter	2 to 3 tablespoons browned
	butter

(1) Clean goose inside and out, removing any patches of fat (which can be rendered and reserved). Rub inside with salt and a little marjoram. Rub outside with salt. Let stand to ripen while preparing stuffing.

(2) Sauté onions in butter. Then add potatoes and sausage meat. Season with pepper and very little salt. Mix well and stuff goose lightly.

(3) Preheat oven to 375 degrees.

(4) Prick goose all over and cook, breast down, on a rack in a covered roasting pan filled with hot water to rack height only.

(5) Cook 1 hour, then turn goose over and prick again.

Finish cooking with cover off. Throughout cooking, baste frequently with pan gravy and a little water, skimming off excess fat (which, again, should be reserved for use in cooking). Allow about 20 minutes per pound (3 hours, 20 minutes). Ten minutes before goose is done, baste with browned butter and turn heat up a little to crisp skin. Serve with spiced crab apples or applesauce.

    Y I E L D: 6 festive portions.

TASTY PASTY:

MICHIGAN'S FINNISH-

CORNISH MEAT PIE

Anyone who thinks that ethnicity in America is a simple matter should make a trip to the copper country of Michigan's Upper Peninsula. There are other reasons for visiting the area: grand stretches of unsullied northern woods, the oceanic expanse of Lake Superior, wild rivers like the Yellow Dog. But eventually the most ardent outdoorsman will stop for a sample of Superiorland's most typical local food, the pasty, a large half-moon of short pastry filled with chopped meat and vegetables.

The pasty (pronounced pass-tee) is as much a feature of the Upper Peninsula landscape as the white pine. In 1968, sidestepping pressure to name it the state food, Governor George Romney went so far as to declare May 24 Michigan Pasty Day. Madelyne's, the pasty world's equivalent of Stouffer's, passed the million-pasty mark years ago at its Ishpeming factory, and independent pasty shops punctuate the fir-lined highways. It was in such a place that I—then just a boy with boyish notions—first bit into a pasty. I stepped up to the counter and asked for a "pays-tee," only to realize from the smirk on the waitress's face that I had made a ludicrous error. The kind of pasty I had asked for was available only in shops specializing in the accoutrements of what is politely termed exotic dancing. My other mistake was more sophisticated: I assumed I was eating a Finnish delicacy.

The copper country is a Finnish enclave. People with Finnish surnames abound, descendants of turn-of-the-century immigrants who came to work the iron and copper mines or to clear the land and farm it. At Hancock, Finnish Lutherans established Suomi College. Suomi is the Finnish name for Finland; it is also the name of a small upper Michigan village. At one time, the Upper Peninsula was a hotbed of Finnish-language theater and newspapers, fraternal lodges, and mutual aid societies. Much of this has vanished, but the Lutheran Church in Gwinn still holds a service in Finnish once a month. In 1976, Central Upper Peninsula Finnish-Americans united in a special bicentennial celebration. And in downtown Marquette, the Upper Peninsula's largest town (population 22,-000), there is a restaurant and bakery called Finlandia.

When I first stopped there in the mid-seventies, the owner had a Finnish name and served Finnish specialties, such as the flat rye bread called *rieska,* as well as excellent pasties. Even today, when the new owner describes himself as "half-French, half-Polack," a sign on the wall thanks customers in Finnish (*kiitoksia*) and sells a sweet Finnish cardamom bread. There are still pasties, too, but they are no more Finnish than lasagne.

The Michigan pasty was long ago adopted by local Finns, but it came to the state with the Cornish miners who arrived about 1850. Their big hot pies were the ideal portable lunch:

you could carry them in your pocket all morning, enjoying their warmth, and then you could eat them with your hands, holding them upright so that the juices drained to the bottom as you worked from one end to the other.

Although there is no real doubt in anyone's mind that the Cornish Cousin Jacks and Cousin Jennies (as Cornish people are known colloquially) were the original pasty makers in Michigan, the inquiring gastroethnographer can uncover earlier, more widespread sources for the dish. Pasties are mentioned in Middle English literature written outside Cornwall. Chaucer and Gower knew about pasties. Later on, Shakespeare's Mistress Page, in *The Merry Wives of Windsor*, offered a "hot venison-pasty" to Falstaff. Neither Windsor nor the Globe Theater of Elizabethan London was a center of Cornish culture. Indeed, the word *pasty* obviously derives from the same Late Latin word for dough as such modern terms as *pasta, pâté,* and *pâte,* all of which have to do with moistened flour, paste. And even the idea of a free-standing meat pie surrounded by dough has been universal in Europe from the medieval period to modern times.

In Finland, for example, in the eastern district of Karelia especially, there are many kinds of small, filled pastries. In *The Finnish Cookbook,* Beatrice Ojakangas gives recipes for rye-flour pasties, sometimes baked, sometimes fried, with a slit in the middle. Some are stuffed with ground meat, some with carrots, some with salmon fillets, some with cabbage. The Finnish name for this family of stuffed pasties is *piirakkaa,* an obvious cognate of the Russian word for filled dumpling, *pirog.* Finland's border with Russia has swung back and forth over the centuries, and the food of Karelia is heavily Russified. But the Finnish culinary imagination has put its own stamp on the Karelian cuisine. No one can say with certainty if *piirakkaa* or *pirog* came first.

But just as the Cornish immigrants to Michigan considered *their* pasties to be theirs, the Finns must have thought that the filled pies they had learned to make in the old country belonged by inheritance and tradition to them. Yet, with the exception of a rarely seen, rye-crusted fish pie called *kalakukko,* the Finnish pasties of Finland do not seem to appear on the tables of Michigan Finns.

Latecomers to the shores of Lake Superior, the Finns found Cornish Cousin Jacks already well established in the mines. The Cornishmen had the advantage of speaking English (or at least a special version of it) from the start, and they were often foremen supervising Finns. Like other immigrant groups, the Finns rapidly adapted to the new culture they found in the Upper Peninsula. One of the lessons they learned was how to cook the locally well-entrenched Cornish meat pie.

Bertha Hill, for example, learned to make Cornish pasties from her mother, who was born in Finland. But she also learned regular Finnish dishes, such as the baked cheese, *juustoa,* and the oven "pancake" called *kropsua.* She grew up in a bicultural world, speaking English and Finnish, cooking in two styles. But in her lifetime, she has felt strong pressures at work undermining the strength of the Finnish component in her background. Her name, Hill, is a translation of a common Finnish surname, Maki. Her son, who learned to speak Finnish at home, was so mercilessly mocked at school that he dropped the language completely and simply refused to use it.

Today, Mrs. Hill runs the kitchen at a nearby country school and lives on an eighty-acre, former homestead farm, where she sometimes bakes in the oven of a white porcelain, old-fashioned Monarch wood-burning stove. Her pasties (see recipe) are better than any of the commercial pies I sampled on a recent trip to the Upper Peninsula, better even than the pasties at Kuz'n Jax in Marquette. This is partly the result of her skill as a baker and partly because all her ingredients—from the vegetables down to the ground meat and lard—are produced on her farm. But in praising Mrs. Hill's pasties, one runs up against the question of authenticity.

In the first place, can a Finn prepare proper Cornish pasties? One local Cornishman who ran a pasty contest disqualified his own wife because of her Finnish blood. This seems indefensible to me on many grounds and even smacks, in a genteel way, of the same anti-Finnish prejudice that has made "Finlander" a term of opprobrium in the Upper Peninsula. As with all traditional recipes, the pasty is a battleground of fiercely disputed culinary theories. Among themselves, the Cornish argue whether the dough should have suet or lard as a shortening, whether the filling should contain rutabaga, whether it is necessary to include pork in the chopped meat, and how coarsely or finely to chop that meat. Some folks pull the crust up from both sides and crimp it together at the top; others pull it over from one side. Some layer the ingredients; others mix them. The pasty controversy recently erupted in the pages of the *Upper Peninsula Sunday Times*. Steamy letters were written to the editor. One liberal Cornishman from Wyandotte, Michigan, a suburb of distant Detroit, plumped for pasty diversity and lamented the disappearance of Cornish culture. "The Cornish-American," he wrote, "has abandoned his folkways with unseemly haste. The only thing that survives in America of Cornish heritage is the pasty, that triumph of the Cornish culinary art, although even here much has been lost."

Perhaps. Nevertheless, the pasty has entered the mainstream of one American region, preserving something of the flavor of Cornwall even when adapted by Finnish hands. It is not clear, however, how much longer the Upper Peninsula pasty can hold its own against the recent, aggressive inroads of the fast-food chains that bestride the highway into Marquette from the airport, but for the moment, to paraphrase a Cornish adage, the Devil seems to have kept out of the Upper Peninsula, "for fear of being made into a pasty."

☞ BERTHA HILL'S PASTIES

3 cups unbleached all-purpose flour	3 carrots, peeled and diced
Salt	¾ pound beef chuck, coarsely chopped
⅔ cup lard	¼ pound pork loin, coarsely chopped
½ cup suet, diced	
1 medium onion, peeled and diced	Pepper
3 medium potatoes, peeled and diced	Butter

(1) Sift flour together with 1½ teaspoons salt.

(2) Cut lard and suet into flour-salt mixture with a pastry blender until well incorporated, so that dough has the texture of coarse meal.

(3) Stir in just enough cold water (a little more than ½ cup) so that dough will pull together into a mass. Let rest for an hour, covered.

(4) Preheat oven to 425 degrees.

(5) Mix together the vegetables and meats to make the filling. Season to taste with salt and pepper. Moisten with ½ cup cold water.

(6) Take one-quarter of the dough and roll it out on a lightly floured surface to a circle 9 to 10 inches in diameter. Trim the edges using an inverted plate as a template.

(7) Fill the circle with a mound of one-quarter of the filling. Dot the filling with butter. Place the filling on one side of the dough and shape into a mound that extends across one semicircle.

(8) Pull the uncovered semicircle of dough over the filling and press it down against the opposite edge. Fold the crimped edge of the dough over on itself and press closed with the fingers. The pasty should look like a bulging half-moon.

(9) Continue in this manner until you have 4 large pasties.

(10) Bake on a greased cookie sheet. After 10 minutes, reduce heat to 375 and continue baking another 50 minutes or until done. The pasties are cooked when a fork will press easily through the crust and into the potato pieces inside.

Y I E L D: 4 pasties.

Two recipes adapted from *Michigan Cooking . . . and other things,* by Carole Eberly, Shoestring Press, East Lansing, Michigan 48823:

☞ UPPER PENINSULA PASTY

4 cups flour	10 tablespoons ice water
2 teaspoons salt	1 pound sirloin, diced
½ teaspoon baking powder	½ pound lean pork, diced
1½ cups beef suet, ground twice	5 potatoes, peeled and chopped

3 turnips, scraped and diced   1 teaspoon pepper
1 large onion   Butter
1 tablespoon salt

(1) In a large bowl, combine flour, salt, baking powder, and suet. Mix well, using fingers, until mixture resembles coarse meal. Pour in ice water and gather into a ball. Add more water if necessary. Divide dough into 6 balls, dust each with flour, and wrap in plastic wrap. Refrigerate for 1 hour.

(2) Combine remaining ingredients, except butter. Roll each ball of dough in a circle on a floured surface to ⅛-inch thickness.

(3) Place 1½ cups filling over half the dough on each circle. Dot with butter. Fold over unfilled side of dough and crimp the edges, sealing by moistening lightly. The pasties look like half-moons.

(4) Preheat oven to 400 degrees.

(5) Place pasties on greased baking sheets and bake for 45 minutes.

Y I E L D: 6 pasties.

☞ ROAST BEAR PAWS

2 large bear paws, skinned   1 teaspoon salt
1 cup flour   ½ teaspoon pepper
3 tablespoons shortening   2 onions, sliced thin
1 teaspoon cinnamon   4 slices bacon
1 teaspoon allspice   ½ cup tomato juice

(1) Preheat oven to 350 degrees.

(2) Dust paws with flour, and brown in shortening. Remove to a casserole dish, and sprinkle with seasonings.

(3) Cook onions in shortening until tender. Place onions around paws and lay bacon on top. Pour ½ cup water and ½ cup tomato juice over paws.

(4) Bake, covered, for 4 hours. (If you catch the whole bear, double the recipe for 4 bear paws.)

Y I E L D: 4 servings.

The South

A SQUIRREL IN EVERY POT:

BRUNSWICK STEW

AND BURGOO

When Dr. Creed Haskins and several of his friends returned from a day's hunting in the woods of Brunswick County, Virginia, in 1828 or thereabouts, they found their loyal black retainer, Uncle Jimmy Matthews, stirring a stew he had concocted in their absence. They ate it, hesitantly at first, then smacked their lips and called for more. By then, it did not dampen their appetites to learn that Matthews's thick and flavorful ragout was made from nothing more than butter, onions, stale bread, seasoning, and a passel of squirrels the same slave had shot that morning.

This, at any rate, is the legend of the origin of Brunswick stew, the most famous dish to emerge from the campfires and cabins of pioneer America. Brunswick stew is still prepared in big caldrons at church suppers, volunteer firehouse fundraisers, and all manner of communal celebrations throughout the Southeast. But it is virtually never cooked according to the original recipe. Dr. Haskins began the eroding of his servant's invention when he added some brandy or Madeira to "give the stew a flavor." Then, probably about the turn of the century, well-meaning cooks domesticated Matthews's squirrel *pot-au-feu* still further by throwing in vegetables.

In his classic statement on the subject, made in 1907, Meade Haskins, a descendant of Uncle Jimmy's master, fulminated against this fancification: "Vegetables are not in the original Brunswick stew. Those who prefer vegetables add them after the stew is done, in their plates."

This Haskins also set down the pure and authentic recipe he had received from his father, Dr. A. B. Haskins:

Parboil squirrels until they are stiff (half done), cut small pieces of bacon (middling), one for each squirrel; one small onion to each squirrel (if large, one to two squirrels), chopped up. Put in bacon and onions first to boil, while the squirrels are being cut up for the pot. Boil the above till half done, then put in butter to taste; then stale loaf bread, crumbled up. Cook then till it bubbles, then add pepper and salt to taste. Cook this until it bubbles and bubbles burst off. Time for stew to cook is four hours with steady heat.

Although this text is not as clear as one might like, it offers adequate proof of what Brunswick stew once was, before modern innovators turned it into a veritable succotash of corn and tomatoes and beans and whatnot (see recipe below). But vegetables are hardly the principal infraction against authenticity currently practiced in Brunswick County and almost everywhere else. Modern Brunswick-stew makers have not only added vegetables, they have eliminated the squirrel.

Now I am not here to claim that a Brunswick stew made with squirrel is superior in any way to Brunswick stew made with chicken. And I certainly have no wish to join battle with those who may have had the opportunity to become fans of variant recipes based on opossum, muskrat, or raccoon. I would merely like to have the chance to taste the original dish. But I doubt I will, unless some hunter favors me with a brace of squirrels. They would have to be wild, woodland squirrels, of course, not urban squirrels that have fed on garbage.

This requirement, which I insist on to preserve my health, did not concern pioneer Virginians, who enjoyed a pristine, rural life style and woods abounding in fat, nut-fed squirrels. Today, however, most of us live in town and our only regular access to traditional game meats is through commercial butchers and restaurants. The law forbids the sale of uninspected game animals that have been shot in the wild. The venison we eat in a restaurant has been produced, like beef or lamb, on a ranch, and lacks the special taste of wild meat. And since no one, so far as I know, has started raising squirrels commercially, that means that even in Brunswick County, Virginia, you will not find traditional Brunswick stew, except perhaps in the home of some backwoodsman with an eccentric passion for gastronomic folklore.

"I couldn't put squirrel in my Brunswick stew even if I wanted to," says Larry of Larry's Lunch, the only restaurant in Lawrenceville, Virginia, the Brunswick County seat. He doesn't even list the dish on his menu, but if you ask him, he will sell you a thick farrago of chicken (cooked until it has fallen apart), lima beans, tomatoes, and potatoes that turns out to be a peppery, sinus-clearing soup of a high order. Larry claims this is a definite improvement over the squirrel-based Brunswick stew he used to eat in his younger days on the farm.

Maybe so, but I wouldn't mind seeing for myself if truly authentic Brunswick stew is worth reviving. I apologize to those who find the notion of eating cute little furry squirrels positively repugnant. And I suspect that this sentimental revulsion is part of the reason that Americans from one end of Appalachia to the other have eliminated squirrel from their hunter's stews. The same thing has occurred in the case of burgoo, which is a stewlike potpourri of meat and vegetables invariably supplied at political rallies and other outdoor gatherings in Kentucky, as well as southern Indiana and Illinois. Some people think that burgoo began during the Civil War, when a soldier with a speech impediment created a stew from blackbirds in a 500-gallon copper caldron normally used for making gunpowder. The soldier meant to call his creation "bird stew," but he actually said "burgoo."

Others have looked for a French etymology. But "burgoo" was undoubtedly in use as early as 1740 to describe a porridge eaten by British sailors. The nautical English novelist Frederick Marryat has a sailor in his book *Peter Simple* (1834) say: "Mark my words, you burgoo-eating . . . trowsers-scrubbing son of a bitch!"

It is not hard to imagine how the British fleet hit upon burgoo as a name for oatmeal. Some sailors on shore leave in a Levantine port must have made contact with the wheat pilaf called burghul (or bulgur) and transferred the name, with a slightly distorted pronunciation, to their oatmeal. This Turkish "burghul" became Peter Simple's "burgoo." And in America, the exotic and faintly pejorative word quite probably attached itself to a similarly mushy mess of pottage concocted ad libitum from available vegetables and meats, one of which was, in Daniel Boone's Kentucky, squirrel.

The modern history of Kentucky burgoo begins with a certain James T. Looney, a retired railroad engineer. At his mother's bidding, Looney gave up the perils of railroading for a grocer's career in Lexington and then turned his hand to burgoo. For forty years he catered burgoo to crowds as large as 10,000. Looney was Kentucky's "burgoo king" and so renowned in the Bluegrass State that a thoroughbred colt was named after him. Burgoo King, the horse, won the Kentucky Derby in 1932.

Success did not spoil Jim Looney. All his long life, he upheld the highest standards of burgoo cookery. He took the meats out of his giant kettles (one of them said to have been used for making saltpeter during the Revolutionary War) midway through the twenty-four-hour cooking process and chopped them up before returning them to the kettles. "You find no strings in my burgoo," he said.

You would find no squirrel either, according to his recipe for burgoo for 5,000 people recently printed in the *Louisville Courier-Journal:*

800 pounds beef, 200 pounds fowl, 168 gallons canned tomatoes, 350 pounds cabbage, 6 bushels onions, 85 gallons tomato purée, 24 gallons carrots, 36 gallons canned corn, 1,800 pounds potatoes, 2 pounds red pepper, ½ pound black pepper, 20 pounds salt, 8 ounces Angostura bitters, 1 pint Worcestershire sauce, ½ pound curry powder, 3 quarts tomato catsup, and 2 quarts sherry.

Today, fiery hot burgoo is available at simple restaurants in Louisville and throughout the Ohio River Valley to the west, always without squirrel or other sylvan beasties. Perhaps this makes no difference. Modern, lunch-counter burgoo is a fine thing, although it owes most of its character to its red pepper. I cannot help thinking, however, that a little gaminess would restore this country dish to a vanished glory.

I came to this conviction in Owensboro, Kentucky, a middling metropolis west of Louisville on the Ohio. Owensboro is the barbecue mutton capital of the world. Every May, carloads of ewes are cooked over pits of hickory at the Owensboro International Barbecue Festival. During the average summer, local Catholic parishes run through 800,000 pounds of mutton at fund-raising barbecues, where exclusively male chefs cook the meat over an open flame for eighteen hours or so. No one knows why the people of Owensboro have chosen mutton as their meat of preference over equally traditional beef, pork, venison, bear, elk, and buffalo. The proprietor of Hardman's on East Fourth Street, one of sixteen barbecue places in a town of 50,000, says: "Mutton stands up to flame better. It has a hard skin. Lamb falls apart."

Mutton also tastes different from lamb. It has a feisty tang to it, a high, almost gamy flavor that can hold its own even against the heady amounts of red pepper commonly added to burgoo. As I sat in the Hardman's dining room, a tiny area with a few tables next to a cold-storage locker containing two dressed ewes, I ate a bowl of superbly muttony burgoo and speculated that when the venison and buffalo became scarce at the end of the last century, Owensboro barbecue chefs, who were even then attracting trainloads of hungry tourists each spring and summer, turned to mutton as the best commercially available substitute for game meats at their famous cookouts.

Once they had established mutton as the main meat for barbecue, it was the natural thing to use some of it for burgoo. Mutton could give burgoo the same oomph that squirrel and opossum had formerly provided. There is no proving this, but if you want to taste a very reasonable facsimile of an authentic American hunter's stew without bagging a squirrel, stop over in Owensboro some time for mutton burgoo.

☞ CISSY'S BURGOO

(Courtesy of the Louisville Courier-Journal)

2 pounds pork shank	2 cups chopped cabbage
2 pounds veal shank	1 quart tomato puree
2 pounds beef shank	2 cups whole corn, canned or
2 pounds breast of lamb	fresh
1 4-pound hen	2 pods red pepper
8 quarts water	2 cups diced okra
1½ pounds Irish potatoes	2 cups lima beans
1½ pounds onions	1 cup diced celery
1 bunch carrots, scraped and chopped	Salt, cayenne, Tabasco, A-1 Sauce, Worcestershire to
2 green peppers, seeded and chopped	taste
	Chopped parsley

Put all the meat into cold water and bring slowly to a boil. Simmer until meat falls from the bones. Remove and chop up meat, discarding bones. Pare and dice potatoes and onions. Return meat to stock and add all vegetables (except parsley). Allow to simmer until thick. Burgoo should be very thick but still soupy. Season as you go along, but not too much, until it is almost done. Stir frequently with a long-handled wooden spoon during the early stages and almost constantly after it thickens. Add chopped parsley at the end.

This is made in a 4-gallon kettle and cooked approximately 10 hours. The time can be broken up by cooking the meat the first day and adding the vegetables the second day.

YIELD: 60 servings.

☞ BRUNSWICK STEW—1975

(A synthesis of several traditional recipes, as compiled by Gay Neale in Brunswick County, Virginia, 1720–1975)

1 3-pound chicken	1 small onion
2 pieces of celery	

Add a quart of water and simmer until meat is tender. Cool. Discard celery. Remove meat from bones and shred into small pieces. Then add:

¼ stick butter	1 quart corn (whole kernel,
1 cup chopped onion	canned or frozen or fresh)
1 quart butterbeans (canned	2 quarts tomatoes
or frozen are good; fresh is	3 medium potatoes, diced
better)	

Continue cooking over medium heat, adding water if necessary and stirring occasionally until separate identity of ingredients is no longer apparent—at least 5 hours. Season with salt, red pepper, and more black pepper than seems sensible—at least 2 teaspoons. Thicken with breadcrumbs, crackers, or biscuit crumbs.

YIELD: 4 to 6 servings.

THE LIME THAT

FAILED

Some people go to Key West for the fishing. Others are attracted by the sunsets in this southernmost American town. Preservationists like to stroll among the island's old homes, visiting the Hemingway mansion or admiring the double elephant folios in the handsomely renovated place where Audubon sojourned while spying on the birds of the Keys and the Dry Tortugas. Many picturesque bars beckon those in search of a bibulous vacation, and in Key West's generally permissive atmosphere, gay people have established a discreet niche. Myself, I drove down from Miami, 160 miles on a highway that arches over the water from key to key, impelled by a lifelong desire to taste an authentic Key lime pie.

As I crossed the last bridge, from Stock Island onto Key West, I assumed I was only minutes from enjoying a rich slice of Florida's most famous regional specialty. But after a week of stuffing down piece after piece of one so-called Key lime pie after another, intermitted by various limeades and lime daiquiris supposedly based on the juice of the small, thin-skinned, legendarily sour and aromatic fruit known as *Citrus aurantifolia*, I came to realize that probably none of these pies or potions contained a single drop of freshly squeezed Key lime juice.

Indeed, after some serious inquiry among local experts, I am now morally certain that virtually all "Key lime" pies and drinks not prepared in private homes in the Keys are actually made with the juice of the Tahiti (or Persian or Bearss) lime, which is not a true lime at all. This hybrid of mysterious origin is the "lime" sold in supermarkets all over the country. Grown primarily in southern Florida and eastern Mexico, it is a satisfactory fruit, but it is not at all the equal of its cousin, *C. aurantifolia* (a.k.a. Key lime, Mexican lime, or West Indian lime).

Roughly twice as large as the Key lime, the Tahiti has a thick skin and looks enough like a small lemon, right down to its pointy end, that it is marketed while its rind is still an immature green. At maturity, Tahitis (and Key limes) turn yellow, and it would be easy for a consumer to confuse Tahitis and lemons. No one, however, would make this mistake with mature yellow Key limes, which are almost perfectly spherical. Sliced open, both varieties of lime are yellow green inside, but Tahitis are seedless, while most Keys have several seeds. Thin-skinned Keys can be easily juiced by pressing them between the thumb and forefinger. And, most important of all, the juice of the Key lime tastes decisively different from the juice of the Tahiti. It is sourer and more complex. In other words, Key lime juice has more personality.

I tested this in a comparative tasting. I also have finally managed to taste a real Key lime pie. And I must insist that, contrary to the opinion of innumerable cookbook authors who claim that "regular" lime juice is a completely adequate substitute, the real thing is far tangier and more interesting than "Key lime" pies made with Tahiti juice. The peel, often grated into pie fillings, may also play a role in this difference, as Key limes have a distinctive essential oil in their peels, which is extracted industrially for cosmetics and for commercial flavoring. You can smell the delicious aroma easily if you hold the fruit to your nose.

It does not take a particularly educated nose or palate to appreciate the superiority and the greater sophistication of the Key lime. The problem is to find a Key lime.

In Key West, I made the rounds of local markets and fancy fruiterers in vain. Restaurants and drink stands used either Tahitis or a bottled juice sold in souvenir stands. This dull beverage, suspiciously labeled "real lime" juice, may, of course, be a chemically stabilized juice of real Key limes, but I doubt it. In any case, it is obviously not fresh juice, and anyone who has ever tasted freshly squeezed orange juice against juice that has been frozen or canned or merely stored in the refrigerator will know that the flavor degrades rapidly after squeezing.

Far and away the strongest argument against the likelihood of any commercial American Key lime product being made from Key limes is that there is no regular commercial source of Key limes in the Florida Keys or anywhere else in the country. According to reliable authority, the last remaining sizable grove of trees is located at Islamorada, about midway between Miami and Key West, in the backyard of a restaurateur who freezes the juice he produces and uses it entirely for his own restaurant.

The persistent gastroethnographer can, nevertheless, lay his hands on fresh Key limes in the Florida Keys. But it helps if you know a Conch. Conchs are indigenous residents of the

Keys (nicknamed after a shellfish abundant in local waters).
Some Conchs have thorny little Key lime trees in their back-
yards. I located a luxuriant fruit-bearing tree on the grounds
of my motel in Key West and two others in a private botanical
garden. Manny and Issa's Restaurant in Islamorada generously
provided me with a bag of fruit. It would evidently not be difficult to find other small-scale private sources. But all these trees
are mere remnants of what was once a thriving agricultural
industry in the Keys and in the southern tip of the Florida
mainland, where tropical weather and the good drainage of
rocky soil are favorable to this idiosyncratic plant.

No one knows when the first Key lime was planted in the
Keys. Citrus historians agree that the tree originated in Ma-
laysia or eastern India. It was first mentioned in Europe in the
thirteenth century, in Italy. Whether Columbus brought seeds
of *C. aurantifolia* with him to Haiti in 1493 is a matter of con-
jecture, but it seems probable, since limes were flourishing on
that island in 1520. Limes then spread gradually across the
West Indies, westward to Mexico and northward to the Florida
Keys, where trees were well established by 1839.

Primarily a home fruit throughout the remainder of the
nineteenth century, the lime became a commercial crop in the
Keys after 1906, when the combination of a severe hurricane
and soil depletion forced Conchs to abandon pineapple culture.
The Key lime was an ideal replacement since it thrives when
meagerly fed. Lime production in the Keys peaked around
1923. Shortly afterward, the hurricane of 1926 dealt the Florida
lime groves a death blow. The groves were never restored. It
was much easier to exploit the same land as residential real
estate for Northern vacationers and retirees or to replant it with
more practical crops. One of these was the anomalous Tahiti
lime. It probably arose from a chance cross in California,
which received large shipments of citrus fruit from Tahiti be-

tween 1850 and 1880. In any case, Tahiti limes were growing in Florida at least by 1883. Today, they are, to all intents and purposes, the only lime grown in the United States. Tahitis are also produced in Mexico, but primarily for export. Mexicans prefer true (Key) limes and pay a premium price for them, nearly twice what they will pay for Tahiti limes. No doubt smiling scornfully, Mexicans send us 16,620 metric tons of Tahitis in a year, but only about 62 tons of real limes, which are shipped into California and Arizona.

Americans, typically, have settled for a hybrid fruit of demonstrably inferior quality, but with ideal qualifications for modern agribusiness. The Tahiti lime is bigger and lends itself to mass-scale agriculture far more easily than the Key lime because it keeps better, has no thorns, and grows a thick skin perfect for machine handling and long truck trips. Of course, life in these United States goes on well enough without the Key lime. The traditional Key lime pie—a graham-cracker shell filled with a sour custard made from juice, egg yolks, and sweetened, condensed milk—tastes almost as good made with Tahiti lime juice. On the other hand, it is undeniably a fake.

Because of agronomic and financial reasons having nothing to do with food quality, we are all duped in a small way every time we buy a lime and get a convenient substitute. We are defrauded whenever we order a Key lime pie and are served a surrogate. And we are the victims of a horticultural shell game if we believe the Key lime is a rare and exotic form of lime. The poorest Caribbean can find real limes in his local marketplace, but in America we can only buy Tahiti limes in our glistening supermarkets. Even, or perhaps especially, in the Keys, the conspiracy to hide this botanical masquerade has succeeded almost completely in perpetuating the myth of a regional dish that actually disappeared, as far as the general public is concerned, almost as soon as it had been invented.

☞ GENE BARNES'S KEY LIME PIE

(Adapted from The Loaves and Fishes Cookbook, *by Susan Costner and Devon S. Fredericks, Wallflower Press, Box 1275, Bridgehampton, New York 11932)*

6 egg yolks, beaten	1 tablespoon grated lime peel
1 15-ounce can sweetened condensed milk	1 recipe graham-cracker crust (see below)
2 tablespoons evaporated milk	½ pint heavy cream, whipped
½ cup freshly squeezed Key lime juice	

(1) Beat together the egg yolks, the condensed milk, and the evaporated milk until smooth.

(2) Stir in the lime juice and lime peel.

(3) Line a 9-inch pie tin with the graham-cracker crust.

(4) Fill the crust with egg-milk-lime mixture.

(5) Freeze.

(6) When the filling has solidified, spread the top with whipped cream.

Y I E L D: 8 servings.

☞ GRAHAM-CRACKER CRUST

1 ¾ cups graham-cracker   ½ cup sugar
    crumbs   ⅓ cup butter, melted

Work all ingredients together. This is meant to be pressed into the pie tin by hand, not rolled.

☞ OLD SOUR

(*From* Conch Cooking, *Florida Keys Printing & Publishing,*
405 *Fleming Street, Key West, Florida* 33040)

2 cups Key lime juice   1 tablespoon salt

(1) Use ripe yellow limes only. Mix the salt and lime juice and let stand for a while. Strain through two layers of cheesecloth as often as necessary to let the juice run through freely.

(2) Then put it into bottles and let stand several weeks before using. Some say the old sour should be put into bottles of brown or green glass; others say it makes no difference.

☞ RAW CONCH SALAD

Skin the conchs and mince very fine. Chop onions very fine. Add salt, pepper, and old-sour or fresh lime juice. Let stand at least an hour to blend. Serve without lettuce. (Note: the recipe lacks quantities, but the resourceful cook will add enough onion to invigorate the salad without overwhelming it. Salt and pepper should also be added "to taste." Use enough old-sour or lime juice to moisten the conch bits and "cook" them, as in seviche.)

☞ CRAWFISH SALAD

1 pound cold boiled crawfish, minced	2 hard-boiled eggs, minced
½ cup minced celery	Salt
¼ cup minced onion	Mayonnaise
	Lime juice or old sour

(1) Cut everything very fine, add the salt and mayonnaise, and mix.

(2) Sprinkle the old sour over the top, and let blend. Just before serving, mix again thoroughly. This is served without lettuce.

YIELD: 4 servings.

☞ EGG LIME SOUP

(*Adapted from* Louise's Florida Cookbook, *by Louise Lamme, Star Press, Boynton Beach, Florida 33435*)

2 tablespoons melted butter	1 tablespoon chopped parsley
1 large onion, chopped	1 cup raw rice
½ cup diced celery	3 egg yolks
1 cup chopped carrots, cooked	1 teaspoon cornstarch
7 cups chicken stock	1 cup milk
Salt	Juice of 2 Key limes
Pepper	

(1) Sauté the onion, celery, and carrots in the butter.

(2) Transfer to a large pot and cover with the stock.

(3) Add salt, pepper, parsley, and rice. Bring to a boil, lower heat, and simmer until rice is chewy but not mushy.

(4) Mix egg yolks with cornstarch and milk. Then stir mixture into soup. Adjust heat when you do this so soup does not boil. As soon as the soup thickens, remove from heat and stir in lime juice.

Y I E L D: 8 to 10 servings.

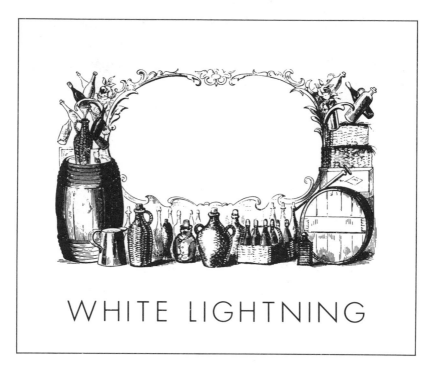

WHITE LIGHTNING

Like most traditional foods, white lightning is fast vanishing from the American scene. Outside of Appalachia, few people under the age of sixty have ever tasted the clear, raw, often sour, almost always illegal alcoholic drink. Moonshine, along with so much else in our comestible folklore, is a casualty of efficient federal regulation, big business, and the homogenizing forces of urban civilization.

In the opinion of many thoughtful observers, the demise of white lightning is a good thing. Howard Criswell, a spokesman for the U.S. Treasury Department's Bureau of Alcohol, Tobacco, and Firearms, the agency charged with rooting out distillers who don't pay federal excise tax on their liquor, points out that moonshiners are criminals who cheat the government of its rightful tithe. Moonshiners have been doing just that since the earliest days of the Republic, when, in 1791, Congress passed the first excise tax to help pay off the debt from the Revolutionary War. This act touched off the violent Whiskey Rebellion. But the government stood firm, and many farmer-distillers decamped for Kentucky's wilderness to escape the tax man.

By the early 1800's, Kentucky had several hundred small distilleries and a two-tiered system of sales—one legal, the other not. The difference between legitimate and illegitimate producers in those days was entirely a matter of tax compliance. They all manufactured essentially the same whiskey, basically a corn liquor sold straight from the still, unaged and brisk on the tongue. They were all fundamentally yeomen farmers far from Eastern markets, who could ship corn as liquor much more conveniently than they could ship plain corn because distillation reduced their grain crop to a manageable bulk with a limitless shelf life.

The whiskey turned out on those frontier farms by the most primitive methods of distillation was clear grain alcohol. It was, in fact, what we would call white lightning. Modern moonshiners often substitute sugar for corn in their mash because sugar increases their yield. But it comes to the same thing.

Bourbon is a sophisticated descendant of this original American booze. The amber, mellow drink, named for a county in Kentucky, came along later in our history than white lightning. The father of bourbon, Reverend Elijah Craig, perfected the first bourbon mash in Kentucky in the early nineteenth century, mixing rye, barley, and corn. The taste of Craig's whiskey won him lasting fame, but the perfection of what we know today as bourbon waited upon the arrival, in Frankfort, Kentucky, in the 1830's, of a Scottish physician named James Crow.

Crow devoted himself to the scientific improvement of our

native potion, which struck his cognac-trained palate as bar-
barously unrefined. Following European practice, Crow took
to aging his whiskey in white-oak barrels. Soon, other distillers
followed Crow's lead. One of them made use of a barrel with
charred staves because he was too parsimonious to throw it
out. Red, caramelized wood under the black surface imparted
a rich color to the whiskey aged in that serendipitously dam-
aged cask. Now, all bourbon is aged in charred oak barrels,
maturing until smooth and mahogany. This refined whiskey
utterly dominates production in the aboveground American
corn liquor industry. It is a better drink, more elegant and complex in taste than white lightning. Moonshine can, of course,
also be manufactured legally. But tax-paying distillers have
ceded the white lightning market, such as it is, to a motley
crew of Snuffy Smiths and thugs, willing to risk jail for a quick
buck selling untaxed alcohol—in Mason jars or by the drink—
to hillbillies and ghetto poor, at unlicensed taverns known as
shot houses or nip joints.

The moonshine industry once flourished on its own turf
and even expanded beyond it during Prohibition years, reach-
ing its zenith about 1950. The product was cheap. Law enforcement was a poor match for wily moonshiners, who in any
case were often acquitted by jurors they knew both as neighbors and as loyal customers. Moonshiners invented dozens of
ruses for hiding their crude pot stills in the woods, in caves,
or in barns, and managed to conceal their tracks by laying
down false trails.

It was an adventurous, romantic life, especially when the
time came to move several dozen cases of finished liquor from
still to point of sale without getting caught by lawmen. Some
moonshiners drove trucks with high sides or concealed the
whiskey under corn. Others used speeding escort cars as
decoys.

Such escapades yielded a rich body of legend that is still an important part of the folklore of the Southeast. Moonshiners even had their own argot for the parts of the still (thumper barrels, worms, heater boxes) and a special jargon anatomizing the process of distillation. As set down in *The Foxfire Book* (Anchor, 1972), this crapulous lexicon includes "dead devils" (tiny beads in the proof vial, which indicate that the whiskey has been proofed or diluted sufficiently), "high shots" (unproofed whiskey running as strong as 200 proof), and "slop" (what is left in the still when the alcohol level of the liquor coming out drops too low to use).

Even in polite circles in moonshining areas, some of this lingo is in current use. And people still joke that a man with a crease on the end of his nose must be a heavy imbiber of moonshine because when you drink straight from a Mason jar, the glass rim hits you in the nose.

But you hardly see a creased nose anymore. Higher levels of education, better jobs, and the greater availability of legal whiskey in once-dry states have all but cut the ground from under the moonshine business. Few young men want to produce it or buy it. Meanwhile, a propaganda campaign run by the Treasury Department has helped to stigmatize moonshining, making people aware that untaxed liquor is a drain on the commonweal and a peril to health. The antimoonshine literature explains that unscrupulous still operators contaminate their whiskey with toxic lead salts from car radiators used as cheapjack condensers instead of the conventional copper tubing.

To make matters worse, by the end of the sixties, courts were handing out moonshining convictions routinely and Treasury men found they could uncover many stills simply by monitoring suspiciously large sales of sugar. Indeed, sugar had become so basic to moonshining that the zoom in world sugar prices, which sent sweet tooths everywhere into a panic, had a lethal effect on marginal moonshiners. Old-timers who had kept working at their stills for lack of another vocation could no longer compete with cheap, legal whiskey. The high cost of sugar had priced them out of the market. These grizzled, folkloric bootleggers did not, by and large, return to moonshining, and few younger men moved in to replace them.

One retired moonshiner, Arthur ("Bad Eye") Williams remembers when he handled 500 cases of illegal whiskey in a week, fetching it from country stills and running it into Richmond, Virginia, where bootleggers like him used to congregate at an all-night restaurant in the Central Market and swap stories about fast chases with revenuers. His last arrest was in 1967, and after five years in federal prison, he finally went straight. Williams, half of his face disfigured from a booby trap that went off when he tried to steal a cache of moonshine as a boy, now finds the whiskey business too well policed, too risky. He hopes to make use of his special skills in a new, legit venture, a gasohol distillery.

Not every moonshiner in America has retired into nostalgia and law-abiding capitalism. Nearly everyone I have talked to in the Southeastern mountain area claims to have a source for white lightning, usually a backwoods practitioner operating on a small scale. In most cases, however, these anachronistic mini-distilleries play as insignificant a part in the overall picture of American liquor production as, say, the homespun wool turned out by individual hobbyists around the country does in the total output of yarn in the United States. But in a handful of rural counties, "homemade" liquor is big business, highly organized and on an industrial scale.

Franklin County, Virginia, just east of the Blue Ridge, is by far the leading center of untaxed whiskey production in the land. Not long ago, the crusading Franklin *News-Post* established this fact in a carefully documented front-page story headlined: "FRANKLIN NO. 1 MOONSHINE COUNTY. No other area even close." The paper's editor-publisher, Kermit W. Salyer, who has been battling local moonshine interests for years, printed official statistics showing that during a two-year period in the late seventies, authorities seized 165 stills in the county with a mash capacity of 125,000 gallons. One still, destroyed by lawmen in 1972 at a site disguised as a cemetery, had a mammoth 16,000-gallon capacity. Since it typically takes only five days to complete a "run" of a single batch of mash, that one site could have produced about 1.2 million gallons a year. With so much at stake, it is no wonder that the still owners do what they can to protect their investment.

Because of Salyer's statistical exposé, published in late 1979, the U.S. Treasury Department and the Virginia Department of Alcoholic Beverage Control staged a raid on stills in Franklin County in January 1980. The national media were invited to bear witness. Salyer, in an editorial, dismissed the raid as a publicity stunt and called for more money to be spent on routine enforcement. He had a point.

Certainly, it did not require national television coverage and a feature in the *New York Times* to reveal what had been common knowledge. Local authorities do not try to conceal or deny the prevalence of moonshining. The casual visitor to the county administrator's office cannot fail to notice that the painting on the wall behind the receptionist's desk is titled *Franklin County Steamer*. It is an attractive picture of a classic still.

When I passed through Franklin County recently, no raids were in progress and I was unable to taste any of the locally celebrated, homemade fruit brandies. But I was invited to try samples of local white lightning by W. Q. Overton, the sheriff, who presides over Franklin County's grim stone jail. There, in a locked closet, which serves as the county's evidence vault, were secreted three nondescript bottles of homegrown hooch. Two of them contained whiskey that was powerfully alcoholic, clear as water, reasonably smooth tasting, almost as refined as commercial vodka. The third was more classic and had the sour taste that aficionados of moonshine prefer. This sourness is caused by a complex of chemicals that "puke" out of the still at the beginning of a run. At legal distilleries, these "sour heads" are drawn off and thrown away. Moonshiners, however, intent on maximizing production, often leave them in. The resultant taste is roughly similar to the characteristic flavor of tequila or those French and Italian spirits distilled from the dregs of wine making, which are known as *marc* and *grappa*, respectively. I mean this comparison only as a rough approximation. It would take a serious chemical analysis of these quite different drinks to establish which of the dozens of possible chemicals lay behind the special taste of each one, but there is definitely a family resemblance. And that has social as well as technical importance. The French, the Italians, and the Mexicans have continued to drink vigorous alcoholic beverages derived from a rural tradition of home distillation. Only in America have we shunned our ancestral liquor, abandoning it almost completely to criminal producers and a shrinking clientele at the fringes of mainstream American life.

☞ MINT JULEP

1 tablespoon sugar	2 ounces bourbon
1 tablespoon chopped mint leaves	1 small bunch fresh mint
Shaved or crushed ice	2 drinking straws, cut short

(1) Put sugar and crushed mint in a mixing bowl. Crush to a paste with the back of a wooden spoon.

(2) Add a tablespoon of water to the mint-sugar paste and stir to produce a green syrup.

(3) Fill a metal cup half full of shaved or crushed ice. (Special julep cups are sold for this purpose, but any silver cup will do. In fact, an ordinary tall glass will suffice, but will not, of course, frost in the same dramatic fashion as silver.)

(4) Pour the green syrup and the bourbon over the ice. Slip in the sprig of mint so that it rises above the ice slightly. Insert the straws.

(5) Carefully place the cup on a tray, trying to avoid leaving fingermarks. Frost in the refrigerator. This will take 30 minutes to 1 hour.

YIELD: 1 julep.

☞ BOURBON BALLS

3 cups vanilla-wafer crumbs	3 tablespoons light corn syrup
1 cup ground pecans	½ cup bourbon
	1 cup confectioner's sugar

Combine all ingredients, form into balls about an inch in diameter, and roll in confectioner's sugar. Store in a tin box. YIELD: 50 to 60 bourbon balls.

☞ PLANTATION SPECIAL

½ heaping teaspoon orange marmalade	2 ounces white lightning
	Cracked ice
Nutmeg	

(1) Dissolve marmalade and a dash of nutmeg in a little water.

(2) Add white lightning, more nutmeg, and ice, and shake well.

(3) Serve in an old-fashioned glass with another dash of nutmeg on top.

YIELD: 1 serving.

LIVING HIGH
OFF THE HOG:
SMITHFIELD HAM

Parke Griffin passes the shaft of an ice pick slowly under his nose. He inhales gently, concentrating as he sniffs. Then he smiles. Griffin is not a homicidal maniac savoring his murder weapon; he is a sixty-one-year-old, tobacco-chewing Virginia farmer testing a country ham. Like his "one-horse" farmer father and generations of other rural folk in the American South, Griffin cures his own hams, smokes them, and then ages them over the summer until they turn dark red and take on a virile tang. The process is crude, does not involve refrigeration, and has been part of human life for as long as there have been hogs and salt. But it is also a subtle method, a gamble against weather, a matter of intuition and experience, a canny fight with bacteria. Parke Griffin is smiling because he is winning his bet.

The ice pick is his "test instrument." He hones it and

probes deep into the ham where it was cut from the haunch of a hog back in January. After a lifetime of testing country hams, he can detect spoilage as easily as a Bordeaux shipper can spot a bad vintage. The long, flat, streamlined, pepper-coated ham he has taken down from the rafters of his smokehouse is doing fine. By Thanksgiving, it will be perfect.

With 1,200 mandolin-shaped hams hanging in several aromatic tiers in two smokehouses behind his spruce- and myrtle-shaded house, Griffin is the very picture of a successful small entrepreneur. He will gross roughly $30,000 from this sideline, but he thinks of himself, correctly, as one of a vanishing breed of old-time ham men. Very few farmers in today's mechanized, competitive agricultural market have the time or the knowledge to cure country hams themselves. And those who do are hemmed in by official regulations that, in effect, keep them from competing with the four packing houses in Smithfield, Virginia, or with other big commercial packers that mass produce old-fashioned country hams. Griffin himself buys "green" (fresh) hams from the packers in Smithfield, the country ham center, a few miles from his house. It wouldn't pay him to comply with federal inspection rules so that he could sell pork he had slaughtered himself. As it is, he can sell his hams only in Virginia, not through the mails or any other avenue of interstate commerce. Indeed, he cannot even sell his hams in local stores or have them sliced on another retail merchant's slicing machine. None of these restrictions keep Griffin from selling out his stock, but they have tended to discourage most farmers from putting money into hams, especially into hams that must hang for a minimum of six months while inflation erodes their value.

Curing hams the old way is also a lot of work. Griffin begins in January. He sets out scalded wood salting racks on the floor of his smokehouse. On these racks he lays out one hundred hams at a time, lays them out flat, with the "face" (the cut side) up, then sprinkles on a small amount of saltpeter. Griffin says he uses only four ounces of saltpeter per hundredweight of ham and lets it soak in all day "until dinner." (Saltpeter colors ham, bacon, and other prepared meats red. It is under heavy attack as a cancer agent, but pork producers, who defend it as a protection against botulism, argue that it has been in common use for centuries, does not present a provable threat to health in normal use, and should not be banned.)

Next, Griffin packs his ham in salt, ordinary table salt that he buys in eighty-pound bags. Some people use flake salt, which does not roll off the ham. In either case, the method is the same, a dry cure.

Old-style country hams, and also Italian prosciutto, are not soaked in brine (salt dissolved in water). They undergo a slower cure with dry salt, which has to dissolve in the ham's natural moisture and therefore penetrates pork more slowly than brine. The dry cure is also riskier because it gives bacteria a better chance of acting if the weather turns suddenly warm. But proponents of Smithfield-style hams and of prosciutto both assert that dry curing is a more refined method that yields a ham of supreme character. Prosciutto is, however, much more lightly salted than Smithfield ham; it is cured in the mountains outside Parma where the constant cool weather and altitude cooperate in lowering the level of natural bacterial activity.

In Smithfield, once a prospering port, the warm climate and low altitude oblige heavier salting. All Smithfield country hams are liberally covered with salt and left to cure for a few days. Parke Griffin generally waits five days. Nancy Warner Dashiell, whose brick smokehouse at nearby Berry Hill Farm is more than 200 years old, waits only four days. At any rate, during that time, the hams "drink" most of the salt. The floor of the smokehouse fills with natural brine that drips down from the hams.

After this first salting, the hams are salted again and left for three to five weeks, depending on the weather. In warm weather, the hams take the salt faster and are cured for a shorter period. Obviously, longer salting gives a saltier final taste. Different palates prefer different degrees of saltiness. In any case, all American country hams are salty, much saltier than prosciutto. But this is only part of the difference between these hams. After it has finished curing, prosciutto is simply hung to dry for six months in the mountain air and then eaten raw.

American country hams, which are normally eaten fully cooked, are much more thoroughly treated than prosciutto. After the curing period ends, the hams are washed off with hot water to remove the salt, then pepper is rubbed into the faces of the hams to seal them off from infection and insect infestation. Finally, they are hung high in the smokehouse, hung carefully so that they do not touch each other, which would cause "bad spots." When the hams have dried for a few days, smoking begins.

The various ham experts I talked to in and around Smithfield each had a different, personal approach to smoking, but they all burned some kind of hardwood—apple, red oak, or even fallen pecan boughs—smothering the fire with wet sawdust and taking their own good time about it. Nancy Dashiell says, "I smoke the meat three times a week, alternating days, for two weeks, then twice a week for a month until it has a good brown color."

Davis Lee Godwin and Tip Spivey, two old farm boys who cure hams in Windsor, Virginia, as a hobby—and a memorial to their youth, when they would trade home-cured hams for groceries during the cash drought of summer—both think that the slow smoking and "individual handling" they give their hams makes them superior to packers' hams. They also favor extremely long hanging, one and a half years or longer, so that the meat ages to an extreme density, turns very red, "marbleizes," and acquires a strong tang.

I was able to buy the last of their 1978 hams, an eighteen-month-old beauty. It was coated with a patina of green mold, a harmless badge of venerability that sometimes fools ham neophytes into throwing out a precious old treasure. I soaked mine longer than standard directions call for (see recipe below), for a day and a half. Because Smithfield hams are long and flat, it took a very large pot to facilitate the cure. They also come with the hock, the long narrow bone just above the foot, still attached. I cut off the hock and used it in pea soup so that I could fit the main part of the ham into my biggest pot. Soaked and slowly cooked, the ham emerged beautifully tender, deep red, and with a taste of powerful sophistication. Was it better than the packers' ham I had tasted at the Wakefield Virginia Diner in Wakefield, a twenty-minute drive from Smithfield? Or the razor-thin slices of estimable ham they serve at the charming old Smithfield Inn, that shrine of Tidewater Virginia cuisine? This is obviously a matter of taste. Perhaps I have not been eating country hams frequently enough or long enough to have formed a clear bias. I liked all those hams. Each one had the flavor impact and directness of a young, rural, pioneer country. Moreover, they all had the paradoxical combination of innocence and refinement that comes from two centuries of practice with an inherently primitive technique. It did, nevertheless, seem to me that the old ham from Godwin and Spivey's smokehouse had something extra, the complexity of taste that, in its entirely different way, a carefully handled great wine can display.

This is certainly the feeling of old-time farmers around

Smithfield, who have watched their way of life erode over the last fifty years, while the packing houses grew into big business. At Berry Hill Farm, which adjoins the Gwaltney packing house, the 300-year-old communal ritual of hog killing continued in the old way until the 1950's. Hogs were slaughtered, hung on gallows to cool, then butchered and trimmed. Lard was rendered in big pots. Nothing was thrown away, from snout to tail. Nancy Dashiell still supervises hog slaughtering for family use, and in her smokehouse, you see not only hams and sides of bacon but also jowls (pronounced "joels" locally) hung by the tongue with the teeth gleaming in the half dark. But the almost tribal ceremony of hog slaughtering is now only a memory from the recent past.

"Then," writes another Smithfield woman, Mrs. Dewitt Griffin, "people worked by the sun and not by the clock and they worked hard so by the time they could eat, they were really hungry. I baked my pies beforehand, and then each day I made large pans of potato pudding, cooked beans, cabbage, and snaps and made cornbread and biscuits to serve with the fresh pork. Everything was eaten, which made me feel good."

Until the twenties, Smithfield was not a major packing center. It was the national peanut capital. But the peanut warehouses burned in 1921, and nearby Suffolk, with its better rail connections, forged ahead as a peanut entrepôt. Smithfield then fell into the big-time ham business almost by default. By 1939, the Gwaltney family and other packers had developed a modern meat-packing industry with dry-cure, aged ham as its emblem.

In the early days of the Smithfield packing industry, farmers would slaughter their own hogs and bring them to Smithfield on flat wagons, hundreds of carcass-laden wagons waiting in line. Federal meat regulations have ended all that, and the packing houses now do their own slaughtering. Each week

90,000 hogs are turned into pork at the two largest packing plants.

Very little of this meat is made into traditional Smithfield hams. At Gwaltney's, now a subsidiary of ITT, only about 50,000 of the company's annual total of more than two million hams are prepared in the canonical way. The Smithfield ham market is a special market. But it is to the Gwaltney company's credit that it persists with its country ham operation in a special building with a gigantic internal wood smokehouse. The old methods are followed with religious devotion and supervised by a Smithfield veteran who has a testing ice pick in his office and who has insisted on traditional techniques despite some initial meddling from the corporate headquarters in Rye, New York.

Have precise temperature controls and mass production in the packing plants cut into the quality of Smithfield hams? Not as far as I could tell. More pertinently, in the opinion of the white-haired butcher who runs the folkloric meat department of West's Supermarket at the end of Smithfield's Victorian main street, packers' old-cure hams are just fine. Although he sells hams he cures himself (as well as cured jowls and tails), the butcher also sells packers' hams and doesn't have a bad word to say about them.

If the country ham is an endangered species, it is not the fault of anyone in Smithfield. It is the result of changes in the outside world, of a new national taste formed by square, water-cured hams in cans, and of naïve people who throw away gift Smithfield hams because they find them too salty. Meanwhile, the old rural life around Smithfield may be vanishing. A newly widened highway will soon bring more commuters from Newport News, twenty miles away. Despite these menaces, the Smithfield ham still hangs on as a savory relic of America's early days. Parke Griffin is still spry enough to perch in his smokehouse rafters in a cloud of pepper, babying his hams. And at least one old-fashioned Smithfield ham will probably survive into the age of fusion. It is seventy-seven years old, woody and inedible, but still intact. One of the Gwaltneys took it with him when ITT bought him out. It is now installed in the office at his Chevrolet dealership, a wizened symbol of the world we are losing.

☞ HAM BISCUITS

2 cups flour

4 teaspoons baking powder

Pinch of salt

½ cup ground Smithfield ham

2 tablespoons shortening

¾ cup milk

(1) Preheat oven to 400 degrees.

(2) Sift flour and baking powder. Mix with salt and ham.

(3) Cut in shortening with knife until all has the consistency of meal.

(4) Add milk, handling as little as possible. Pat out with hands or roll on floured board. Cut out and bake on a greased cookie sheet until brown.

YIELD: About 1 dozen biscuits.

PLANTER'S LUNCH

North of Charleston, in that swampy paradise for waterfowl known as the South Carolina Low Country, is a 9,000-acre, quondam rice plantation I will call Tara. It began as a cypress swamp where Indians fished. Toward the end of the seventeenth century, European settlers discovered that rice would thrive in the murky waters that ran through it to the Atlantic. Slaves who spoke the West-African/English Gullah patois extirpated the cypress and dug the dikes for rice impoundments. The crop was so lucrative that it took two centuries before a combination of hurricanes, competition from more economical rice fields in other states, and Reconstruction brought an end to Carolina riziculture. The coup de grace came in 1942, when hydroelectric damming let sea water flow inland and turned the Low Country into a brackish fen.

By then, certain rich Yankees had bought control of many

of the old estates. They converted the impoundments into game preserves and managed their salty waters so that they produced food for shootable birds. The only constant in this man-churned environment was the black population. Some descendants of the old slave communities remained, while rice mills and whole "streets" of slave cabins collapsed.

One such black retainer was on hand, early in this century, when Tara's new Yankee owner arrived, unannounced, in a private plane and landed in a field. The black servant had never seen a plane before, never heard of one, but he gathered his courage and walked forward to greet the young visitor from the sky.

"Hello, Massa Jesus," he said. "And how's your Pa?" Today, that man's grandson carries on the family tradition at Tara. He lives by the old and crumbling rice mill, and he speaks Gullah with his wife, who cooks plantation meals in the big house. Her fried chicken is a paradigm of the best in Southern cooking. Her hot biscuits define delicacy in baking. When this dignified, taciturn old woman makes crab cakes, they are almost pure crabmeat and light and crisp.

Like other traditional Low Country cooks, she uses rendered pork fat, from bacon or hog jowl, where most of us would use butter or oil. When she makes shrimp stew, she begins by frying bacon in the pot.

There is nothing more fundamental to a cuisine than its fat. In his classic study of French regional cooking, *The Food of France*, Waverley Root divides France into three parts, the "domains" of butter, olive oil, and lard (meaning any kind of pork fat as well as goose fat).

In the Old South, salt-cured pork was the standard source of cooking fat, even in seafood dishes. Oysters were prepared this way, for example, in brown oyster stew with benne (sesame) seed (see recipe). Benne was introduced by slaves, who considered it a lucky plant. Modern versions of this Afro-American dish are done with more readily available bacon, instead of cured "side meat" or jowl.

Oysters continue to be a mainstay of Low Country seafood. At Tara, on special occasions, local gentry gather for an open-air oyster roast. This feast is similar in type to the New England clambake, but it is far simpler. Indeed, a Low Country oyster roast requires nothing except a charcoal fire, a grill, bushels of single select McClellanville oysters from just down the coast, and burlap sacks. You dump the oysters on the fire, cover them with burlap, and as soon as they start to open, you shovel them onto a table covered with paper.

Guests are provided with one work glove, to protect the hand that holds the oyster, and an oyster knife to cut the bivalve loose. I consumed several dozen juicy charcoal-roasted oysters one nippy evening. As if this were not enough, the natural order of things in the Low Country supplies an extra bonus for the omnivorous diner at an oyster roast. Every so often, one of the oysters contains a small, pink softshelled crab.

Pinnotheres ostreum, called oyster or pea crab, is a tiny creature that attains a maximum width of one and a half centimeters. At an early stage, it crawls inside an oyster and installs itself for a lazy, commensal existence. Harmless to its host, the oyster crab merely uses the larger animal as an apartment. Male oyster crabs do migrate in search of a female residing in another oyster, but once the male visitor has copulated, he dies.

Our forebears prized these tiny shellfish. Alan Davidson, in *North Atlantic Seafood,* reminds us that George Washington loved them so well that *P. ostreum* was almost renamed the Washington crab. The first President often saw them served floating on top of an oyster stew. And in palmier days, Americans frequently ate oyster crabs sautéed or deep-fried, with or without oysters. Davidson also mentions two recipes from a Philadelphia cookbook published in 1901: an omelet containing twenty-five to forty oyster crabs and a "real extravaganza" called Canopy à la Lorenzo, which consists of a bell-shaped crouton stuffed with fifty oyster crabs, one quarter of a truffle, crab meat, chicken meat, and cream, all dusted with "green" breadcrumbs.

I doubt that anyone in the South Carolina Low Country still serves oyster crab as a separate dish, but the culinary past persists at old homes like Tara, because the memory of how to live off local products lives on. And the old cypress swamps still produce most of the old-time foods, including a yellow-bellied turtle called terrapin or cooter. Certain foods common all over the South—Jerusalem artichoke, mustard pickle, pickled okra—are widely available in Charleston supermarkets. You can buy folkloric, if foxy, wine fermented from the juice of the scuppernong grape in the gourmet shop in the shopping arcade in Charleston's boutique-filled former slave market.

Meat counters routinely sell shreds of bacon, for rendering. And the local predilection for rice has more than survived the demise of South Carolina's own rice production. Local cookbooks are filled with recipes for pilaus, elaborate risotto-like dishes of rice garnished with okra, chicken, or shrimp. The prevailing local pronunciation of pilau, no doubt a Gullah adaptation, sounds like "perloo."

So Low Country cooking traditions are not all shriveling up in the face of competition from the mainstream culture. But culinary tradition in and around Charleston can only be as vigorous as the people who cook it. And eat it.

The ideal mode of transmission of traditional food knowledge is from an expert cook to an apprentice, in the same household, in a culturally and agriculturally stable situation. This perfect set of circumstances obtained in the South in general, and on large Southern plantations in particular, for generations. And even after Low Country plantations were sold to Yankees during the "second reconstruction" following the 1929 crash, kitchen staffs still carried on the practices of their mothers and grandmothers. Only a generation ago, there were still blacks at Tara who had never set foot off the property.

Today, the Tara cook is probably the last in her line. And even her cooking shows signs of a corrupting contact with the outside world and its convenience foods. Her shrimp stew, for example, contains bottled ketchup, bottled Texas Pete hot sauce as well as bottled Lea & Perrins steak sauce.

In Charleston, the same discontinuity is detectable even in places where tradition is most militantly affected. A woman on the local Junior League committee responsible for the group's cookbook, *Charleston Receipts,* told me the book contained old-fashioned terminology, such as "1 blade of mace," which she didn't understand.

Actually, it is a good thing that the texts of these recipes have been preserved with their antique references to "blades" and "pecks." The honest scribes at the Charleston Junior League have reproduced on paper the practice of their mothers and their mothers' cooks without so much as a phrase of modern revision. But how much longer the women in Charleston's stately and well-kept homes will continue to cook that hearty combination of rice and cow peas (small legumes resembling miniature black-eyed peas, also called field peas) called Hoppin' John on New Year's Day is not clear. The dish, which gets its special flavor from rendered hog jowl or bacon, dates back at least as far as 1841, when, by oral tradition, it was hawked in the streets of Charleston by a crippled black who identified himself as Hoppin' John.

This superb concoction will continue to stick to Low Country ribs as long as someone keeps on growing cow peas in response to the demands of those astute enough to crave this savory source of protein. Other aspects of South Carolina Low Country cooking are more fragile, more dependent on social context and culinary skill. I have in mind the lunch that took place after Tara's most recent oyster roast.

Inevitably, some of the roasted oysters were left over. With consummate delicacy, the old cook breaded them lightly and fried them. They came out crisp, but still succulent and full of the smoky taste of the previous night's outdoor feast.

At Tara, they can still pull off this sort of culinary magic, but it is a special place, costly to maintain. It is also gravely menaced by a plan to redredge neighboring rivers, which will desalinify Low Country rice impoundments and make them unfit for supporting the carefully nurtured plants that attract the game birds that currently attract wealthy Yankee owners. The trend, in any case, is for such Low Country plantations to be donated to the public as nature conservancies. In one such 20,000-acre tract that I toured, the endangered red-cockaded woodpecker finds a safe niche, and a protected herd of deer feed on corn set out for them in troughs. The former black staff is long gone, their church abandoned. Nature stands still in this place, embalmed by vigorous and ingenious human efforts to maintain a hunter's paradise, but the human presence has dwindled to a small band of environmental biologists, gifted at providing a welcome for the semipalmated plover, but not primarily concerned with the survival of shrimp stew.

☞ HOPPIN' JOHN WITH HOG JOWL

(Adapted from Rice Recipes, *Georgetown County Historical Commission, Georgetown, South Carolina 29440)*

2 cups cow (field) peas or black-eyed peas, soaked overnight	Salt
	Pepper
	1 cup rice
½ pound smoked hog jowl	

(1) Drain and rinse peas in a colander. Set in a large pot with the hog jowl. Cover with 8 cups water. Add salt and pepper to taste and boil until peas are tender.

(2) Remove jowl. Cut off skin and discard. Cut meat into small pieces. Reserve.

(3) Drain peas, reserving cooking liquid.

(4) Put 1 cup of cooked peas in a pot with the rice and 2½ cups cooking liquid. Bring to a boil, reduce heat to low, cover, and cook until rice is tender.

(5) While rice is cooking, fry jowl pieces until crisp. Drain and reserve.

(6) On a serving platter, combine pea-rice mixture, remaining cooked peas, and cooking liquid. Place fried jowl pieces on top.

YIELD: 8 to 10 servings.

Eleven recipes adapted from *Charleston Receipts,* collected by the Junior League of Charleston, P.O. Box 177, Charleston, South Carolina 29402:

☞ MRS. RALPH IZARD'S "AWENDAW"

1½ cups cooked hominy	1½ cups milk
1 heaping tablespoon butter	¾ cup cornmeal
3 eggs, lightly beaten	½ teaspoon salt

(1) Preheat oven to 375 degrees.

(2) While hominy is still hot, add butter and eggs.

(3) Gradually, stir in milk and, when well mixed, stir in cornmeal and salt. The batter should be like thick custard.

(4) Pour batter into deep, greased pan and bake 10 minutes.

YIELD: 6 to 8 servings.

☞ LOUISA STONEY'S BROWN OYSTER STEW

WITH BENNE (SESAME) SEED

4 slices bacon	2 tablespoons sesame seeds
1 large onion, sliced	parched in a heavy pan on
2 tablespoons flour	the stove until browned
1½ cups oyster liquor,	2 cups shucked oysters
approximately	Cooked rice or hominy

(1) Fry the bacon and onion until brown, then remove them from the pan with a slotted spoon.

(2) Shake the flour into the hot grease and stir vigorously until flour is brown.

(3) Remove from heat and gradually add oyster liquor until the mixture is smooth.

(4) Pound the sesame seeds, using mortar and pestle.

(5) Return flour mixture to heat and stir until slightly thickened. Then add sesame seeds.

(6) Lastly, add oysters and poach until the edges curl. Serve over rice or hominy.

Y I E L D: 6 servings.

☞ TURTLE SOUP

1 large or 2 small yellow-bellied rice-field "cooters" (*Pseudemys scripta scripta*), preferably female	Salt Pepper, red and black 1 teaspoon thyme 1 large onion, chopped

(1) Butcher turtle, chop off head. Let stand, head end down, until completely bled. Scald in boiling water for 5 minutes. Then crack or cut through shell with a hatchet, taking care not to damage eggs. Reserve eggs. Cut away hind and forequarters, the liver, and a strip of white meat adhering to the back of the shell. Peel off outer skin and discard.

(2) Bring 4 quarts of water to a rolling boil. Add skinned turtle meat and liver, along with seasonings and the onion. Reduce heat and simmer for 2 hours or until meat begins to fall off bones.

(3) Remove meat and liver with a slotted spoon. Pull off bones and discard.

(4) Chop or grind meat. Chop liver roughly. Return meat and liver to the soup. Correct seasoning. Return to the boil, reduce heat, and add turtle eggs. Continue cooking for 20 minutes.

Y I E L D: 6 to 8 servings.

☞ FREDERICK A. TRAUT'S RICE WINE

1 large box seeded raisins	1 orange, sliced
1½ pounds raw rice	1 yeast cake
2½ pounds granulated sugar	1 gallon tepid water

(1) Put all ingredients in stone crock and cover 3 weeks to 1 month, depending on temperature. In hot weather, the process goes faster.

(2) Stir with wooden spoon daily for a week, every other day the second week, then not at all. Strain. Next day, pour through filter paper. Bottle and set aside 6 months to 1 year.

☞ RUTH WALKER GASDEN'S

BLACKBERRY WINE

7 quarts blackberries, mashed	1 egg white
	7 pounds sugar

(1) To blackberries, add 3½ quarts water and let stand for 24 hours, then strain through thin cloth.

(2) Beat egg white, add sugar and 2 quarts water. Boil 5 minutes. Skim. When syrup is cool, add to blackberry juice. Stir well and place in jar.

(3) Skim each morning for 10 days, followed by a good stir each time; then put in demijohn. Do not cork. Cover with cloth and leave until it ceases to ferment.

(4) Siphon off and bottle.

☞ MARGARET WALKER'S

SCUPPERNONG WINE

8 quarts grapes   3 pounds sugar

(1) Mash the grapes.

(2) Pour on 2 quarts boiling water.

(3) Let stand 36 hours. Strain and add sugar.

(4) Bottle and let stand uncorked until all fermentation is over, keeping bottles full.

☞ CAROLINE DARDEN HURT'S SMITHFIELD-

HAM STUFFED CHICKEN BREASTS

2 to 3 chicken breasts, deboned and halved	2 tablespoons melted butter
4 tablespoons melted butter	1 cup bread crumbs
Salt	2 tablespoons parsley
4 to 6 slices Smithfield ham (or ¾ cup ground ham)	1 teaspoon sugar
	¼ teaspoon sage

(1) Preheat oven to 350 degrees.

(2) Pound chicken breasts skin side down to a thickness of ¼ inch.

(3) Brush with melted butter. Lightly salt. Place a ham slice or 2 tablespoons ground ham over each breast.

(4) Meanwhile mix remaining ingredients and toss well. Spread 1 to 2 tablespoons resulting mixture over ham-covered chicken.

(5) Roll up chicken breasts, dip each in melted butter

and then in topping mix. Place in lightly greased baking pan. Drizzle any leftover topping mixture and butter over chicken. Bake for approximately 1 hour or until done.

   Y I E L D: 4 servings.

☞ DOLLY WARD BATTEN'S VEGETABLE

HAM BONE SOUP

5 small potatoes, diced	Salt
2 carrots, diced	1 teaspoon pepper
2 ribs celery, diced	1 tablespoon sugar
1 quart butterbeans	1 quart tomato juice
1 medium onion, diced	1 ham bone
2 cups corn	

   (1) Cover potatoes, carrots, celery, butterbeans, and onion with water and cook for 45 minutes.

   (2) Add remaining ingredients and simmer for 1 hour or until done.

   Y I E L D: 6 to 8 servings.

☞ JOSEPHINE WALKER'S GREAT-GRAND-

MOTHER'S WHOLE ARTICHOKE PICKLE

1 peck (32 cups) Jerusalem artichokes	1 cup brown sugar
	2 tablespoons celery seed
Salt	2 tablespoons allspice
1 small lump alum	2 tablespoons cloves
4 tablespoons mustard seed	1 cup powdered mustard
1 gallon vinegar	

(1) Wash and scrape artichokes and let them stand overnight in water to which salt has been added (1 tablespoon to each quart).

(2) Drain. Soak for a day in water to which the alum has been added.

(3) Rinse well.

(4) Soak mustard seed in small amount of vinegar.

(5) Boil rest of vinegar and sugar and spices a few minutes. Let cook.

(6) Add mustard and mustard seed.

(7) Put artichokes in a crock and add liquid mixture. Let stand at least a week before using. Dip artichokes out as desired. When supply is exhausted, more brine-soaked artichokes may be added to same liquid.

☞ HARRIET MAYBANK ROYALL'S

CHOPPED ARTICHOKE PICKLE

3 quarts Jerusalem artichokes	1 large cauliflower
4 cups onions	2 cups salt
6 bell peppers	

SAUCE	1 tablespoon turmeric
1 cup flour	4 cups sugar
6 tablespoons dry mustard	2 quarts vinegar

(1) Slice or chop artichokes and onions. Cut peppers fine and break cauliflower into flowerets.

(2) Mix all together and cover with salt and 1 gallon water. Let stand 24 hours.

(3) Pour into colander and drain well.

(4) Mix all dry ingredients for sauce and add enough vinegar to make a paste. Heat rest of vinegar and pour over mustard mixture. Return to stove and boil until it thickens, stirring constantly.

(5) Add vegetables, bring to boil, and seal in sterilized jars while hot.

YIELD: 16 to 20 cups.

☞ ESTHER GREGORIE GRAY'S

ICED GREEN TOMATO PICKLES

7 pounds green tomatoes	1 teaspoon ginger
3 cups powdered yard lime	1 teaspoon allspice
dissolved in 2 gallons water	1 teaspoon celery seed
5 pounds sugar	1 teaspoon mace
3 pints vinegar	1 teaspoon cinnamon
1 teaspoon ground cloves	Green vegetable coloring

(1) Soak sliced tomatoes in lime water 24 hours.

(2) Drain. Soak in fresh water for 4 hours, changing water every half hour. Drain well.

(3) Make a syrup of sugar and vinegar and add spices. Bring syrup to a boil and pour over tomatoes. Let stand overnight.

(4) Next morning, boil for an hour or until tomatoes are clear. Add several drops of green vegetable coloring to the liquid. Seal in sterilized jars while hot.

YIELD: 8 pints.

Three recipes adapted from 200 *Years of Charleston Cooking* (New York: Harrison Smith and Robert Haas, Inc., 1930):

☞ SHRIMP PILAU

4 slices bacon	1 cup raw rice
1 small onion, finely chopped	1½ cups peeled cooked shrimp
2½ cups canned tomatoes	Salt

(1) Cut the bacon into inch pieces and fry until crisp. Remove from the pan, reserve, and brown the onion in the bacon fat. Add the tomatoes and let cook for a few minutes.

(2) Add the rice and steam in the upper part of a double boiler until the rice is cooked —about 45 minutes.

(3) Preheat oven to 350 degrees.

(4) Add shrimp and bacon and turn into a baking dish. Bake for about 15 minutes. This should be rather solid in texture, and the rice, while perfectly cooked, will not be as soft as when cooked by our usual method of boiling in quantities of water.

YIELD: 6 servings.

☞ JOE ROBERTSON'S CALAPASH

(TERRAPIN IN THE BACK)

(1) The rice field "cooter" or terrapin is first killed and allowed to drip, head down. In extracting the meat, remove the bottom of the shell. Care should be taken to get this out in pieces as large as possible.

(2) Then boil for at least 4 to 5 hours over a slow heat, depending upon age of the terrapin, when a rich brown thick soup or stew is obtained. Seasoning should be added at time of boiling, such as salt, pepper (red and black). Some prefer a small quantity of white or Irish potatoes and a little onion.

(3) When thoroughly cooked, the meat should be cut

into small pieces with a sharp knife or scissors (across grain, for if cut otherwise, it will have a tendency to become stringy).

(4) The back of the "cooter," having been cleaned thoroughly both inside and out, is then used as the container for the stew, to which bread or biscuit crumbs and ample butter are added. This is placed in the upper part of the oven, a slow heat (300 degrees) rather than a fast one being preferable, for about ½ hour, after which time the top will form a brown and crispy crust. Particular care should be exercised to serve very hot.

☞ CALAPASH II

(Caroline P. Rutledge, Hampton Plantation, Santee River, South Carolina)

(1) Prepare the terrapin as for soup, put it on to boil with just enough water to cover it (long boiling makes it stringy), season with black and red pepper, salt, onion, and a little thyme. When the flesh becomes tender, remove all bones and thicken with wheat flour or cornstarch which has been mixed with cold water to the consistency of cream and which is free from lumps. Let the terrapin boil long enough to cook the flour.

(2) Remove from the fire and add 1 good tablespoon of butter, a wine glass of wine or good whiskey, a pinch of cloves and mace to taste, and lemon to taste. Have the back of the terrapin ready, which must be scalded and scraped, make a stiff dough of flour and water, form a bank around the shell, pour the mixture in, and dust the top well with pounded biscuit crumbs. Place several terrapin eggs, which have been boiled and removed from the shell, over the top, and heat in the oven until the top is of a light brown.

HOT CAJUN SAUSAGE

Dudley Hebert stirred the big pot with a short-handled canoe paddle, gently prodding thirty-five pounds of pork and pork innards, while they cooked almost to the point of disintegration. Standing in the improvised kitchen at Arceneaux Park in Broussard, Louisiana, some little children and adults watched as he ground that meat and mixed it with rice and lots of red pepper. Then he showed them how to stuff this "rice dressing" into sausage casings. Mr. Hebert and his collaborator, Elmer Girouard, used a hollow, open-ended cow horn to do the stuffing. The horn once belonged to Mr. Girouard's grandfather, who had always used it to stuff sausage on his farm in southwestern Louisiana, when he and his family slaughtered hogs in the preserving cold of a winter day and processed every shred of the animal, from head to hock. Being Cajuns, they spoke

French, and called this gala pork butchering event a *boucherie*. And the loose sausage they made—a fiery, pale-colored specialty with a strong taste of liver and kidney—they called *boudin blanc*. Traditional Cajun *boudin blanc* can still be found in Cajun country. Indeed, last February in Broussard, it was impossible to avoid.

Broussard is somewhere in between being a drab, post-Depression farm center and a suburb of bustling Lafayette, ten miles to the north. This year the Broussard Jaycees and Jaynes sponsored the second annual Louisiana Boudin Festival. Local *boudin* factories worked overtime to produce thousands of pounds of sausages. Hebert and Girouard did their demonstration. Several young men and women competed in the *boudin*-eating contest, slurping stupendous quantities of pork and rice stuffing out of long, drooping casings.

I myself consumed an immoderate number of *boudins*, warding off the chill of an incessant winter drizzle with their warming spices. I ate *boudins* from all the booths, including a seafood *boudin*, heterodox but delicious. Somewhat bloated with all this gorging, I began to see the justice of an opinion expressed by John Norbert, a professional *boudiniste* at one of the booths. "The secret of a good *boudin*," he averred, "is seasoning plus more meat than rice."

With these words fresh in mind, I joined forces with *boudin* aficionado Barry Jean Ancelet, a young and impassioned Cajun folklorist at the University of Southwestern Louisiana in Lafayette, who introduced me to the higher arcana of *boudin* at a nearby supermarket called Dud Breaux's. The pork-rice ratio seemed just about ideal as Ancelet, his family, and I worked our way through a few pounds of sausage hot from the pot at Dud Breaux's. We threw the casings to the Ancelet dog and launched into the vexed question of Cajun culture.

The *boudin* is a spongy but natural platform from which to rise to the larger issue of Cajun identity and survival because *boudin*—ungainly, wildly spiced, and messy to eat—has become part of the stereotype of the Cajun in our time.

"Cajun" itself is an emblem of cultural misunderstanding, corrupted from the French *acadien,* the name given to French settlers driven out of Nova Scotia (then called Acadia) in 1753. As they made their way south, an unfriendly Anglophone North America dubbed them Cajuns. Arriving in southwestern Louisiana's malaria-infested bayous and isolated lowlands about 1765, they found a refuge where they could carry on peacefully as an ignored, French-speaking majority. "They were the melting pot here," says Barry Ancelet.

They were the mainstream society. All through the nineteenth century, other groups came in and adopted French, people with names like Johnson, Segura, and Schneider. The original Cajuns were not immigrants to the United States. They were here before there was a United States. My grandmother objected when a nephew of hers married *"une américaine."*

As late as the turn of the century, Cajun culture was all there was around here. Hell, everyone was eating *boudin.* Then the Anglo-American world began to press in. Oil was found in Jennings, at the so-called Evangeline field. (I really resent the whole Evangeline business, having the rest of the world learn about us through that poem. Longfellow never met a Cajun. And he wrote in English.) Oil brought in a money economy and an English-speaking population. Then the mandatory education act established a school system that forced our kids to learn English. And World War I took a whole generation of Cajuns away from home, where they saw for the first time that they were a minority. The mass media finished the job of putting our culture in danger, by providing slick programming that was much better than anything coming from here. People began to feel their culture was low class, something to leave behind.

With all these external pressures on them, it was no wonder that many Cajuns fled into assimilation or as far away as they could from the traditional life of the Cajun "coonass," a local pejorative probably drawn from the French slang term *conasse*, meaning a stupid person or, as Vaughan Burdin Baker puts it in the Junior League of Lafayette's Cajun cookbook, *Talk About Good*, "an ignorant and superstitious individual speaking ungrammatical and thickly accented English, eating *boudin* and two-stepping to a cacophonous accordion."

Currently, Ancelet estimates that there are about one million French-speaking people in Louisiana, of whom only one-third to one-half use French primarily. This is a sharp decline from the 100 percent of a few decades ago. But there are counterforces at work. Cajun music has undergone a serious revival. French, albeit standard French, is now promoted officially in local schools. And the University of Southwestern Louisiana fosters Cajun traditions through the Center for Acadian and Creole Folklore, which employs Barry Ancelet, who is militantly at work trying to foment a literary and cultural renaissance conducted in the dialect of his forebears.

Food plays no small part in Ancelet's plans. Cajun food is especially threatened by outside influences. The homogenizing forces of American agriculture and corporate food production compete with Cajun rural cuisine, just as they do with every American food tradition rooted in the folkways of old-time farm life. In a world of supermarket meat departments, the Cajun *boucherie*, once a focal point of Cajun communal existence, now happens only here and there, and just rarely enough so that people turn out for a staged hog slaughtering just as they would for a special event.

Perhaps the Louisiana Boudin Festival itself is a sign of incipient decline. No figures exist for comparing *boudin* consumption today with its consumption fifty years ago. But it is safe to say that *boudin*, more than any other feature of Cajun life, apart from the French language, symbolizes the French-speaking community of Louisiana and its complicated, imperiled identity. When you taste a *boudin blanc*, you know you have come into contact with Cajun culture, unapologetic and unlike anything else.

Well, not quite. Like Cajun French, the Cajun *boudin* has firm roots in France. The heavy amount of rice in the stuffing reflects the overwhelming traditional local commitment to rice as a crop, and the powerful spice in the Cajun *boudin* may bring tears to the eyes of French visitors; but those same visitors can undoubtedly lay claim to a paler but older recipe for a recognizably similar *boudin blanc*.

Indeed, the roots of the *boudin* go very deep, right to the bedrock of European civilization. The etymology of the word is not altogether certain, but it probably derives from a Latin word for sausage, *botulus*. The philosopher Seneca speaks, in a letter, of a *botularius*, a "sausage seller." And our word *botulism* is the name of a lethal disease first demonstrably caused by infected sausages.

The *Larousse Gastronomique*, with its usual certitude, declares that the *boudin* is a sausage consisting of a hog's large intestine filled with hog's blood. In English, we would call this concoction (which *Larousse* fancifully ascribes to the cuisine of ancient Assyria) a blood pudding.

It takes no great leap of phonological imagination to see the bond between *pudding* and *boudin*. They sound somewhat alike, and they both originally referred to sausages that had to be cooked so that their stuffing would solidify and become edible. Our modern sense of pudding developed because dessert puddings used to be boiled in casinglike bags. In England, the practice still continues.

In France (which somewhat later received the word *pouding* as a loan from England to describe molded desserts such as English plum pudding), *boudin* retained its original sense of blood sausage, but was extended to include a sausage of minced pork meat mixed with egg and cream and then poached until the eggs firmed up the stuffing. This is the most probable ancestor of the Cajuns' *boudin blanc*.

But if Cajuns carry on this secondary tradition of white *boudin,* what happened to the primary one, the pseudo-Assyrian blood pudding still so popular in modern France when grilled and accompanied with sautéed apple rings or mashed potatoes? Barry Ancelet thought the Cajun version of this, called *boudin rouge,* had died out completely. But at least one enterprising food retailer, LeBouef's of Broussard, still produces Cajun blood pudding on a daily basis in a sausage factory tucked away behind a big conventional American supermarket.

The LeBouef family opened shop many years ago as a *boudin* and crackling store. The current Mrs. LeBouef's grandmother made the sausage at home. Today, the LeBouefs have their own abattoir a short drive from the market, where they slaughter all kinds of meat for their butcher department. And so they are in a position to collect fresh blood legally for *boudin rouge.* Pork blood is too hard to keep free from hairs, so they use veal blood; this satisfies the meat inspector but isn't, in theory, as tasty.

On a typical day at the *boudin* factory behind LeBouef's supermarket, Jacques Benjamin, a French-speaking black, finished up his day's work on several hundred pounds of white *boudin* and turned his attention to the red. Wearing an orange apron, he poured two gallons of blood and cooked rice and seasonings, pork fat, and a scoopful of cayenne into his sausage-stuffing machine. The little room was filled with a haze of red pepper. Tripping the motor switch, he babied a casing as it filled and turned dark purple. He knotted and twisted it into a string of resilient sausages and then started another casing. Eventually, he completed the batch and put it in a pot of water to poach for a half hour, testing for doneness by poking through the skins with a toothpick. By the time he was done, a crowd of workmen and truck drivers were lined up outside at the meat counter to buy their lunch. Hot *boudin blanc*, hot *boudin rouge*. Hot enough to make a Frenchman cry. Hot enough to make a Cajun weep for joy.

☞ CAJUN BOUDIN BLANC

2½ pounds boneless fresh pork, butt or shoulder

¾ pound pork liver

¼ pound pork kidney

Salt

2 cups long-grain white rice

2 tablespoons butter

1 large onion, peeled and coarsely chopped

2 bunches scallions, chopped

1 handful parsley

Black pepper

2 teaspoons cayenne pepper

3 yards small sausage casing, approximately (see note)

(1) Cook pork, pork liver, and pork kidney in lightly salted boiling water to cover until meat falls apart, about 2 hours. Reserve the meats and the broth.

(2) Meanwhile combine rice, butter, 2 teaspoons salt, and 4 cups of water in a heavy saucepan. Bring to a boil, stir once, cover, reduce heat to low, and cook for 15 minutes. Empty rice into a bowl and reserve.

(3) Grind the reserved meats, onion, scallions, and parsley together in a meat grinder, using the coarse blade, or grind coarsely in a processor, using the metal blade.

(4) Mix the ground meat mixture with the rice, black pepper to taste, salt to taste, and the cayenne pepper. Add the cayenne gradually. The amount recommended may be impractically torrid for non-Cajuns, although it is ethnographically correct.

(5) Mix in enough of the reserved broth to make the stuffing moist but not soggy.

(6) Rinse the casings to leach out the salt they are preserved in. Cut them into 20-inch lengths with a scissors.

(7) If you have a traditional metal sausage-stuffing "horn" or an attachment for a mixer or meat grinder, any one of them will work well for this recipe. Even a large household funnel will suffice. Work one end of the casing over the tube. Then pull on the rest of the casing in a series of folds. It is not necessary to knot the casing. Merely press the free end of the casing and pull it an inch or so off the tube. Then push the stuffing through the tube into the casing, which, with some assistance from you, will pull off the tube as it fills. When the casing is filled (with an inch of free space at either end), twist the ends and set aside. Continue until all stuffing is used up. Prick the casings here and there to release any trapped air. The filling is dense enough so that only minor amounts of filling, if any at all, will leak out during the final cooking.

(8) *Boudins blancs* are usually served steamed. In other words, heat up a batch in barely simmering water and serve.

Eat them by holding the casing in your hands and sucking the insides from the casing. Discard emptied casings.

Y I E L D: About 8 servings.

Note: For $10 postpaid, casings are available from Standard Casings, 121 Spring St., New York, N.Y. 10012, in 100-yard hanks that keep almost indefinitely under refrigeration. Paprikas Weiss, 1546 Second Ave., New York, N.Y. 10028, will mail syringelike sausage horns for $35.00 postpaid.

The East

AN ORIGINAL OLD-FASHIONED YANKEE CLAMBAKE

The most exclusive and elaborate event in the American culinary calendar takes place on a tree-lined plot of land near Dartmouth, Massachusetts, in August. Last year, Wilfred Morrison, the proprietor of Davoll's General Store in the nearby hamlet of Russells Mills, was the *chef de cuisine*. He presided over a brigade of more than one hundred *sous-chefs*, who had worked for days to get this multicourse extravaganza onto the plates of five hundred lucky guests, who had signed up in time to secure a seat at one of the long wooden picnic tables across the path from Morrison's al fresco kitchen. Two thousand eager gourmets were turned away.

Unlike most modern chefs, Morrison did not cook with gas on a massive professional range. Indeed, he had no range at all, but insisted on a traditional, one might even say aboriginal, oven constructed, *à l'improviste*, from rocks, wood, and canvas. No wire whisks, copper pans, or Cuisinarts were allowed on the premises, only the canonical utensils sanctified by ninety previous years' experience: long-handled steel shovels.

The Allen's Neck Clambake began as an outing for the Sunday school of the local Quaker meeting in 1888. Originally held on Horseneck Beach, it moved slightly inland after 1903, but it is still within smelling distance of the Massachusetts shore in the state's biggest surviving agricultural region, just to the east of the Rhode Island line. Getting lost in the maze of winding country roads running around farms is inevitable the first time you visit the area. The rational highway system of modern America is only minutes away, but just far enough to preserve the area from creeping exurbia. And because of this isolation from the socioeconomic mainstream, the life of the region has been spared the worst, most deracinating shocks that have shaken much of the rest of New England. A community of dirt farmers and gentry with a conservative outlook is holding its own on the east branch of the Westport River. And the Allen's Neck Clambake is its high-water mark, a historic ritual that transcends its official purpose of raising funds for the Friends Meeting House.

When working folk and local Brahmins sit down side by side over paper plates filled with steaming clams and ears of corn redolent of rockweed, there is a spirit of old-time, small-town democracy in the salt air, the same spirit that once animated town meetings in New England. Perhaps the mood is mainly symbolic, but at least the symbolism is pure and unadulterated by slickness, shortcuts, and Chamber of Commerce hoopla. The genius of this clambake is its unremitting, stiff-necked fidelity to a method of cooking and a menu that have not changed since the dawn of the Republic, when settlers learned to cook the corn and shellfish of their newfound land in ad hoc ovens the Indians had invented and perfected on the rocks and sand of that same coast.

The New England clambake has as much claim to the title of our national feast as Thanksgiving, except that Thanksgiving flourishes everywhere, while the clambake has mostly fallen into neglect and been distorted by modern notions. Even some of the clambake's most devoted adherents will succumb to the proddings of their sensual natures and embellish the bake with lobsters. Others, hoping to simplify the cumbersome, labor-intensive process of watching and controlling the bake, conduct this chthonic cookery in a metal prison that started out as a washtub.

At Allen's Neck, the bakemaster has always held the line against lobster fancification. And teams of willing weed-rakers and rock-pilers have been turning out early and late for more than fourscore years. This combination of abundant manpower and a menu codified right down to the tripe (see recipe) has preserved the original Yankee clambake in as rugged and pristine form as modern conditions will allow.

Today, it is true, the menfolk no longer sail a catboat into Buzzard's Bay for fresh fish. And clams are no longer dug locally. The fish (mackerel) comes already filleted from a wholesaler. Clams arrive from Maine, where they were dug commercially in Machias Bay. But the corn is picked in a local field the morning of the bake. And the process of the clambake itself is militantly unchanged.

On the eve of the bake last summer, some twenty volunteers, men and boys, waded into the east branch of the Westport, collecting rockweed under the watchful eye of Karl Erickson, a retired schoolteacher with twenty years' experience on the clambake committee. He picked up a handful of rockweed and pointed out the blisters all over it. "They're full of water," he explained. "When they're heated, that water makes our bake into a natural steam pressure cooker."

It was almost nightfall before the pickup truck on the

riverbank was full of rockweed. Meanwhile, other volunteers had been gathering the rocks and the hardwood for the fire.

By 7:15 a.m. the day of the bake, all of the raw materials had been assembled at the site, except for the corn, still to be picked, and the clams, which would soon be laboriously sorted and washed in a boat filled with seawater on the sand at Horseneck Beach.

At the site, a team of teenagers started building the huge fire. They began with a concrete apron covered with a platform of long green oak stringers, on which were laid alternating levels of cut hardwood and stones. One girl, hefting a granite rock as big as her head and passing it on down the line, said, "This is great. All these years we've been coming here and we never knew this was how it was done."

Eventually, she and her friends had built an oblong rock and wood structure that stood five feet high and measured about twelve feet long and four feet across. There was kindling on top and gasoline-soaked paper underneath. At 8:45 the fire was lit and roared away brightly. "Utopia," said Karl Erickson, "is when it burns so there's not a stick of wood left, just charcoal and stones." By 9:00, all the food was cut and trimmed, bagged and racked, ready to cook. J. T. Smith, ninety-one years old and a former bakemaster, looked on approvingly.

By 10:45, the fire had burned down to a pyramid of rocks. It was time for the pullers. With their long-handled shovels, they dragged the hot rocks off the cement apron so that the charcoal and ash could be cleaned away. No wood smoke should defile the bake.

Speed was crucial so that the rocks wouldn't cool any more than absolutely necessary. As soon as the cement was clean, back went the rocks. On top of them came the rockweed. The food was set out in layers on the rockweed: the racks of clams first, the delicate corn last. Then the whole sizzling pile was covered with a soaked sheet and six layers of canvas; the edges of these cloths, where they met the ground, were caulked with rockweed. Clouds of vapor rose when the sheet went on, but the extra canvas shrouding and the rockweed sealed in the steam. The last edge was tamped down at 11:45. Twenty minutes later, steam pressure made the canvas billow up taut as a sail in a good wind.

Now Ralph Macomber could rest while the clambake baked. This burly sawyer had supervised the trickiest part of the ritual, the breaking down of the fire and the piling up of the hot stones. And at 1:00, as 500 eager guests gathered round, it was his job to reach down, pull up a corner of the canvas, and gingerly extract a finger-burning clam. Out of the shell it came, and into his mouth it went. Macomber pronounced it done.

Off came the six canvases and the sheet. Ravenous diners took their places at the tables, and efficient teams of servers moved about, distributing the mountain of food. On my paper plate was a feast without equal. The clams, especially, were remarkable—fresh and tender and permeated with the aroma of rockweed and ocean. I was happy. Wilfred Morrison was happy. Karl Erickson was happy. Ralph Macomber was happy. We stuffed ourselves with an abandon that itself is part of the clambake tradition. The late Skipper Howland, a chronicler of New England life and the grandfather of my host at Allen's Neck, wrote the classic description:

The first bowl of clams disappears with surprising speed. Another relay appears, reinforced with fish, corn, and potatoes from the bake, and slices of brown bread and helpings of onions from the center of the table. But from this point on how can I attempt to set down in words, which after all are poor things, the disposal of all these gifts of God, which have been for the most part cooked in the good earth, seasoned by the salts thereof, uncontaminated by the impurities of civilization, fresh as the dawn; in such abundance that no one has to bolt his first helping to ensure a second, third, or even a fourth—except to say that, when every soul here gathered has filled himself or herself to comfortable capacity, and those who smoke have ignited the butt ends of Manila cheroots that have come tied in bunches with buttercup-yellow ribbands in leaden chests from the Far Eastern Isles, the day sinks softly and peacefully down toward its end in a pale blue smoky haze of contentment; a contentment that can come only from the know-how of making the most of Nature's gifts and the satisfaction arising from such knowledge, which has been acquired, not from endowed institutions of learning, but from attendance at that greatest of all universities, the outdoor world.

☞ CLAMBAKE TO FEED 500 PAYING

GUESTS PLUS 125 WORKERS

(*From the* Allen's Neck Friends Cook Book)

A safe, smooth, convenient site	1 truckload of rockweed
1 cord of dry hardwood in	1½ tons of stones about the
4-foot lengths	size of a cantaloupe melon

All clambakes are not alike; they vary in menu. Allen's Neck always has the same menu:

22 bushels clams	100 pounds onions
200 pounds sausage	20 large watermelons
75 pounds fish fillets	85 homemade pies
150 pounds tripe	50 pounds butter
75 dozen sweet corn	Coffee
3 bushels sweet potatoes	Milk
30 pans of dressing	

SPECIAL REQUIREMENTS

A group of enthusiastic workers willing to work from Monday through Thursday; without these people no clambake of this size would succeed.

The clams must be culled and washed in fresh seawater, in a boat at Horseneck Beach.

The sweet corn must be fresh and sweet—harvested the day of the clambake. The rockweed must be fresh and kept moist.

After all the food from the bake has been consumed, it is hard to imagine how 20 large watermelons and 85 pies can disappear, but they do! No person should ever leave an Allen's Neck Clambake unless he or she is "full to the gills."

Now the last, and most important, ingredient of all is to ask our dear Lord for good weather.

Four recipes by Harriet Tucker, adapted from the *Allen's Neck Friends Cook Book:*

☞ STEWED SQUASH À LA NANTUCKET

1 large Hubbard squash	Molasses

(1) Cut a large Hubbard squash into 6 pieces. Peel hard part off.

(2) Place in large skillet, tender side down. Cover with ⅓ part molasses, ⅔ part water. Stew uncovered for 1 hour. Turn shell side down. Continue to cook until tender. Serve hot.

Y I E L D: 6 servings.

☞ CORN PUDDING

12 ears raw corn, grated	1 tablespoon butter
¾ cup milk	Salt
2 eggs	Pepper
1 tablespoon sugar	

Combine all ingredients and bake in a shallow dish for 1 hour at 350 degrees.

Y I E L D: 6 to 8 servings.

☞ CAPE COD BAKED BEANS

1 pound pea beans	3 tablespoons molasses
3 tablespoons brown sugar	½ teaspoon dry mustard
1 teaspoon salt	3 tablespoons catsup
1 teaspoon onion	2 cups strong coffee
¾ pound lean salt pork, slashed through rind	

(1) Soak beans overnight.

(2) Preheat oven to 325 degrees.

(3) Add all ingredients and boil for 1 hour.

(4) Then bake for a few hours or until done, adding water as needed and pushing salt pork down into beans.

YIELD: 6 to 8 servings.

☞ LOBSTER STEW

Salt	1 bay leaf
4 1½-pound lobsters	2 cloves
1 tablespoon sugar	4 tablespoons butter
2 cups clam juice	Flour
1 sprig parsley	Pepper
1 rib celery	Cayenne
1 carrot, scraped and cut in rounds	Dry Sherry
	4 cups light cream
1 small onion, peeled and finely chopped	

(1) Boil lobsters for 15 minutes in lightly salted water to cover, with the sugar.

(2) Remove all meat from shells. Reserve both meat and shells.

(3) In a large pot, combine clam juice, 2 cups water, parsley, celery, carrot, onion, bay leaf, and cloves. Bring to a boil, add lobster shells, and simmer for 30 minutes.

(4) While the shells are simmering, cut the lobster meat into chunks (leave the claw meat whole).

(5) In a skillet, heat the butter until it foams. When the foam subsides, add the lobster meat and sauté at low heat. While you do this, sprinkle the meat lightly with flour, salt, pepper, and a dash of cayenne. When the pepper has browned lightly, add 2 tablespoons of sherry. When that comes to a boil,

add a cup of the shell cooking liquid without straining out any coral or tomalley.

(6) Add cream. When the stew is heated throughout, add more sherry and/or broth or other seasonings to taste.

Y I E L D: 6 to 8 servings.

BLUEBERRY BLUES

Passing through Washington County, Maine, in August, even the least-informed traveler knows that he is in the right place for cheap, fresh lobster and that he cannot go any farther east in the United States than this bleak, coastal pocket of poverty. The alert visitor also notices that many apparently abandoned fields are littered with string. That's how it looks at first. Then it becomes clear that the string has been purposely arranged, stretched in a pattern of roughly parallel lines. Sometimes, people are hunched down along those lines of string. Watch long enough and the people move, slowly making their way down the string rows, and then heading back to the road, to blue machines set up on the shoulder. The machines are for winnowing, and the people are picking blueberries, but the neophyte wonders, "Where are the blueberry bushes?"

Those accustomed to highbush blueberry shrubs (*Vaccinium corymbosum*), which grow as tall as six to eight feet, have to look twice before they make out Maine lowbush plants (*V. angustifolium*), flourishing at ankle level, camouflaged by grasses, alder shoots, and sweet fern. The berries themselves are tiny, roughly half the size of the cultivated highbush fruits sold in supermarkets. Lowbush berries are almost never sold as whole, fresh fruits outside New England, and they are not cultivated in the normal sense of the word, that is, planted by man from a selected stock. Lowbush berries are wild, naturally occurring, not adapted to mechanical harvesting, difficult to ship or store fresh, and generally impractical. But they are superb berries, tastier by far than the comparatively insipid highbush cultivars grown commercially in Michigan and other states with more hospitable climates.

Highbush plants and the even taller rabbiteye blueberries (*V. ashei*) grown in the Southeast have two crucial advantages over the undeniably more delicious lowbush fruits. Because of selection and hybridization begun by U.S. Department of Agriculture botanist Frederick V. Coville in 1909, the cultivated berries are very large and therefore appealing to consumers, who tend to taste with their eyes. Furthermore, highbush plants are high. Machines can harvest them easily and, perhaps more important, each plant can be picked selectively several times, so that only perfectly ripe berries are taken during each pass. This means that markets get an ideally uniform crop. Lowbush shrubs, on the other hand, can only be harvested once because the hand rake takes all the berries as it combs through the brush. Pickers have to wait until all the berries in a given patch have ripened. By the time this happens, the early-ripening berries on each plant are turning senescent, getting soft. Rough handling from the rake and the winnowing machine, which separates the berries from the leaves and stems pulled in by the rake, further degrades the appearance of the berries and diminishes their keeping quality.

These factors have seriously reduced the lowbush berry's appeal as a marketable fresh fruit. Also, the big Maine blueberry companies, located at the edge of vast, flat stretches of blueberry patches known as the Barrens, have had little incentive to bother with shipping the lowbush berries fresh, for they have traditionally been able to sell almost the entire crop to large baking companies for use in muffins as well as muffin and pancake mixes. Even the mass-market consumer prefers the little lowbush berry in his muffins. Unlike the bigger highbush berries, which turn into large blue blots when baked, lowbush berries don't look messy after baking, and the manufacturer can put more of them in each muffin—an advertising plus.

Recently, however, even the baking industry has been forced to look with increasing favor on the highbush berry. Lower production costs make the bigger berries roughly thirty cents a pound cheaper. Moreover, besides yielding berries that are easier to harvest and clean, highbush blueberry bushes are far more efficient producers than the wild Maine species. In Michigan, growers have been able to pick an average of two to three tons of berries per acre every year. In Maine, the average yield is only 800 to 1,000 pounds per acre every other year, and most of those acres have to be as laboriously tended as if they were conventional cultivated fields.

"I don't know what they mean when they talk about Maine wild blueberries," says Mary Ellen Bailey, an independent blueberry producer based in Columbia Falls, Maine. "We fertilize. We mow out weeds. We run oil burners over the fields."

Indeed, the only thing "wild" about Maine blueberry production is that the plant propagates itself, spreading its rhizomes underground and producing its own seed. Growers encourage the process with a battery of land-management techniques designed to reduce competition from other plants and from pests, as well as to improve the vigor of the blueberry plants themselves.

Native blueberry fields are really forests artificially held back at the low-shrub state of old-field succession by weed control. After the harvest, growers burn over their fields, a process that eliminates all surface growth but that leaves the blueberry rhizomes unharmed below ground. In effect, moreover, the burning prunes the blueberries and spurs their growth.

Meanwhile, birds spread new seed over the cleared fields, and established rhizomes take over more territory. By July, new growth begins to show above ground. Buds appear but do not blossom in the first year. Because of this biennial cycle, growers rotate their harvests so that only half their fields are in the nonfruiting stage at one time. Yearling shrubs turn red in the fall. Then growers hope for a good snow cover, which will shelter the plants from freezing winter weather. Finally, in the spring of the second year, they have the pleasure of seeing their blueberries blossom. Each bud puts forth several white or pink-tinged blossoms in late May or early June.

At this point, growers have to contend with various pests and diseases, the worst of which is the blueberry maggot. Its larvae attack the berries and feed on their flesh. To eradicate the larvae, many growers spray infested fields at the end of June.

By the end of July, the lowbush blueberry crop has ripened. Day after day, local people—schoolteachers, students, whole families—collect in the fields early in the morning, stooping over the bushes with the short-handled rakes that resemble cranberry scoops. Made from galvanized metal, these tools have long, thin teeth and a reversed handle that extends over the teeth, so that when the picker tilts a rake, berries roll into a collecting area at the back. One Abijah Tabbutt of Columbia Falls invented the blueberry rake in 1883. The first one, designed for the rough ground of unimproved fields, had only eight teeth. On today's flatter fields, on the Barrens, pickers use rakes with forty to sixty teeth. Tabbutt's grandson Clarence Drisko carries on the business at 86, selling most of the 3,000 rakes he produces in a year to the giant blueberry companies, Jasper Wyman of Millbridge and A. L. Stewart and Sons of Cherryfield.

Both companies bus in Micmac Indians from Nova Scotia for the harvest, but many of the pickers are Washington County residents earning extra cash for back-to-school clothes or for plain subsistence in the bleak economy of rural Maine. On the Barrens, where picking conditions are ideal, a large family can make up to $400 a day. But the work is very hard and completely anachronistic in the general context of American agriculture. The largest machine at a picking site is the winnower, which is a portable conveyor belt device usually run by a lawn-mower motor. Some are still operated by hand.

"Every year for fifteen years, I've stood on the Barrens and said to myself, 'I don't believe that people will pick 20 million pounds of blueberries like that,'" says Amr Ismail. Dr. Ismail, an expatriate Egyptian, is no casual observer of the lowbush blueberry scene. He is the Maine Blueberry Professor of Horticulture at the University of Maine in Orono. Ismail also supervises the Blueberry Hill Environmental Farm, a research facility in Washington County. There, in scientifically managed, mulched plots, this exuberant, rotund botanist and a small team of colleagues are developing lowbush blueberry clones that will produce a bigger crop of berries than the average wild types. More important, these clones are lowbush cultivars. At Blueberry Hill, there is now actually a cultivated patch Ismail has developed. The clone spreads slowly, taking a decade to cover a field. But Ismail says that "this may be the future. Perhaps we will compromise and go to existing fields to put desirable clones in open places left by herbicides." He also anticipates that, as the cost of hand picking rises, "they'll invent a picking machine." In fact, the University of Maine has already developed a rake head suitable for machine harvesting on level fields that are weed free.

In general, Amr Ismail is an optimist. He sees a bright commercial future for lowbush blueberries, although he concedes that "once we get to propagating and planting, we won't be dealing with the native, natural plant anymore." Ismail, of course, has faith in his clones. But Tom Rush, general manager of A. L. Stewart and Sons, thinks hard times are ahead for the lowbush blueberry. He told the *Wall Street Journal* that by 1985 half of all Maine growers will be forced out of the blueberry business by low prices. Ismail and Rush may actually be talking about a similar future, since only well-capitalized blueberry operations will be able to survive in a market dominated by Ismail's cultivated clones.

The ordinary consumer should be concerned about the future of *Vaccinium angustifolium*, but there is really no legitimate position for most of us to take, except to hope that the cultivated lowbush berries of the future will continue to taste as good as the experimental varieties I sampled at Blueberry Hill. For the time being, the only sensible thing is to cross your fingers and make the trip to Washington County in August to taste the quintessential American berry in the only place you are sure to find it fresh.

Once you are in Maine, you can even arrange to pick your own berries. For me, this foraging, which is almost always technically a trespass on somebody's land, is one of the most exhilarating things to do in the outdoors. Robert Frost caught the beauty and mild mischief of it in his horticulturally precise poem, "Blueberries":

> *You ought to have seen how it looked in the rain,*
> *The fruit mixed with water in layers of leaves,*
> *Like two kinds of jewels, a vision for thieves.*

☞ BETH AND MILLIE GARDNER'S

BAKED BLUEBERRY PUDDING

(Adapted from Cutler Cookery, *United Methodist Church, Cutler, Maine 04626)*

½ cup plus 1 tablespoon shortening	1 egg, lightly beaten
Salt	¼ cup milk
½ cup brown sugar	1 cup flour
2 cups blueberries	1 teaspoon baking powder
½ cup white sugar	Whipped cream

(1) Preheat oven to 350 degrees.

(2) In a saucepan, combine 1 tablespoon shortening, a pinch of salt, and the brown sugar. Cook over medium heat until the sugar melts. Then stir in the blueberries and pour mixture into a greased baking dish.

(3) Beat together the remaining ½ cup of shortening with the ½ cup white sugar until smooth. Then beat in egg and milk.

(4) Sift together flour, baking powder, and ¼ teaspoon salt. Mix with mixture from step 3 to make a batter.

(5) Cover blueberry mixture with the batter and bake for ½ hour. Serve with whipped cream.

YIELD: 8 portions.

☞ BLUEBERRY MUFFINS

(Adapted from a recipe submitted to All Maine Cooking *[edited by Ruth Wiggin and Loana Shibles, Courier of Maine Books, 1 Park Drive, Rockland, Maine 04841] by the late Margaret Chase Smith, senator from Maine)*

1½ cups fresh blueberries	1 egg, lightly beaten
1½ cups flour	¾ cup milk
½ teaspoon salt	3 tablespoons melted
3 tablespoons sugar	shortening
1 tablespoon baking powder	

(1) Preheat oven to 400 degrees.

(2) Wash the blueberries and drain thoroughly.

(3) Sift together the flour, salt, sugar, and baking powder.

(4) Stir the beaten egg and milk together and then stir into the flour mixture. Add berries and melted shortening.

(5) Mix well and pour into a greased muffin tin, filling each compartment three-quarters full.

(6) Bake for 20 minutes.

YIELD: 9 to 12 muffins.

☞ SUSAN'S BLUEBERRY COTTAGE

CHEESE CAKE

1 tablespoon butter	1 egg, separated
4 cups blueberries	¾ cup milk
2 envelopes (tablespoons) unflavored gelatin	1 teaspoon grated lemon peel
¾ cup sugar	3 cups cottage cheese (mashed, sieved, or
¼ teaspoon salt	blended)

2 tablespoons fresh lemon
 juice

1 teaspoon vanilla extract or
 kirsch

¾ cup heavy cream

(1) Butter a shallow, 1⅓-quart dish. Arrange 3½ cups blueberries in dish to form a shell.

(2) Off heat, in top of double boiler, mix together gelatin, sugar, and salt. Separately, beat together egg yolk and milk and add to top of double boiler. Cook over simmering water, stirring, for 6 minutes. Add lemon peel and cool.

(3) When mixture has cooled, stir in cottage cheese, lemon juice, and vanilla or kirsch. Chill until slightly thickened.

(4) While cottage cheese mixture is chilling, combine egg white and heavy cream in a chilled mixing bowl, beat until stiff, and fold into chilled cottage cheese mixture. Pour filling into shell. Arrange remaining blueberries on top. Chill.

Y I E L D: 6 to 8 servings.

☞ MELT-IN-YOUR-MOUTH BLUEBERRY CAKE
(Suzanne Moore, Port Clyde, Maine)

2 eggs, separated
1 cup sugar
½ cup butter
¼ teaspoon salt
1½ cups sifted flour

1 teaspoon baking powder
⅓ cup milk
1½ cups blueberries
1 teaspoon vanilla

(1) Beat egg whites until stiff. Add ¼ cup sugar to whites.

(2) Cream butter; add salt and vanilla. Add rest of sugar, egg yolks. Beat until light and fluffy.

(3) Sift flour and baking powder. Add alternately to

creamed mixture with milk. Fold in egg white mixture, then blueberries (mix 1 tablespoon flour with blueberries—this supposedly keeps the berries from sinking to the bottom).

(4) Grease 8 by 8 pan. Pour in batter. Sprinkle top liberally with granulated sugar.

☞ WALT'S FRUIT-NUT BREAD

(Adapted from The Compleat Blueberry Cookbook *by Elizabeth W. Barton, Phoenix Publishing, Canaan, New Hampshire 03741)*

2 cups fresh or dry-packed frozen blueberries	3 eggs, at room temperature
3 cups all-purpose flour	¾ cup milk, at room temperature
1 teaspoon salt	1 cup crushed, drained pineapple
2 teaspoons double-acting baking powder	2 teaspoons grated lemon rind
2 teaspoons baking soda	1 cup chopped English walnuts or pecans
½ cup shortening or margarine	
1½ cups granulated sugar	

(1) Preheat oven to 350 degrees. Grease three 4 by 6 by 3 loaf pans, or two 9½ by 5½ by 3 loaf pans.

(2) Wash, drain, and dry fresh blueberries between paper towels, or thaw just to separate frozen ones. Toss berries in a small amount of flour to cover.

(3) Sift and measure flour. Resift with salt, baking powder, and baking soda. Cream shortening and add sugar gradually, beating until light and fluffy. Beat eggs until frothy; then add milk. Turn into the shortening bowl and blend.

(4) Drain pineapple. Add pineapple and lemon rind to liquid ingredients. Stir the liquid ingredients into the dry in-

gredients, mixing until dry ingredients are completely moistened. Fold in blueberries and nuts. Pour dough into greased pans.

(5) Bake for 40 to 50 minutes. Test with cake skewer. If tester does not come out clean, bake for 10 minutes more, or until golden brown. Cool on cake rack for 5 to 6 minutes before removing from pans, and loaves will come out easier.

Y I E L D : About 20 servings.

MOSES AND MANHASSET: THE KOSHER KITCHEN

When Solomon Carvalho explored the Rocky Mountains in 1853 as the daguerrotypist on John Charles Frémont's last expedition, this Jewish adventurer did not obey the dietary laws of his religion. He ate horsemeat and mule. Similarly, Sigmund Schlesinger found no ritually pure butcher shop after he survived the Battle of Beecher Island, Colorado, in 1868, when he and fifty other scouts held off 700 Cheyenne and Sioux Indians for nine days. "Killt a Coyote & eat him all up," he wrote in his diary.

Many other Jewish immigrants ate nonkosher food in America with far less justification than Carvalho or Schlesinger. Indeed, for some refugees from Eastern European *shtetlach,* one of the attractions of America was the chance it offered to throw off the constraints of kashrus, the elaborate system of biblically based food customs and prohibitions that had been mandatory in the pious homes of their parents. My paternal grandfather emigrated to Utah in search of a secular utopia on homestead land in an agrarian commune.

Thousands of other immigrants did continue to maintain kosher homes in America. But even the Lower East Side of Manhattan, in its Jewish heyday before World War I, did not provide the same isolation as Russia's Pale of Settlement, where orthodox Jewish practice had flourished undisturbed except by czarist pogroms and oppression. One of my mother's grandfathers, a rabbi with the highest standards of talmudic observance, refused to follow his congregation to New York, convinced that the holy life was impossible there. Because of Hitler, we will never know whether he and millions of other exterminated traditional European Jews would have continued eschewing pork, separating meat and milk in the same meal, and otherwise eating orthodox Judaism's idea of pure food had they made it to the United States.

Statistically speaking, my great-grandfather's fear has been borne out by history. Given ample opportunities to assimilate into the American diet, millions of American Jews have done so. Even among those affiliated with Jewish congregations, the majority (1.1 million families) are Reform Jews, who are not required to keep kosher homes. Orthodox and Conservative congregations, which officially demand the observance of kashrus, claim at least 775,000 families. These figures leave out Jews with no formal synagogue membership, most of whom presumably do not adhere to dietary tradition. Obviously, then, kosher keeping has declined. But surely more remarkable in this era of conspicuous consumption and intermarriage is that more than three-quarters of a million American households still profess allegiance to the spiritual and practical ideal of maintaining a kosher home. Indeed, some American Jews raised without any kosher principles are now converting their lives and homes to kosher practice.

Zelda and Irving Leibowitz, who live in the New York

suburb of Manhasset Hills, raised their five children in a non-kosher home. Although they belong to a Conservative synagogue, their only nod to kashrus until recently had been to avoid bringing *trayf* (nonkosher foods such as pork and shell-fish) into the house. Then they went with a group from their synagogue to a weekend retreat in Morristown, New Jersey, a sort of conference sponsored by the Lubavitcher hasidim, a sect of Orthodox Jews very active in wooing less observant Jews back to strict forms of piety.

"I was very impressed," says Zelda Leibowitz. "I wanted something more than Conservative Judaism."

At the retreat she learned that the Lubavitcher Women's Organization was ready to help her kosher her home. Late last year, Mrs. Leibowitz, with the support of her husband, embarked on a strenuous process that turned her kitchen upside down and completely changed her life and that of her family.

Lubavitcher representatives went through every cabinet and closet, eliminating all foodstuffs not stamped with a seal of rabbinical approval. They scrubbed her countertops and rinsed her pots with boiling water. Men took the metal pots and pans outside behind the house and burned them with a blowtorch to remove any lingering traces of food. They also took the pots in cartons to a ritual bath in Brooklyn for consecration. Unfortunately, utensils made of earthenware, glazed china, Pyrex, or Corning Ware cannot be koshered, and Mrs. Leibowitz had to give them all away. When I visited her, she was using paper plates and intending to replace her china with two new sets: one for meat dishes, the other for dairy foods.

Like all kosher principles, the separation of meat and milk is the result of divine ordinance enunciated in scripture and interpreted by rabbis over the centuries. The basic idea sounds simple, but it has ramified into a system of daunting practical complexity. To keep meat and dairy products from contaminating each other, Mrs. Leibowitz divided her kitchen down the middle—with one side reserved for meat, the other for dairy—and installed a second sink for her dairy dishes. Meat utensils are tagged with red tape, dairy with blue. She has kosher kitchen soaps, also in red and blue. She is not using her dishwasher, pending expert advice on whether it can be salvaged. Many Orthodox Jews have two dishwashers to eliminate any doubt about milk-meat contamination through a common machine.

The principle of meat-milk separation also introduces complications into cooking and eating. A serious kosher keeper does not want his body contaminated by internal mixing of meat and milk in the digestive tract, so he eats no dairy products for six hours after eating meat. After a dairy meal, on the other hand, the wait before eating meat can be much shorter, unless one has eaten a hard, aged cheese.

Then there is the basic question of which raw materials and basic food products are kosher and which are not. Kosher meat comes only from animals that have cloven hoofs, that chew their cud, and that have been properly slaughtered. Ritual slaughter—slitting the throat swiftly with a knife—must be performed by specially trained people under strict rabbinic supervision, and about half of each animal cannot be used. Hindquarters are not kosher, because the forbidden sciatic nerve is too deeply embedded in the muscle tissue to be removed except with great difficulty. Ergo, sirloin steaks are *trayf*. So is forequarter meat from an animal with internal defects such as adhesions on its lungs. And even bona fide kosher meat has to be rinsed and salted (see recipe) or broiled, sometimes both, to extract the blood, a forbidden substance.

These requirements are only the most basic of the koshering rules for meat. The average person in modern society is simply not in a position to comply with all the provisions. As a result, it is commonplace to rely on kosher butchers. Mrs. Leibowitz goes to one near the Lubavitcher headquarters in Crown Heights, Brooklyn.

When it comes to seafood, she faces an entirely different set of perplexities. To be kosher, seafood must possess both fins and scales. (Clearly, this means that lobster and shrimp and clams are taboo.) But a kosher fish scale is special: it must be easily removable and has to form a separate integument on top of the fish's skin. Mrs. Leibowitz must therefore be able to distinguish between species of fish with kosher scales, and others (eels, swordfish, sturgeon, and catfish) with no scales or scales that are embedded in the flesh. For guidance, she can turn to a handlist of fish prepared for the Union of Orthodox Jewish Congregations of America by James W. Atz, curator and dean bibliographer in the Department of Ichthyology of the American Museum of Natural History.

Mrs. Leibowitz and other strict kosher keepers also have to be particularly concerned about packaged foods and food additives. In effect, they depend on the judgment of professional kashrus supervisors who work for food manufacturers. These experts have to judge the kosherness of chemicals undreamed of by the authors of the Talmud, and they are not without their critics.

"Kashrus supervision has become 'big business' with big business practices," wrote Rabbi M. D. Tendler, faculty advisor to a student group at New York's Yeshiva University, which has published a brief *Guide to Kashrus*. Rabbi Tendler, in his introduction to the pamphlet, sounds like a Hebraic Ralph Nader campaigning for truth-in-labeling: "The secret process, the half-truth or actual misleading information, and the privileged information clauses written into kashrus-supervising contracts forbidding manufacturers from even answering questions related to the kashrus of their products, are . . . alien to our

Torah community and rejected even by our secular society which now emphasizes the 'right of the consumer to know.' "

For her part, Zelda Leibowitz looks for the seals of rabbinic approval on packaged foods without puzzling over what Rabbi Tendler calls "the interface of food technology and kashrus laws." But even this much scrutiny adds to the special labor of her kosher shopping in modern America.

Why go through all this? What reason did the Lubavitcher hasidim give Mrs. Leibowitz that could possibly justify the daily contortions of kashrus? "No rational explanation is given in the Torah," says the author of the Lubavitcher Women's Organization's cookbook. The rules of kashrus produce health only as a "fringe benefit," but the text continues, "we observe them because they are the will of G-d and were given to us for all time at Mt. Sinai."

As a practical matter, however, the elaborate ritual of kashrus sets Jews apart from non-Jews, making it virtually impossible for them to eat comfortably with Gentiles. By the very arduousness of its requirements, kashrus encourages the preservation of a separate Jewish identity in a non-Jewish world. To worry if a cheese was coagulated with kosher rennet is to affirm one's Jewish identity in a small but profoundly unambiguous way.

☞ CHOPPED LIVER

(Adapted from **The Spice and Spirit of Kosher-Jewish Cooking,** *published by the Lubavitcher Women's Organization, 770 Eastern Parkway, Brooklyn, New York 11213)*

1 pound beef liver	½ teaspoon salt
Coarse kosher salt	¼ teaspoon pepper
3 hard-boiled eggs	1 tablespoon lemon juice
1 large onion, peeled and	(optional)
chopped	½ tablespoon mustard
2 tablespoons oil	(optional)

(1) Since liver has too much blood in it for salt alone to do an effective job of koshering, it is not salted in the regular way. It is salted on all sides (with coarse kosher salt) and also must be roasted over an open fire or over the open flame of a gas range (not an electric fire). If roasting a whole beef liver, cut into it across its length and width before roasting. Thoroughly wash off all outside blood and remove all visible blood clots. Salt the liver immediately before the roasting. Roast over an open fire with nothing between the fire and liver so that the blood can flow out freely. A thin wire net with large holes may be used to hold the liver over the fire. Rotate the liver a few times, so that all sides will be exposed to the fire and become roasted. If you use an open fire from a gas range, cover all sides

around the open fire so that no blood can splash on the stove and render it unkosher.

(2) Grind liver, eggs, and onion. (For added flavor you can sauté onion in oil first.)

(3) Mix together well.

(4) Add oil and seasonings, and mix again.

☞ CHALLAH RECIPES

Most Jews today think that "challah" refers to the braided bread commonly served at the Sabbath meal. This is true, but the word itself originally meant a small piece of dough removed before baking and used for ritual purposes. During the time of the temple in Jerusalem, the separated *challah* was given to the Kohanim, the priestly tribe. Today, it is no longer possible to perform this ritual in the old way, but Orthodox women do still separate *challah*. They separate the raw dough and then burn it, because, once separated, the *challah* is a priestly portion that no longer belongs to them, and they have no right to enjoy it.

There is no standard challah recipe or even a standard way of forming the loaves. Here are several methods adapted from *The Spice and Spirit of Kosher-Jewish Cooking*.

☞ FAMOUS CHALLAH

2 ounces fresh or 4 packages dry yeast

1 cup sugar

2 tablespoons salt

13 to 14 cups flour

2 eggs, beaten

1 cup oil

(1) Dissolve yeast in 4 cups warm water. Water temperature should be 80 to 90 degrees when using fresh yeast,

95 to 105 degrees for dry yeast. When dissolved, add sugar, salt, and half the flour. Mix well. Add eggs and oil, then slowly stir in most of the remaining flour. Dough will become quite thick. (Until kneading stage, dough can be mixed in electric mixer.)

(2) When dough pulls away from sides of the bowl, turn onto floured board and knead for approximately 10 minutes. Add only enough additional flour to make dough manageable. Knead until dough has acquired a "life of its own"; it should be smooth and elastic, springing back when pressed lightly with fingertip.

(3) Place dough into a large, oiled bowl. Turn it over so that the top will be oiled as well. Cover with a damp towel and let rise in a warm place for 2 hours, punching down in four or five places every 20 minutes.

(4) Preheat oven to 375 degrees.

(5) Separate *challah*. Shape loaves (see shaping directions below), and place into well-greased bread pans or onto greased cookie sheet. Allow to rise again until doubled in bulk. Brush tops with beaten egg and sprinkle with poppy or sesame seeds. Bake for approximately 20 minutes, or until nicely browned.

☞ BIG CHALLAH RECIPE

5 pounds flour	6 eggs
1½ cups sugar	¾ cup oil
4 ounces fresh yeast	2 tablespoons salt
4 cups water	

(1) Sift flour into large pan. In another bowl, dissolve yeast in ½ cup lukewarm water and 1 teaspoon sugar. Form a

well in flour and add yeast mixture. Mix in enough of the flour to form a paste. Let stand for 5 minutes, or until yeast paste rises and little bubbles form.

(2) Meanwhile, in a glass bowl, beat eggs and add oil, salt, and remaining sugar. Mix. Slowly add the remaining water, then gradually stir the liquid mixture into flour. Use a wooden spoon. Knead for 25 minutes, adding flour if necessary. Cover and let rise until double in bulk.

(3) Preheat oven to 300 degrees.

(4) Take a piece for *challah*. Shape challahs and bake for 50 minutes.

☞ CLASSIC CHALLAH

1½ to 2 ounces yeast	¼ cup oil
1¼ cups lukewarm water	4 eggs, beaten
1 tablespoon salt	9 cups flour
½ cup sugar	

(1) Dissolve yeast in water for 10 minutes. Add salt, sugar, oil, and eggs. Mix. Add 3 cups of flour at a time and mix after each addition. (Make sure all 9 cups of flour are in.) If you need more flour to work the dough, add it in.

(2) Knead the dough until smooth, then knead for an additional 7 minutes. Place in a large greased bowl and leave in a warm place (perhaps near stove) for 1½ hours, or until it has risen to double its original size.

(3) Punch down completely so there are no air pockets. Take off a piece for *challah*. Divide dough, braid, and shape as desired. Place onto greased cookie sheets. Let challahs rise again until double in size.

(4) Preheat oven to 350 degrees.

(5) Brush with egg yolk and water mixture and bake for 30 minutes.

☞ RAISIN CHALLAH

4 packages dry or 3½ ounces fresh yeast	1 whole egg
	4 egg yolks
1 teaspoon honey	1½ to 2 cups raisins
½ cup oil	5 pounds flour
2½ teaspoons salt	

(1) Mix yeast and honey in 1 cup lukewarm water.

(2) Add oil, salt, and eggs.

(3) Pour 2½ cups hot water over raisins, steep until plump, drain, and add to mixture. Mix together well.

(4) Next, add all the flour.

(5) Knead dough. Brush all sides with small amount of oil. Let rise until double in size.

(6) Preheat oven to 375 degrees.

(7) Take *challah.* Shape challahs. Bake for 30 minutes.

☞ ILLUSTRATED DIRECTIONS FOR

SHAPING YOUR CHALLAHS

Here is a simple suggestion to help avoid confusion when braiding challahs the first few times (especially when making the six-braided challah): PRACTICE WITH STRINGS FIRST.

(1) Take some string, cut off six strips approximately 9 inches long each. (Use only three strips for the basic braided challah.)

(2) Take Scotch tape and connect all the pieces at the very top.

(3) Take small pieces of paper and number the pieces 1 to 6.

(4) Again with Scotch tape, attach a number to each string, according to the illustrations on the next page.

(5) Practice the procedure over and over again until you have it correct throughout the whole process.

Note: It is best to do the practicing during the day or on an evening when you are not baking so that you won't be pressured for time.

THREE-BRAIDED CHALLAH:

This is a very simple procedure, identical to any braiding procedure.

(1) Roll out three long, thin pieces (Fig. 1). The pieces should be a bit longer than the size of the pan in which the challah will be placed, for once it is braided, it will be smaller than the pan.

(2) Pinch the tops of all three pieces together (Fig. 2).

(3) Take the one on the outer right (#1), cross it over #2 and bring it into the middle (Fig. 3).

(4) Now take the one on the outer left (#3), cross it over the middle strip (#1) and let it rest in the middle (Fig. 4).

(5) Repeat this procedure until the end, alternating bringing the one on the outer right to the middle, and then bringing the one on the outer left to the middle, until you have completed shaping the challah (Fig. 5).

(6) Some people also make a thin braid over the large braided challah (Fig. 6), so that the challah is made with a total of six pieces, and together with the second challah on the table, there will be a total of twelve.

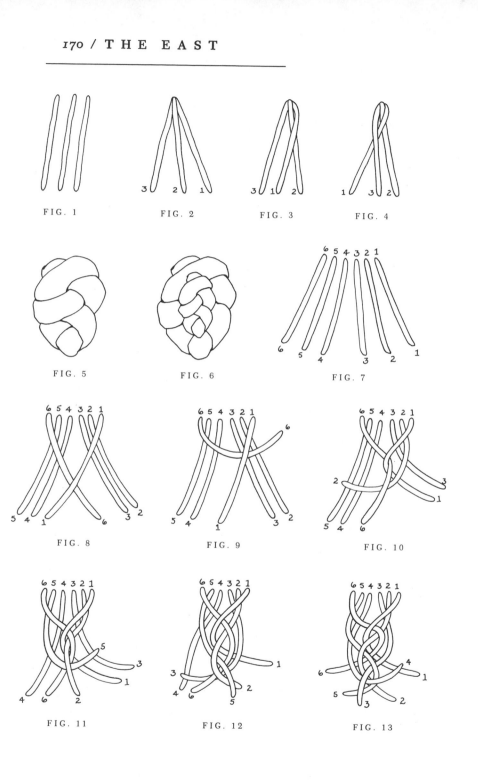

FIG. 1   FIG. 2   FIG. 3   FIG. 4

FIG. 5   FIG. 6   FIG. 7

FIG. 8   FIG. 9   FIG. 10

FIG. 11   FIG. 12   FIG. 13

SIX-BRAIDED CHALLAH:

(1) Roll dough into six equal strips approximately ten inches long each.

(2) Lay out strips evenly and pinch them together at the top. (Place a knife on top of the pinched section to keep it down and make it easier to maneuver the strips.)

(3) Push the three strips on the right farther to the right; and the remaining three, more to the left (Fig. 7). Now you are ready to braid.

(4) With right hand, take #6 and with left hand take #1 (left hand is crossed *over* right hand), moving right and left hands simultaneously. Cross #1 *over* #6 inside the center (thus uncrossing your hands (Fig. 8).

(5) Swing #6 over the pinched section and rest it upon the pinch and beyond. Bring #1 down to the right-side group, placing on the left side of #3 (making #1 the innermost strip of the right side group and #2 the outermost strip). Now the strips are in this position (Fig. 9). From now on, the right and left sides will have two or three strips alternately, while there will always be one strip above and on top of the others.

(6) Now to have three strips on the left side do the following: With your left hand, take the outermost strip, #2, from the side that already has three strips (the right side) and with your right hand take the uppermost strip, #6 (crossing the right hand *over* the left). Simultaneously, bring #2 under #6 and place it on top and beyond the pinch (replacing #6) and bring #6 to rest in the left-side group, on the right side of #4 (Fig. 10). All the steps thereafter take on the same pattern, merely alternating between right and left sides—making the right-side group have three strips while the left has two and then the left-side group have three strips while the right has two. The outermost strip of the three-strip side is always placed on top of and beyond the pinch, while the strip

which is on top of the pinch and beyond it is always brought
to the innermost place of the two-strip side, thus making it a
three-strip side. To illustrate further: (Figs. 11 to 13).

(7) Take #5 with right hand and #2 with left hand
(left hand *over* right), moving #5 and #2 simultaneously.
Bring #5 under #2 and swing it (#5) around, placing it on
top of the pinch and beyond (so that it takes the place of #2)
while bringing #2 down to the right-side group and placing
it on the left-hand side of #1. Now the right-side group has
three strips—#2 is the innermost strip and #3 the outermost
(Fig. 11).

(8) Take #3 with left hand and #5 with right hand
(right *over* left) and simultaneously bring #3 under #5. Place
#3 on top of pinch and beyond, while bringing #5 to the left-
side group, to the right of #6 (Fig. 12).

(9) Place #4 on top of pinch and beyond and bring #3
to right-side group, making it the innermost strip (Fig. 13).
Continue until strips are too short to work with. Then pinch all
the ends together—and you have a six-braided loaf!

JUPITER'S WALNUT

IN THE NEW WORLD

Faced with starvation in the harsh winter of 1609–10, the desperate colonists at Jamestown fed themselves with roots and herbs and other wild foods. They ate what the land gave them, including, it is recorded, walnuts. But these walnuts were not the easily cracked nuts the colonists remembered from pleasant evenings in England. The English, or more properly the Persian, walnut (*Juglans regia*) is a civilized, mild-tasting, easily extracted fruit; the native American black walnut (*Juglans nigra*) is an untamed recluse, lurking inside a tough husk, clinging to its shell like a limpet to a rock.

Modern fanciers of this powerful-tasting nut attack the husks with hammers. Some folks even run them under car wheels. The black walnut is definitely a delicacy, with its dark, earthy flavor. Specialty stores and mail-order houses sell it, but the black walnut is too troublesome to rival its old-world cousin,

Juglans regia, or its American relative, the pecan (*Carya illinoensis*) as a commercially cultivated nut tree.

All of these trees, as well as hickories and butternuts, are in the walnut family (Juglandaceae), and they all produce true nuts—hard-shelled fruits with sizable food sources. The family name comes from the Latin word for walnut, *Juglans,* a syncopated form of the original phrase, *Jovis glans,* the acorn of Jupiter. The Romans seem to have borrowed the word from a Greek word of identical meaning, *diosbalanos,* that referred to the European chestnut (*Castanea sativa*).

All the nuts in the walnut family have obvious similarities, but the black walnut is special and it is in danger. There was a time when hardy native trees, some still producing bushels of nuts after useful lives of as long as 250 years, ornamented the landscape with comforting frequency across their huge natural range, from Ontario to Florida and west to the Great Plains. They formed part of the staple diet of various Indian tribes, who knew the nuts would last through the winter.

Indians ate the nuts raw. They also pounded them into "butter," which they sometimes flavored with herbs or used in baking. Recipes survive for cranberry walnut cakes and for maple black-walnut cookies made with cattail flour. One Indian cooking method for black walnut butter, described in Barrie Kavasch's *Native Harvests,* would still be a clever way of separating the nutmeats from the shells. You simply smash the nuts and boil them in water until the meats and oils rise to the surface and can be skimmed off for pounding. Shell pieces settle to the bottom of the pot.

Native Americans were experts at utilizing the Juglandaceae trees around them. They enlivened pumpkin soup with black walnuts and took the sap from *Juglans nigra* for syrup as readily as they tapped maples. The Creeks even prepared hickory milk for their corn dishes. The Indians also taught what they knew to the white settlers, who liked black walnuts as much as any Iroquois. But the colonists unfortunately looked beyond the sap and nuts to the trees themselves and quickly discovered that black walnut wood was a wonderful material, hard and lovely. It made fine furniture and resilient gun stocks.

Today, most of the great old trees, over 100 feet high, have been cut for timber. The champion black walnut reported to the American Forestry Association is in the redwood country of Humboldt County, California. It is 132 feet high, has a circumference of 22 feet, and an average crown spread of 133 feet. Most big walnuts that remain are now so valuable that lumbermen stalk them in rural areas, offering top dollar to cut them down and turn them into luxurious planks. This is the end of a process that began in the seventeenth century. Word had reached Europe well before the naturalist-explorer John Tradescant (1608–1662) gathered black walnuts in Virginia for Charles I. The trees were established in England some time after 1650, but the black walnut never became widespread abroad.

In North America, on the other hand, the black walnut was until recently an important feature of rural life. Jasper Woodroof, author of *Tree Nuts,* writes of "annual pilgrimages to the woods before Thanksgiving with baskets, buckets and bags." The black walnut crop provided work, in harvesting and cracking, all through Appalachia.

Wild trees were meanwhile cultivated and hybridized for easier harvesting. The Stabler variety is an example of a strain whose nuts are fairly easy to crack. Descendants of the original tree sprang up twenty miles north of Washington, D.C., and produce nuts that come out of the shell in unbroken halves; some even emerge whole. Other improved varieties, such as Thomas, Ohio, and Myers, start bearing nuts in the second or third year after planting, seven or eight years earlier than native trees. The new varieties, which also have thinner shells, are propagated by grafting scions onto native seedlings.

Anyone willing to plant a black walnut is obviously a saint of horticulture. In a climate of overall decline in production (despite the development of commercial cracking methods), what could be more useful, even patriotic, than to devote some land to this vanishing yet estimable national treasure?

People with a good stretch of well-drained, rich, loose soil of limestone origin at least four feet deep should consider planting a few black walnuts. Because of their extensive root system, trees should be set a minimum of sixty feet apart. And don't plant them near vegetable gardens. Because of an allelopathic interaction with certain plants in the neighborhood of their roots—probably having to do with a toxin, called juglone, produced by black walnut roots—black walnuts will kill alfalfa, tomatoes, potatoes, blackberries, blueberries, and rhododendrons. On the other hand, the growth of beets, snap beans, sweet corn, black raspberries, grapes, and alas, poison ivy is either unaffected or actually improved by contact with black walnut roots.

Black walnuts are monoecious: each tree grows both male and female parts. The male catkins are carried on the previous year's wood, while the female flowers appear on the current spring's new wood. By July, the little flowers have burgeoned into tough, green spheres. These nuts ripen by late September or early October. After the leaves have fallen, the nuts drop to the ground and can be gathered. But this is only the beginning for the black walnut forager.

Those freshly fallen green nuts, big as limes, surrounded by pulpy husks, are not at all ready to be eaten. Soon, however, the tight exterior begins to soften, blotches spread, color fades, and then the mess starts. You have to get the husks off. They are magnificently indehiscent. Nature does not lend a hand. A government publication suggests: "The rear wheel of an automobile can be an effective hull remover. Fit one of the rear wheels with a tire chain and jack up the rear with just enough room beneath the tire for the nuts to pass. The chain will remove the hulls as the nuts are forced through the trough formed by the turning wheel." Another expert, R. L. Scheffel, advises crushing them with your heels on flagstones.

Whichever method you use, be sure to wear work gloves and dispensable clothes, for black walnut husks are rich in black dye. Pioneers used it to tint homespun textiles. Because it is indelible, you have to deal with it as best you can. Some of the husk pulp will persist in clinging to the nut. Pick off what you can. Then wash the nuts to remove the remaining black matter. Harry Lesher of Middleburg, Pennsylvania, who processes black walnuts at home, by hand, and does a small business with them, hoses down his nuts.

Still they are not ready. If you cracked a black walnut just after it had come out of its husk, it would be mushy and bitter. Lesher takes the inch-high nuts, with their thinly furrowed, rough, sharp shells, and dries them in shallow racks at the top of his garage. After six weeks to two months, the time finally comes to crack the nuts. Lesher uses a rubber mallet. Other people use metal hammers.

It often takes several blows of the hammer to make a crack. The edible kernel is then exposed and will normally come away from the convoluted shell in several pieces.

At this point, black walnuts can be treated like other walnuts. They are rarely eaten salted, as a snack, but they can be substituted in any recipe that calls for ordinary walnuts. Perhaps the most popular traditional American black walnut dish is black walnut ice cream, a delicacy for the gods, made with our native, feisty acorn of Jove. Proceed as you would for vanilla ice cream, add one cup chopped nuts per quart of ice cream, freeze, and be glad we have not yet turned all our black walnuts into shotguns and chests.

☞ MRS. VIOLA BRICKER'S

BLACK WALNUT CAKE

½ cup (4 ounces, or 1 stick) salt butter, at room temperature	2 cups flour
	¾ cup cold water
1½ cups sugar	5 ounces black walnuts
1 teaspoon baking powder	4 egg whites
	1 recipe icing (see below)

(1) Grease two 8-inch cake pans.

(2) Preheat oven to 350 degrees.

(3) Cream butter. Gradually beat in sugar and continue beating until smooth.

(4) Sift together the baking powder and flour. Mix into the sugar-butter mixture with the cold water.

(5) Chop all but ½ ounce of the walnuts and add to the cake batter. Reserve the unchopped nuts.

(6) Beat egg whites until stiff but not dry. Fold into the batter.

(7) Pour equal amounts of the batter into the prepared layer pans.

(8) Bake for 30 to 35 minutes.

(9) Cool on rack.

(10) Unmold the cake layers. Set one on a serving plate. Ice top sparingly. Set the other layer on top of it. Ice top and sides of cake. Decorate with reserved walnuts.

Y I E L D: One 2-layer, 8-inch cake, about 8 servings.

I C I N G

8 ounces cream cheese, softened	2 tablespoons vanilla extract
4 tablespoons salt butter, melted	1 pound confectioner's sugar

(1) With an electric mixer, beat the cream cheese until it is light and fluffy.

(2) Gradually add the melted butter, beating until it is completely absorbed. Add the vanilla and the sugar, beating well after each addition so that the icing is smooth.

STALKING

THE CULTIVATED

GOOSEBERRY

*I am going to turn over a new life and I am
going to be a very good girl and be obedient to
Isa Keith, here there is plenty of gooseberries
which makes my teeth watter.*
—Marjorie Fleming (1803–1811)

Before her untimely death at the age of eight, the precocious British diarist Marjorie Fleming had already acquired her nation's taste for the tart and hairy fruit of *Ribes grossularia*. For my own part, as a more or less typical American, I did not even try a gooseberry until, as a nominally mature twenty-two-year-old Fulbright student, I sat down to dinner at Wadham College, Oxford, and having picked desultorily at the main course, braised ox heart, fell upon the dessert—gooseberry compote—with a gusto that diminished after the first bite.

Adelaide de Menil

COUNTY FAIR,
INDEPENDENCE, IOWA (*page 13*)

Adelaide de Menil

MORELS, MICHIGAN *(page 45)*

COUNTRY HAMS,
SMITHFIELD, VIRGINIA *(page 101)*

Adelaide de Menil

WILD AMERICAN PERSIMMONS,
INDIANA *(page 23)*

LOWBUSH BLUEBERRIES, MAINE *(page 147)*

LAMB ON THE HOOF,
COLORADO *(page 188)*

Adelaide de Menil

Adelaide de Menil

WILD RICE, MINNESOTA *(page 36)*

Dan Seifert

FINNISH-CORNISH PASTIES,
UPPER MICHIGAN *(page 64)*

Dan Seifert

CAJUN <u>BOUDIN</u>,
BROUSSARD,
LOUISIANA
(page 126)

BURGOO,
KENTUCKY
(page 74)

CLAMBAKE,
MASSACHUSETTS
(page 136)

SALMON ROAST,
PACIFIC NORTHWEST (*page 250*)

The once-green and translucent berries had lost their shimmer in the canning process, but I could still make out the delicate, longitudinal striping on their skins. The actual flavor did not then mightily attract me. Over the years, however, I have put away this childish phobia and ceased to be a gooseberry fool. Now, back in the United States, I have a new problem. Fresh gooseberries are almost as rare as the great auk.

Prepared gooseberry products are easy enough to find in this country: on a recent visit to a specialty store, I turned up two kinds of gooseberry preserves (one English, one from Oregon) and a jar of canned whole gooseberries from Germany. But fresh gooseberries seemed to be only a midsummer's dream until a hot tip from a horticulturally alert friend sent me out to the eastern tip of Long Island and beyond, by ferry over Gardiner's Bay, to Shelter Island.

Stalking the cultivated gooseberry on that seagirt and historic summer mecca was soft work, but I got there just in time. Kathleen Brown, who had been tending her opulent garden on the island for seventeen years, was just packing the last of her belongings and preparing to move to a planned retirement community in southern California.

The berry patch was still in place, however, on a small plot behind a cheerful yellow ex-privy in the middle of a sunlit lawn bordered by a mob of lilies. Tangled branches with long thorns and curly green leaves were tied off in sections to make it easier to pick fruit during the short season that runs, on Shelter Island, from the end of June until late July.

The stand of shrubbery wasn't particularly imposing but for years it provided Mrs. Brown with enough berries for a cash crop. In 1977, her best year, she picked twenty-seven quarts and sold most of them at a local farm stand. You couldn't call it a phenomenal output, but the outsider, knowing how unlikely it is to find such a thing at all, wondered why

Mrs. Brown had turned her green thumb in this unusual direction. Was it a case of anglophilia or a yearning for the exotic?

"I didn't know there was such a thing as a gooseberry," she said. "A friend gave me a bush. She had a lot. I layered more every year. Gooseberries are no trouble at all."

In the mild climate of her garden, under her watchful eye, this may be so, but the fact is that the gooseberry has had a hard time of it in this country, even though, in the beginning of British colonization, there was every cultural reason for it to have prospered on American soil.

Apparently, early settlers did try to transplant European gooseberries, but they failed. *Ribes grossularia,* which had been cultivated in northern Europe since as early as the sixteenth century, did not adapt to our climate. Imported shrubs succumbed to a fungus known as gooseberry mildew, which attacked the leaves, twigs, and fruit of the plant, covering it with its weblike mycelium in the spring.

All was not lost, however. In the nineteenth century, a native wild gooseberry turned up in New Hampshire and Vermont. By 1846, Abel Houghton, Jr., of Lynn, Massachusetts, had cultivated it, probably from seed of the plant now called *Ribes hirtellum.* Subsequent hybridization with European strains led to viable cultivars with commercially exploitable fruit, inferior in flavor to the European gooseberries, which can be eaten out of hand, but still a delectable berry for jams and cooked desserts (see recipes).

High hopes for the American gooseberry soured when it transpired that it, like its *Ribes* cousin, the black currant, played host to a virulent fungus, *Cronartium ribicola,* which attacks five-needle pines. In fact, the so-called white-pine blister rust is such a threat to the timber industry that federal and state laws regulate shipment and cultivation of gooseberries and black currants.

Clearly, the white pine has a far more important role in American life than the gooseberry. And in the conflict between the two plants, the gooseberry has lost out. Production figures for American gooseberries are hard to come by, but the annual crop is not large. In its statistical tables the U.S. Department of Agriculture lumps gooseberries together with "miscellaneous fruits and berries." The department did publish numbers for frozen gooseberries until 1970, when 540,000 pounds of the fruit were processed, as compared with some 29 million pounds of blackberries and 202 million pounds of strawberries.

It would be unfair to lay the blame for the meager gooseberry harvest entirely at the door of the timber lobby. Fruit growers would, I am sure, have found a way to grow gooseberries safely and in quantity if there had been a strong public demand for them. But the high acidity of domestic gooseberries has undoubtedly played a real part in making them unpopular. A sweet-toothed populace eager for convenience foods will opt for sweeter fruits that can simply be popped into the mouth.

And then there is the matter of the name "gooseberry" itself. It makes the fruit sound funny, especially the way we Americans pronounce the word. In England, they disguise the poultry aspect of their gooseberries with a pronunciation that sounds like "guzbry." When you hear it you don't think of a goose. This is etymologically reasonable, since the term may very well have nothing to do with geese at all. No one knows for sure, but it is not hard to see how "gooseberry" may have evolved from the Dutch *kruisbezie,* the German *Krausbeere,* or the French *groseille.*

Even if gooseberry does have some fanciful connection with geese, the domestic species and hybrids still offer an alternative to more familiar berries for anyone who wants to try a complex and distinguished summer fruit. Some farm stands and fancy fruiterers carry them. And the home gardener can find shrubs for sale at nurseries. I recently saw a small plant for sale in Manhattan at $5.99.

The standard method of propagation is mound layering. After severe pruning, so that the plant has been cut back almost to the ground, heap soil around the bases of the stems, which will send out roots. Then set out the rooted stems and let them develop into new plants.

Mrs. Brown layered her gooseberry patch by cutting into long stems on the bias, painting the cut with a commercial rooting chemical and burying the cut area underground. A brick was placed over each buried piece to hold it in place. She did this at the end of the season and never cut her plants back, thereby probably reducing her overall crop, since the heaviest output normally occurs on wood under three years old.

But Mrs. Brown has a green thumb. She knew how to keep gooseberry maintenance to a minimum. In early May, she fed her patch with 5-10-5 fertilizer. She sprayed the bushes with Sevin, one tablespoon per gallon of water, to hold down insect infestation. Then, all she had to do was wait and pick the berries before the birds got to them. As she explains:

You pick them when they're half green, with a red blush. When they've turned solid red and started to fall on the ground, it's too late. In the beginning, I waited until they were all red and picked them very carefully. Then I learned that earlier was better. I was so amazed that you could take these green gooseberries and cook them and then see them turn red.

Color will vary among varieties, but the result is the same, plenty of fruit for ten to twenty years, after two or three years of waiting for the patch to take hold. Gooseberries will not do well in hot, dry climates. But these are hardy plants, whose range extends nearly to the Arctic Circle. Many people leave them alone altogether. With any luck, Mrs. Brown's patch will survive and continue to bear fruit, even after she leaves for Chula Vista and abandons her beloved gooseberries to a new, possibly uninterested owner.

☞ MARY PEACOCK

AND AMANDA STINCHECUM'S

ILLINOIS GOOSEBERRY FOOL

1 quart gooseberries	1½ cups scalded milk
1¼ cups sugar	1 teaspoon vanilla
5 egg yolks	1 cup heavy cream, whipped
1 pinch salt	

(1) Cook the gooseberries until soft with ¾ cup sugar and ¼ cup water. Mash a bit.

(2) Beat the egg yolks lightly together. Then gradually beat in the remaining ½ cup sugar and continue beating until the mixture lightens in color and forms a ribbon.

(3) Beat in the salt, then the scalded milk in a slow stream.

(4) Heat the egg mixture over boiling water or over low

to moderate heat until it thickens. If some scrambling of the yolks occurs, pour the mixture through a fine strainer.

(5) Stir the vanilla into the egg mixture. Cool. You will get a light, pourable custard sauce.

(6) Pour the custard sauce (crème anglaise) over the fruit mixture.

(7) Top with whipped cream just before serving.

Y I E L D: 4 to 6 servings.

☞ GOOSEBERRY FOOL

(Traditional English recipe adapted from Elizabeth David's Summer Cooking, *Penguin Books, New York)*

1 pound hard green gooseberries	½ cup heavy cream, whipped
10 tablespoons sugar, approximately	

(1) Cook the gooseberries and sugar in a double boiler until the berries are quite soft. There is no need to top and tail the gooseberries.

(2) Push the gooseberry mixture through a strainer or run through a food mill. Chill.

(3) Stir in the whipped cream. Add more sugar if the fool is too acid. Serve very cold.

Y I E L D: 3 to 4 servings.

The West

FLEECE AFOOT:

COLORADO LAMB

Way back up in the hills, high above the Colorado River, high above the tourists in rafts and kayaks, but less than fifty road miles from Doc Holiday's Bar in Glenwood Springs, with its Old West trappings and mean-mouthed barmaid, you get to the top of an anonymous mountain in the White River National Forest and turn left through the aspens and Engelmann spruces onto a dirt track they call the Bar H-L Road. You'd better go in with a four-wheel drive, because when it rains, the gradually descending trail, marked with U.S. Department of Agriculture Forest Service mileposts, can turn to quagmire. On a dry day in early July, maybe ten miles after the turn and just as you are getting used to the bumping ride and the lush, fabulously expansive meadows, spattered with flowers and empty against the big sky, you hear the noise, as loud as a city of untuned bells or a jungle of monkeys.

Five thousand sheep are on the march up to their sum-mer pasture where the grass stays cool and green. They are heading along an official stock driveway, through cattle-grazing country to higher pasture where only sheep can survive, for a two-month session of nomadic fattening. Ewes and lambs bleat as they walk—mothers trying to find their babies, babies separated from their mothers calling out, and eventually, since each animal has its own special bleat, they locate each other, bounding through the flock and then, al-ways moving, the lambs "mother up" joyfully on the ewes' teats. The flock trudges on, guided by instinct but also shooed forward by shepherds on horseback and little dogs that keep the sheep from straying off into the woods. The herders whistle and hoot and head off the ragged edges of this woolly white mob. The flock flows over the tan road like a huge, low cloud.

Idyllic? Why, of course it is. Theocritus coined the word "idyll" for his bucolic poems, which for the first time in Western literature described just such a scene. All pastoral poetry hymns the life of the shepherd (Latin *pastor*). And this pro-cession of lonely men and gregarious animals (Latin *grex* = "herd") from low pasture to high, this transhumance, is older than literature, older even than settled agriculture and the sedentary life we call civilization. But even the ancient tradi-tion of the pastoral contained a darker strain, epitomized by the famous Latin tomb inscription that crops up in pastoral paintings by Guercino, Poussin, and Reynolds: *Et in Arcadia ego*, "I [death] am even in Arcadia," the mountainous tradi-tional haunt of Greek shepherds in the Peloponnesus.

And even in late twentieth-century Colorado, mortality lurks behind the peaceful and picturesque surface of the annual sheep drive. Nobody knows this better than Gus Halandras, whose survival as a sheepman is threatened by forces far more complex than the natural risks that menaced the pastoral livelihood of his Greek ancestors Thyrsis and Corydon in Arcadia.

On the surface, Halandras and his 5,000 sheep are doing fine. He and his wife, Christine, both of them children of Greek immigrants, live in a big house in Meeker, Colorado, and raise fat sheep on open rangeland. But like all other American sheep producers, the Halandrases operate in what might be called a hostile environment. The statistics are eloquent.

In 1979, the national sheep flock numbered 12.5 million animals, a mere fifth its peak size of 56 million in 1942 and only a quarter what the flock was at the time of the first U.S. sheep census in 1867, when the human population was under 40 million. Last year's lamb slaughter yielded only 294 million pounds or 1.6 pounds per person. Compare this to an annual beef gorge of 120 pounds per capita, and you have to conclude that lamb is, relatively speaking, an endangered species.

Ironically, in the eleven Western states where 60 percent of America's sheep are raised, mostly on open range, virtually no lamb is consumed. The South is also a desert for lamb. Two-thirds of American lamb is shipped to the Northeast, half of that to the New York City metropolitan market, where people of Mediterranean and Jewish background persist in bucking the national trend toward an all-beef meat diet. Gus Halandras says that 90 percent of his lamb goes East.

No one, however, can say for sure why Americans don't all love lamb with the fervor of Greeks and Jews. Halandras speculates that a whole generation of GI's were subjected to bad Australian mutton during World War II and afterward wouldn't touch so much as a lamb chop. Then there is the fact that beef cattle were convenient machines for gobbling up the postwar grain surplus and turning it into cheap, easy-to-prepare meat, while most sheep continued to eat plain grass. Also, Americans who did indulge in lamb limited their consumption to the most expensive cuts, the chops and the leg. As a result, lamb has an expensive image, although these days the average price "across the carcass" is running about $2.50 per pound, as compared with $2.33 for beef.

To help educate the American consumer about efficient use of the whole lamb in cooking, Christine Halandras recently compiled a booklet of recipes for the American Sheep Producers Council (see recipes below). She is a skillful advocate of lamb consumption from tripe to head and has even taken to preparing Rocky Mountain oysters (lamb testicles) in an ingenious if improbable modern manner. Oysters are normally very hard work to clean, but as delicate as sweetbreads afterwards, when breaded and fried. To simplify the cleaning stage, Mrs. Halandras drops them in her garbage disposal, which miraculously removes the tenacious mucous coating and leaves a perfectly white and unharmed oyster.

On the trail, she cooks more conventionally, but with a practical brilliance that made me think of pioneer women improvising meals out of their Conestoga wagons. In fact, the home economics of cooking for thirteen people in a modern sheep camp are not too different from pioneer conditions. For five days on the trail, the Halandras family, their two herders, and their guests all live in two tents and two metal-clad, home-made vehicles called sheep camps. Jim Atencio and Tomás Magaño, the herders, normally live by themselves in the camps, which look like gypsy wagons with stovepipes coming out of the roofs. Years ago, the ancestors of today's camps had long-spoked wooden wheels and were pulled by horses. In our time, pickup trucks do the hauling and the camps roll on inflated rubber tires. Otherwise, inside the camps, history stands still.

Ingeniously fitted out with wood bunks and a slide-out tabletop, as well as cupboards and stowage compartments, the

Halandras camps reminded me of ships' cabins. The kitchen area, near the doorway, centers on a cast-iron wood stove, fired by fallen timber picked up along the way. On its surface and in its little oven, Christine Halandras managed to turn out impeccable pancakes, hot biscuits, and eggs with chopped venison. One day, she made a lamb stew from "rough cuts" that Gus Halandras sliced off the partly butchered yearling lamb he had slaughtered just before they left. The meat kept remarkably well in an unrefrigerated screened box. Year-old lamb is technically mutton, but this meat was tender and very flavorful, not muttony. The stew simmered during the midday break and then had to be hauled inside the camp to the place where we were going to spend the night. To keep the stew from spilling, Mrs. Halandras put the pot in a big metal washbasin. Barely a drop splashed out along the way.

On another night, we ate wheat tacos rolled out that afternoon by the Mexican herder, Tomás, and filled with venison chili. And at every meal, there was something produced in Christine Halandras's canning kitchen back in Meeker, where she puts up two thousand jars of spicy pickles and peach jam and tomatoes in a good year. At breakfast, for instance, she brought out some cherry syrup, a sweet-and-sour concoction she makes from the juice left in the large containers of pitted cherries she buys from a ladies' aid society.

The whole family collaborated on these meals, feeding the stove, chopping, and peeling. Gus Halandras turned out to be a mean egg fryer, and his smoked mutton, sliced for an afternoon snack, was as sophisticated a use of a normally maligned meat as you could imagine.

All this cooking takes place in the middle of the day, while the sheep are grazing, waxing fat and not exerting themselves in the full sun. The herders rouse the sheep at 5 a.m., while it is still cool, nudging the flock from behind to get the animals moving in the right direction, herding them along the road for a couple of miles or so, then resting them until 4 p.m., when they move them on for a similar distance and then stop them for the night. The pace is slow and orderly, to save the sheep's energy and prevent injury or loss. And all the way along the Bar H-L Road—which follows the migrational path of earlier nomads, the Ute Indians—other flocks belonging to other ranchers are ambling, in a federally controlled order of march, up to their grazing allotments on Forest Service lands.

This system was set up by the Taylor Grazing Act of 1934, which established firm official control of grazing on public lands. The Forest Service now regulates which sheep go where and when, in order to eliminate trampling of pastures still wet from spring runoff and to prevent the overgrazing that once exacerbated the traditional enmity between cattle and sheep producers all over the West.

Plenty of grassland is required in rough country above 8,000 feet to pasture sheep adequately. In the old days, free-ranging herds left wastelands behind them and earned the name "hoofed locusts" from cattlemen who retaliated by shooting whole flocks or driving them off cliffs. Under the modern system, which he finds overregulated and costly, Gus Halandras pays $2,700 for grazing rights on 20,000 acres of USDA forestlands in the summer. In the winter, he uses 60,000 to 70,000 acres of desert controlled by the Department of the Interior's Bureau of Land Management. Halandras has been driving sheep to these pastures for thirty years, and before him, his father had the same allotments. Understandably, he feels possessive about the vast meadows and resentful when bureaucrats regiment his drive.

Federal regulation is a rich topic of embittered discussion at the Halandras camp during the leisurely middays of the drive. Not only do the authorities control grazing, they also hinder Halandras's ability to import experienced herders. At the moment he has the men he needs. Jim is a U.S. citizen and Tomás has a green card that permits him to come in legally from Mexico to work most of the year in complete isolation, thousands of miles from the wife and children he has to leave in the state of Michoacán. Few Americans are willing to endure a shepherd's solitude and fewer have the training necessary to supervise sheep. And the immigration laws are a roadblock in the way of sheep producers who want to import experienced shepherds on a permanent basis.

From Halandras's point of view, an even more galling threat to his kind of traditional mountain grazing comes from environmentalists who, at their most radical, want to keep sheep out of public lands altogether, protecting the fragile alpine ecology from everything human except perhaps a controlled form of tourism. "What could be more sensible, environmentally, than open-range grazing?" he asks, while loading four orphan "bum" lambs, which have to be bottle-fed, into his overloaded pickup. "It takes no grain, no supplementals. We produce prime meat with grass feed. Is this country so affluent it can abandon a renewable resource and keep it just for recreation?"

Later, after a bath in a stream, Halandras fulminates some more against meddling wildlife preservationists who don't share his hatred of the coyote. Like other sheep producers, Halandras would like to use poison to control the coyotes, which, according to him, kill 10 to 15 percent of his lambs. But since 1972, when President Nixon ordered a ban on predator poisons on public lands, sheepmen have had to depend on traps, guns, and guard dogs. Last year, Jim Atencio did manage to trap or shoot sixty-three coyotes, but the Halandras flock still lost 250 to 300 lambs, "maybe more." Assuming that those figures are accurate, the loss from predation (figuring each lost lamb as a lost market potential of $70) ran Halandras from $15,000 to $20,000.

Environmentalists hotly dispute the standard figures that sheep producers give for their predator losses. And since most of the data available from official sources comes out of possibly self-serving questionnaires solicited from sheep producers, it is hard to prove that the apparent rise in coyote-caused lamb deaths since the poison ban is a real one. Furthermore, the figures can be read in two ways.

Even if the percentage of predator kills has doubled since the 1950's, the rise could be explained simply as an arithmetical result of the decline in absolute numbers of sheep on open-range pastures. If, for instance, the number of kills remained constant over time, the percentage loss would rise inevitably as the sheep population fell for a host of unrelated reasons, ranging from producers going into other lines of work to adverse market pressures. Obviously, coyotes do kill lambs, but the coyote controversy will never be resolved until a very thorough and disinterested study is made of coyote populations and the cause of lamb deaths on the range. Meanwhile, sheepmen seem to be fighting a losing battle against both *Canis latrans* and environmentally minded lawmakers.

The political weakness of sheep producers is, however, easily explained by their small numbers, distance from Washington, and lack of economic significance. And underneath all of these factors lies the fundamental stigma that sheep and sheepmen bear, both out West and in all America's folklore. As Halandras puts it, "No American child ever plays shepherds and Indians."

Gus Halandras hopes his own children will get out of the sheep business. "I want them to get an education," he says, "and train for a profession." Regas Halandras, fifteen, plans to become a lawyer. He and his younger brother are both accomplished herders, but if they sell their father's sheep and go to work in offices, their children will never know about the splendidly familial, outdoor, gypsy way of life on the range.

Perhaps open-range grazing is an anachronism and a threat to the pristine quality of the Western mountains. But it is still a vigorous tradition, locally symbolized by the initials that generations of herders have carved on aspens at campgrounds along the Bar H-L Road and nationally represented by meltingly tender domestic lamb raised on grass and thin air.

Unfortunately, through some Gresham's law of meat marketing, beef seems to have driven lamb virtually out of circulation. Lamb production rose slightly this year, but the basic picture is still dim. Regas Halandras knows that. His family may eat ground lamb, but MacDonald's doesn't serve it. And he must have learned another lesson about the low status of sheepherding when he went up to the edge of the family grazing allotments, at glorious Meadow Lake, and found the access road blocked with a log and posted with a sign forbidding automobile traffic. The ranger who put up the sign must have meant to keep tourist vehicles out. He apparently forgot that the sheep camps were coming.

☞ LAMB CHOPS

10 to 12 lamb chops
½ cup olive oil
Juice of two lemons
1 to 2 cloves garlic, peeled and
   finely chopped

Worcestershire sauce
1 teaspoon oregano leaves,
   crushed
Salt
Pepper

(1) Place chops in a flat baking pan.

(2) Mix remaining ingredients and pour over chops. Marinate overnight or longer.

(3) Broil or barbecue chops, basting with sauce.

Y I E L D : 10 to 12 chops.

☞ LAMB SHANKS KAPAMA

4 to 5 lamb shanks
2 garlic cloves, minced
1 large onion, peeled and
   chopped
½ cup chopped celery
1 to 2 bay leaves

1 teaspoon oregano
1 cup tomato paste
½ cup olive oil
½ cup red or white wine
Salt
Pepper

(1) Preheat oven to 350 degrees.

(2) Mix all ingredients in a roasting pan.

(3) Add 2 cups water. Cover and bake for 1½ hours.

(4) Uncover and bake 1 hour or until tender and sauce thickens. Serve sauce over rice or noodles.

YIELD: 4 to 5 servings.

☞ LAMB AVGOLEMONO

2 pounds lamb, stewing meat or shoulder, cut in chunks	1 teaspoon salt
	Pepper
2 tablespoons olive oil or butter	3 large eggs
1 large onion, chopped	1 tablespoon cornstarch
5 to 6 celery ribs cut in 2-inch sections	Juice of 2 lemons

(1) Brown meat, a few pieces at a time, in very hot oil, in a heavy pot. Reserve.

(2) Reduce heat and brown onion and celery lightly in the same oil. Return browned lamb to pot, add salt, pepper, and 3 cups water. Bring to a boil, reduce heat and simmer, covered, for 1½ hours or until meat is tender.

(3) To make sauce, remove 2 cups hot cooking liquid and reserve. Then, beat eggs in a bowl until frothy. Add cornstarch and beat until thoroughly incorporated. Add lemon juice gradually, beating as you add it. Pour in reserved cooking liquid in a slow stream, beating constantly.

(4) Pour finished sauce over meat, which should still be hot. You can heat this gently, or keep it on the stove over low heat until ready to serve, but do not boil. The best thing is to serve it immediately.

YIELD: 4 to 6 servings.

☞ KEFTETHES (MEATBALLS)

1 cup bread	½ teaspoon cumin
½ cup milk	1 tablespoon chopped parsley
2 pounds ground lamb	1 teaspoon dried or
1 clove garlic, minced	1 tablespoon chopped
2 eggs	fresh mint
1 large onion, chopped	Flour
½ teaspoon cinnamon	Oil

(1) Soak bread in milk. Mix with remaining ingredients.

(2) Form into small balls and roll in flour.

(3) Sauté in hot oil until browned and cooked through.

YIELD: 6 to 8 servings.

Note: These may be served in a spaghetti-type sauce, but they are delicious served as is or served on toothpicks as hors d'oeuvres.

☞ STUFFED TOMATOES

10 to 12 tomatoes	1 tablespoon chopped parsley
1 pound ground lamb	1 teaspoon cumin
½ cup cooked rice	2 tablespoons olive oil
1 medium onion, peeled and chopped	Salt
1 tablespoon fresh chopped or	Pepper
1 teaspoon dried mint	

(1) Preheat oven to 350 degrees.

(2) Cut top from tomatoes so that pulp can be scooped out. Save the pulp, push it through a sieve, and reserve.

(3) Mix ground lamb and remaining ingredients. Stuff the tomatoes with this mixture.

(4) Set the stuffed tomatoes in a greased baking pan. Pour reserved juice from tomato pulp over tomatoes. Top with dried bread crumbs.

(5) Bake for 1½ hours.

Y I E L D: 4 to 6 servings.

Note: Green peppers may be used, following the same method.

☞ LAMB LIVER IN SALSA

Oil
1½ pounds lamb liver, cut in narrow strips
Flour
1 large onion, peeled and chopped
1 clove garlic, peeled and chopped

1½ cups tomato sauce
2 tablespoons chopped fresh parsley
1 teaspoon dried oregano
Salt
Pepper
1 lemon, sliced thinly (optional)

(1) Heat oil in a skillet. Meanwhile, dredge liver strips in flour. Shake off excess flour and brown in hot oil. Remove strips with a spatula as soon as they brown and drain on paper toweling.

(2) Add all remaining ingredients to the drippings in the skillet, along with 2 cups water. Bring to a boil, reduce heat, and simmer 15 minutes.

(3) Return liver strips to skillet and cook at a slow simmer. Test the liver after a few minutes and remove it to a serving platter as soon as it has absorbed the sauce's flavor. Do

not overcook. Use excess sauce with spaghetti served on the side or at another meal.

YIELD: 4 to 6 servings.

CHILI CON BLARNEY

Looking like a giant egg with eyebrows, a stranger came up to me in the lobby of an Austin, Texas, motel in 1971, proffering a plain brown carton. I looked puzzled. He showed me his driver's license, which was Vietnamese, but gave his name as Wick Fowler. The carton contained several packets of pre-mixed spices boldly labeled "Three-Alarm Chili." Fowler had created the jocular product to capitalize on his fame as the chief cook of the Chili Appreciation Society International (CASI), an outfit that sponsors the Annual World Championship Chili Cookoff in a Texas mining ghost town called Terlingua.

Fowler was not profaning the pristine sanctity of the Terlingua cookoff. His chili mix was by no means contemptible. And self-advertisement lies at the heart of the cookoff itself, which began as a publicity stunt in 1967. A Dallas restaurateur and journalist, Frank X. Tolbert, had concocted the contest to promote the sale of his book, *A Bowl of Red: The Natural History of Chili with Recipes*. Originally, Tolbert had planned to pit Fowler against Dave Chasen, the Beverly Hills restaurateur, whose chief stirrer was to have been Elizabeth Taylor. But Chasen fell ill, and the humorist H. Allen Smith of Mount Kisco, New York, author of a boastful mock attack on Texas chili cooks, stood in for him. The result was called a draw, but the cookoff itself was a decisive success, spawning what Tolbert has called "an international subculture" involving thousands of "chili heads" who compete in CASI-sponsored local tourneys from Manila to Connecticut. Winners trek to Terlingua on the first Saturday in November for "the big showdown," which is probably the biggest, grossest, booziest, most self-inflated, and certainly most entertaining of all the thousands of American regional food events that each year purport to commemorate and preserve the hallowed and embattled dishes of yesteryear.

Second to none in my hunger for authentic American food, I traveled to Terlingua for the Fourteenth Annual Wick Fowler Memorial World Championship Chili Cookoff. Getting to the remote patch of desert on the banks of the Rio Grande where the contest is held isn't easy. Essentially, you drive through the 8,000-foot, lunar Chisos Mountains in the Big Bend National Park, and turn right. Road runners skitter and bob across the highway. The sky is big, and the nearest town of consequence, Alpine, is eighty miles away. For cookoff weekend, Alpine's motels are full, all their rooms having been reserved several weeks in advance. There aren't really many other places to stay in the rest of Brewster County, the state's largest, which at 5,935 square miles is bigger than Connecticut and very empty.

A century ago, when its mines provided 40 percent of the

country's cinnabar, or mercury ore, Terlingua itself had 2,000 or so inhabitants. But foreign competition closed the mines, and only four permanent inhabitants remained when CASI staged the first cookoff. By now, however, the word has spread worldwide. On cookoff weekend, Terlingua hosts hundreds of chili heads and camp followers who arrive with tents and vans for the rowdiest weekend this side of Fort Lauderdale.

The contest site looked like a Hollywood mock-up of a Western town. But the real-life action was a bit more "adult" than the movie industry tends to allow. Dancers in Old West costumes gyrated at the Ball Buster Bar. They were the show business aspect of the Ball Buster Chili team. The cookoff gives an award for the best variety act of the day, which explained the frontier revival church in full swing at one end of the patio. Brother Willie and Sister Lilly's Salvation Chili team led the pagan hordes in a hymn sung to the tune of "Amazing Grace": "Salvation chili came to me/ And saved my soul from grief./ It cured my pimples, healed my toe/ And put me on relief . . ."

The crowd was dressed in a variety of costumes, ranging from obscene T-shirts to the height of urban cowboy dandyism —an all-rattlesnake-skin vest decorated with several huge rattles and fossilized shark's-teeth all set about with turquoise and silver. The crowd, restless with anticipation and primed with Texas beer, gathered to watch young women vie in a wet T-shirt contest and young men take their pants off for the "equal opportunity" hairy legs competition. At the height of the frenzy, a voice on the public address system announced: "Matt Butler lost his pistol. Nickel-plated. Whoever finds it, there's a reward. If that's necessary."

Meanwhile, at the edge of the festivities, a motley collection of men and women were devoting themselves with solemnity to the preparation of chili. For them it was a serious day of judgment.

Connecticut champ Jim Hibbits, wearing a frock coat and top hat, stirred and tasted his Ugly Butcher Chili. Wayland Walker of Ardmore, Oklahoma, told passers-by how he had turned to chili out of desperation, when a slaughterhouse mis-cut a whole beef he had purchased from the local sheriff. Some sixty contestants labored over their pet chilis all through the forenoon, hoping that greatness would be thrust upon them by the CASI judges. Most of the cooks used whole chili peppers, not prepared powder. And they followed CASI rules, which in-sist on beef and forbid all vegetables except onions. This not only eliminates exotic ingredients such as pineapple but also excludes beans. At Terlingua, beans are viewed with alarm, as a contaminant of what Texas Governor Bill Clements hailed in an official proclamation as "unadulterated Texas chili."

My own random tasting of the chilis in progress reminded me how much variation there can be on an apparently simple culinary idea. Even with the CASI restrictions, no two chilis tasted alike. Recondite spice combinations and varying dos-ages produced a wide spectrum of flavors, as well as levels of hotness ranging from mild to infernal.

Judges assembled at lunchtime on a protected upper level and began their tongue-singeing task, clearing their palates with beer between tastes, doing their best to rate each entry on a ten-point scale based on five criteria: aroma, red color, consistency, taste, and aftertaste.

No one disputed their final decision to award the world championship to Brother Willie and Sister Lilly's Salvation Chili. But any objective bystander who had not entirely suc-cumbed to the soporific powers of Texas sun and brew was left wondering what it all meant. Was Terlingua merely a ribald exercise in boosterism and self-parody or did the cookoff really help to maintain the purity of one of the nation's best known and most polymorphous regional dishes?

At issue is the whole vexing problem of authenticity in

food. CASI's rules are a laudable attempt to codify and preserve what one of its members asserted to me was an invention of the frontier, a simple beef stew seasoned with regionally abundant capsicum (chili) peppers and other spices (usually cumin, oregano, and garlic) and onions (see recipes). Also, the Terlingua chili heads are certainly right to abominate *outré* variations such as Cincinnati three-way chili or the bland bowls of ground meat and beans served at every nondescript lunch counter in the land.

On the other hand, all the Lone Star chauvinism at Terlingua overlooks certain obvious factors that must have contributed to the evolution of chili con carne. The dish obviously did not originate entirely among English-speaking Texas ranchers. The influence of Mexico, within sight across the river from Terlingua, shows itself in the part-Spanish, part-Nahuatl name. "Chili" is a descendant of the Aztec term for capsicum peppers. And it simply must be the case that modern chili arose through the contact of nineteenth-century white immigrants with native Indians and Mexicans. This of course is where all of the so-called Tex-Mex foods began. Chili is merely the most popular among them, mixing the Mexican tradition of sauces flavored with chili (and other spices typical of Mexican food) with the European notion of a beef stew based on chunks of browned meat.

All through the American Southwest different variations on the same theme have sprung up and prospered. Consider chili with beans, green chili made from green chili peppers, or chili with ground meat. You will find chili served at Indian pueblos and at the Tigua Indian Reservation in El Paso. There is even quite "authentic" chili in Arizona and other non-Texas locations in the Southwest.

To be fair, the Terlingua cookoff is not purely isolationist. It promotes the worldwide proliferation of its kind of chili. But the motive behind CASI is still intrinsically self-contradictory.

CASI wants to protect traditional Texas chili, as if it were a dish handed down over generations by a coherent culture, fixed as to its ingredients and style of preparation in one basic ancestral recipe. But the very essence of chili con carne is its cultural diversity and lack of culinary fixity. At Terlingua, the chili heads, while claiming to preserve a traditional recipe, are in fact trying to create one. So remember, the next time you start to put beans in your chili, the eyes of Texas are upon you.

☞ FRANK X. TOLBERT'S

"SIMPLIFIED TEXAS CHILI"
(Adapted from a text in Flying Colors *magazine)*

3 pounds lean beef	½ cup paprika
2 ounces suet (or substitute vegetable oil)	1 tablespoon cayenne (optional)
2 to 4 chilis anchos	1 sprig fresh coriander
2 tablespoons cumin	(cilantro), chopped
1 tablespoon oregano	⅓ cup finely chopped garlic

(1) Cut the beef into bite-sized chunks.

(2) Render the suet in a heavy skillet, and sauté the beef chunks until they turn gray.

(3) Pour the liquid from the skillet into a heavy pot, leaving a small amount in the pan. Continue cooking the meat until it is well browned on all sides.

(4) Meanwhile, remove stems from chilis and puree in a blender with a small amount of water. Add puree to chili pot.

(5) When meat is browned, add it to the chili pot and simmer for 30 minutes.

(6) Add remaining ingredients and simmer for another 30 minutes or until meat is tender. (Use choice chuck. That old myth about bull meat is not for the Tolberts.)

(7) Keep the chili overnight; in the morning, scrape off the grease that comes to the top.

Y I E L D: 6 to 8 servings.

☞ LONE STAR TEXAS CHILI WITH BEANS

2 tablespoons vegetable oil
2 pounds stewing beef, cubed
1 cup chopped onions
1 green bell pepper, seeded and chopped
1 clove garlic, minced
1 12-ounce can tomato paste
2½ cups water
2 pickled jalapeño peppers, rinsed, seeded, and chopped

1½ tablespoons chili powder
½ teaspoon crushed red pepper
½ teaspoon salt
½ teaspoon dried oregano
½ teaspoon cumin
1 15½-ounce can pinto beans, drained

(1) In a large, heavy pan, heat oil and brown beef cubes on all sides. Add onions, bell pepper, and garlic and fry with beef for about 5 minutes.

(2) Add all the remaining ingredients except beans, and simmer the chili for 1½ hours or until the meat is tender.

(3) Add beans and simmer 30 minutes longer.

Y I E L D: 4 to 6 servings.

☞ CHILI CON CARNE

8 pounds lean beef, cubed	1 teaspoon dried oregano
4 tablespoons lard	½ teaspoon cumin
4 large onions, peeled and chopped	4 cups fresh green chili, chopped
4 garlic cloves, minced	Salt

(1) Brown the meat in the lard (lard produces the most authentic flavor in New Mexico cookery).

(2) Fry the onions along with the meat until translucent.

(3) Add the garlic, oregano, cumin, and chili. Pour in 6 cups hot water and simmer for several hours. Salt to taste. Other meats such as pork, mutton, deer, moose, elk, and goat, may be substituted or combined.

YIELD: 16 servings.

☞ CHILI CON CARNE WITH TOMATOES

1 pound lean ground beef	1 cup fresh green chili, chopped
½ cup chopped onion	
2 tablespoons lard	2 garlic cloves, minced
1 tablespoon flour	½ teaspoon oregano
1 can tomatoes (number 303) with liquid	¼ teaspoon cumin
	Salt

(1) Brown the meat along with the onions in the lard. Stir in the flour.

(2) Mash the tomatoes and add along with the liquid. Add the chili, garlic, oregano, and cumin. Salt to taste. Add 1 cup water and simmer covered for 2 to 3 hours.

YIELD: 6 to 8 servings.

☞ CHILI CON CARNE WITH BEANS

1 cup pinto beans
2 tablespoons lard
½ cup chopped onion
2 pounds lean ground beef

2 cans tomatoes (number 303)
 with liquid, mashed
2 tablespoons chili powder

(1) Boil the pinto beans in plenty of water until tender.

(2) Heat the lard in a large skillet and brown the onion. Add the ground beef, brown, and simmer for a few minutes.

(3) Drain the beans and add along with tomatoes and their liquid. Stir in the chili powder and bring to a boil.

(4) Reduce heat and cook until meat is tender and the flavors well blended.

YIELD: 10 to 12 servings.

☞ PUEBLO GREEN CHILI STEW

(Adapted from the Southwestern Indian Recipe Book, *by Zora Getmansky Hesse, Filter Press, Palmer Lake, Colorado 80133)*

Oil
2 pounds pork, mutton, lamb,
 or beef, cut in small pieces
Kernels scraped from 3 ears
 corn
2 ribs celery, without leaves,
 diced

2 medium potatoes, peeled and
 diced
2 medium tomatoes, diced
5 roasted green chilis, peeled,
 seeded, and diced

(1) In large pot, put in enough cooking oil to prevent meat from sticking.

(2) Add meat and cook until lightly browned.

(3) Add rest of ingredients. Add water to cover all. Cover pot and simmer for 1 hour or until done.

YIELD: 8 servings.

☞ GREEN CHILI STEW

(*Adapted from* Pueblo and Navajo Cookery, *by Marcia Keegan, Earth Books,* *145 Palisade Street, Dobbs Ferry, New York 10522*)

1½ pounds boned lamb, cut
    into 1-inch cubes
Flour
  2 tablespoons lard
  ½ teaspoon freshly ground
    black pepper
  3 dried juniper berries,
    crushed
  1 medium-sized onion, peeled
    and chopped

2½ cups canned hominy
1½ tablespoons red chili
    powder
  ½ teaspoon salt
  1 clove garlic, peeled and
    mashed
  1 teaspoon oregano
  3 green chili peppers, peeled,
    seeded, and chopped

(1) Coat lamb lightly with flour.

(2) Brown lamb slowly on all sides in lard in a large heavy saucepan. While meat browns, add black pepper and juniper berries.

(3) Transfer meat to a plate. Sauté onion in pan until slightly wilted. Return meat to pan. Add remaining ingredients, plus 2 cups water, and simmer, covered, for 1½ hours, stirring occasionally.

YIELD: 6 servings.

Three recipes adapted from the *Pueblo Indian Cookbook,* edited by Phyllis Hughes, Museum of New Mexico Press, P.O. Box 2087, Santa Fe, New Mexico 87503:

☞ CHILI STEW WITH CORN DUMPLINGS

2½ cups diced, peeled potatoes
  2 cups cooked pinto or other
      dried beans
  2 teaspoons salt
  1 large onion, chopped
  1 tablespoon lard
  1 pound ground beef or lamb

2 teaspoons chili powder or
    ⅓ cup red chili pulp
3 large fresh tomatoes or one
    can tomatoes (number 303)
1 recipe corn dumplings
    (see below)

(1) Mix potatoes, beans, salt, and 3 cups water in good-sized kettle.

(2) Sauté onion in melted lard. Add beef and cook until meat loses red color. Add chili and tomatoes, stir thoroughly, and add to first mixture. Bring to boil and simmer for 30 minutes.

(3) Drop dumpling mixture by heaping tablespoonsful on top of stew, cover, and simmer 8 to 10 minutes.

Y I E L D: 4 servings.

☞ CORN DUMPLINGS

1 cup corn kernels
1 cup flour
1 teaspoon baking powder

3 tablespoons cornmeal
Salt

(1) Mash corn thoroughly or grate in blender.

(2) Mix all ingredients until well blended. Add water if necessary but keep dough fairly stiff.

☞ JUNIPER LAMB STEW

2 pounds lean lamb, cut in small cubes

1 tablespoon flour

1½ teaspoons salt

2 teaspoons chili powder

2 tablespoons lard

6 ears fresh corn

6 scallions with tops, chopped

3 green bell peppers, seeded and chopped

2 teaspoons dried wild celery (⅓ cup chopped celery tops may be substituted)

5 dried juniper berries, crushed

(1) Dredge lamb in mixture of flour, salt, and chili powder.

(2) Brown in hot lard in heavy kettle. Cut corn from cobs and add with other ingredients and 4 cups water to meat. Cover and simmer for 1 hour or until meat is tender.

Y I E L D: 4 servings.

TILLAMOOK CHEDDAR

First there were the mountains of the Coast Range and, in between them, lush green meadows. The climate was mild, and grass grew thick all year. This dairyman's utopia was what Joe Champion saw when he landed by whale boat in Tillamook Bay one April morning in 1851. Champion had sailed down the Oregon coast from Astoria at the mouth of the Columbia River to settle this remote but lovely corner of the earth.

"The Indians," wrote Champion, "generally seemed pleased with the prospect of having the whites to settle among them [poor fools].

"They showed me a large hollow Spruce Tree into which we conveyed all my property."

He lived in the tree for a month and then built a cabin. That same year, other rugged pioneers followed Champion to Tillamook, driving herds of cattle that waxed fat on the pristine pasture and gave milk in wonderful abundance. But there was no practical way to ship the milk out of Tillamook. The only land route over the summit of the Coast Range was an Indian track. The county did not get a rail connection with the outside world until 1911. Boats were undependable and slow. Milk was bulky and perishable.

Cheese was the answer. It was compact and kept extremely well. So the Tillamook pioneers made cheese from their milk and in 1855 built a ship called the *Morning Star* to carry it up the Columbia River to market.

Little cheese factories sprang up everywhere, amateur operations that resulted in a bewildering array of cheeses— some good, some bad. Eventually, in 1894, an itinerant cheesemaker from Ontario, Peter McIntosh, introduced the standard cheddar process he had learned back East.

By 1894, cheddar was already an established part of life in many parts of North America. The first cheddar factory in the United States had been set up in 1851 by Jesse Williams near Rome, New York. This hard, bacterially cultured whole-milk pressed cheese was British in origin, having been invented there some time before 1664, in the Somersetshire village of Cheddar, near Bristol. Yet it assimilated itself in the New World so well that it was often known as American cheese. New Englanders spoke of it familiarly as rat cheese or store cheese.

Tillamook cheddar ought to have been just another example of the same ubiquitous product. But those sturdy Pacific Northwest yeomen who made it aged their cheddar longer than the standard six or seven months. They liked their cheese as sharp and mature as possible. Two whole years of curing was not unusual.

Something else crucial separated the Tillamook cheesemakers from their competitors in other places, even from those in other locations along the Oregon coast. The Tillamook factories had a flair for modern marketing. As early as 1909, they banded together as the Tillamook County Creamery Association, standardized their production, and adopted Tillamook as an exclusive trade name.

Today, you can learn all about the progressive consolidation of the Tillamook factories in the museum at the giant plant on Highway 101 just north of the town of Tillamook. Out in front is a full-scale replica of the *Morning Star,* which is the Tillamook logo.

The plant itself is now the only factory producing cheese for the Tillamook label. It is a model of spotless, automated mass production and worlds apart from the cheesemaking of olden days commemorated in the exhibit of antique cheese vats and tools in the plant museum or from the battered fifty-gallon copper cheese kettle in the Pioneer Museum in town.

In the visitors' observation area of the plant, you can watch the cheesemaking process through a glass wall. Oregon's strict health laws forbid visitors going out on the plant floor, but the overhead view of the five 15,500-quart vats is dramatic all the same. A sea of milk cultured with lactobacilli and rennet curdles while automatic stirring devices sweep slowly through the vats. Whey gradually drains out of the vats, leaving behind curds that remind you of scrambled eggs. Then a man appears. He cuts a lengthwise ditch down the middle of the vat, leaving the curd packed together on either side. In a few minutes, the curd is firm enough to be turned without breaking, and it is time for him to "cheddar" the cheese. He cuts the curd into slabs several inches wide. He works with machinelike precision, cutting dozens of identical loaves of curd, then turning them so that whey runs out uniformly and rapidly. The firm slabs then travel on a conveyor belt to a milling machine that cuts them into fingerlike pieces, washes them, adds a small amount of salt, and packs them in hoops.

Each hoop holds forty pounds of curd, which is pressed for three hours. The pressed blocks go into a curing area with a ten-million-pound capacity, where the temperature is always 38 degrees Fahrenheit. Federal law requires that cheddar be cured for sixty days. Medium Tillamook is, in fact, cured for three months. The sharp cheddar ages for seven months.

On my way out of the observation area, I walked through the factory gift shop and bought some sharp cheese. In the parking lot, I cut into the package, feeling in direct contact with Tillamook pioneer days as the annatto-colored cheese emerged. The Coast Range loomed on the horizon. *Morning Star II* was only a few feet away. I tasted the cheese.

It was mediocre. Not bad. Clearly a cheddar, with a respectable tang to it, but not the stellar cheese I had once tasted in the home of a New York epicure whose Oregonian wife had imported it from a special source in her home state.

But I had been warned. James Beard, himself an Oregonian, had told me I would probably not find old-fashioned, aged Tillamook cheese in Oregon. The demand is too great these days. The cost of holding the cheese in the curing room for two years is prohibitive. M. Wayne Jensen, Jr., director of the Pioneer Museum and the son of a cheesemaker, told me much the same thing. He remembered when farmers used to leave cheeses in the factory curing area to age like cigars in the Dunhill humidor room. He even remembered tasting a cheddar that had been cured right through World War II. "It was a bit crumbly," he conceded, "but good, good and sharp." Nevertheless, he didn't know where I would find even a two-year-old cheese today.

James Beard had suggested that I might ask around at the factory. Some of the employees might be aging cheese at home. I left my car and accosted the first worker I saw. "Yes," she said, "I've got some in my refrigerator right now. I keep it sealed in the back of the vegetable drawer for two years. Just turn it once a week."

If I wanted to buy some old cheddar, she said, I might try at the market up the coast in Bay City.

The C & W Markette is a little country store in a very small town. You would not ordinarily stop there on your way north along the gorgeous coastal highway. And even if you did, you would probably notice nothing special about the place except for the homemade beef jerky in the meat department. But the well-informed turophile at the C & W walks briskly to the back of the store and snaps up some peculiar little packages of cheddar in plastic bags. They sell for more than the brand-name cheddar in the same display area, but the price is not at all outlandish: $3.45 per pound. They look just like other cheddars, but they are sublime. Not aggressively sharp, yet undeniably vigorous, these special cheeses are luxuriously dense but not at all crumbly. They are, indeed, curiously smooth, with a complexity of taste that would make Peter McIntosh proud.

"I buy medium cheddar from the factory by the ton," says Frank Walz, proprietor of the C & W. "Then I age it at 32 degrees for three years. It's easier that way. It would go faster at 55, but I'd have to turn it all the time."

Tradition dies hard in Oregon. The Tillamook central plant keeps the legend of its cheese alive, and it manufactures the raw material for traditional aged cheese. Frank Walz, who migrated west from Minneapolis twenty years ago, does the rest. And in my New York refrigerator, five pounds of factory-sealed cheese sits quietly in the back of the vegetable drawer. I turn it from time to time, thinking of pacific cows, thick grass, and Joe Champion in his hollow spruce.

☞ OREGON FISH AND CHEESE CASSEROLE

(Adapted from Carol Cate's Clam Dishes and Rock Fishes, *available from Carol's Cookbooks, P.O. Box 795, Winchester, Oregon 97495)*

1½ pounds rockfish (fleshy white fish) fillets
1 teaspoon salt
¼ teaspoon pepper
1 cup whole-kernel corn
1½ cups green beans, cooked
2 cups cooked potatoes, sliced
¼ cup butter or margarine
2 tablespoons lemon juice
2 tablespoons grated onion
1 tablespoon chopped parsley
2 medium tomatoes, peeled and sliced
¼ cup grated cheddar cheese (1 ounce)

(1) Cut fish into 3 or 4 serving-size portions and sprinkle with half the salt and pepper. Preheat oven to 350 degrees.

(2) In a large, well-greased casserole, place in layers the corn, green beans, and potatoes, sprinkling each layer with the remaining salt and pepper.

(3) Combine butter or margarine, lemon juice, onion, and parsley. Dip fish into mixture and arrange on top of potatoes. Cover with tomato slices and cheese.

(4) Bake 1 hour and 15 minutes or until fish flakes.

YIELD: 3 to 4 servings.

☞ WELSH RAREBIT

(From Bert Greene's Kitchen Bouquets, *Contemporary Books, Inc., Chicago, Illinois)*

2 tablespoons unsalted butter
3 egg yolks
1 teaspoon Dijon mustard
½ teaspoon beef bouillon
    powder
1 teaspoon imported soy sauce
Dash of hot pepper sauce

Pinch of ground allspice
¾ cup light beer
10 ounces sharp cheddar,
    grated
1 tablespoon heavy cream
1 teaspoon Scotch whisky
4 slices hot buttered toast

(1) Melt butter in a double boiler.

(2) Beat the egg yolks with the Dijon mustard, bouillon powder, soy sauce, hot pepper sauce, and allspice. Stir in the beer.

(3) Add the beer mixture to the melted butter; place over simmering water. Stir until hot. Add the grated cheese, ¼ cup at a time, stirring constantly in one direction with a wooden spoon until mixture is smooth.

(4) Stir in the cream and Scotch. Do not let mixture stand more than 5 minutes before serving over hot buttered toast.

YIELD: 4 servings.

THE GIANT SNAIL OF
LA JOLLA: DIVING
FOR ABALONE

Emma Stark Hampton, Daughter of the American Revolution and the distinguished Michigan lady after whom my Detroit elementary school was named, had in her time put together a stylish amateur collection of rocks and fossils, fish bills, and shells, which came eventually to rest in an unlabeled heap in a disused closet at the Hampton School. The principal, a canny bureaucrat who had been frequently pressed by my mother to "enrich" my educational program, seized upon the neglected Hampton trove as an ideal extracurricular project that would occupy my vaunted intellectual curiosity and also give the school its own museum of natural history.

While other children sat in class, studying the art of the paper wad, I attended to my curatorial duties. Completely ignorant of biology and geology, I spent many happy hours leisurely familiarizing myself with the objects but not making much progress toward their positive identification. Fortunately, an older boy named Larry Fishman, who had a modest grasp of the relevant science, was my co-curator. He knew a trilobite when he saw one, and he was also able to tell me that certain large, flattish, nacreous shells with holes in them were abalones.

In that inland setting, where even clams and oysters were exotic beasts, it never occurred to me that the gastropods that had once lived in those iridescent shells were edible. But like many other Midwesterners, when I grew up, I made my way to California, off whose shores various species of the abalone genus, *Haliotis,* cling to underwater rocks and feast on kelp. Californians justly prize the muscular flesh of the foot—sometimes almost twelve inches long—that holds this marine snail in place. Indeed, abalone is such a delicacy along our southern Pacific coast that it is possibly the most expensive indigenous American food, at roughly $15 a pound in markets, because it is so scarce. Commercial divers and sportsmen with scuba rigs have pursued abalone so avidly that good beds are harder and harder to find. And now that the sea otter is environmentally protected, this natural predator of abalones is extending its range and further depleting the haliotian supply.

This abalone dearth sounds like a typically modern problem in which overfishing, high population density, and ecological tampering have decimated a mollusk that had happily carried on its vegetarian life cycle in American waters for millenniums before the coming of our advanced civilization. This scenario is true enough as far as it goes, but the wholesale assault on the abalone actually began very long ago and must qualify as one of the earliest human depredations of the American biomass.

In the kitchen middens of Indians who lived on what is now Catalina Island, west of Los Angeles, about 4000 to 3500 B.C., Clement W. Meighan found shell remains indicating that even then, without benefit of high technology, the abalone had started its up-and-down career as a sometimes endangered species.

In the lower strata that he excavated, Meighan found a predominance of abalone shells. They outnumbered the next most abundant genus, *Mytilus* (mussels), by a ratio of 4 to 1. In the upper levels, the ratio had reversed. Evidently, the Indians, preferring the abalone to other shellfish, had eaten their way through the abalone beds and then switched over to mussels when abalones became scarce.

Although contemporary Californians may seem to be re- peating the process, they have not yet switched to mussels because of toxic pollution and a dietary phobia against them. Fortunately, they also have taken some measures to turn the tide in favor of the abalone. In a former sardine cannery in Monterey, George S. Lockwood is at work perfecting a com- mercially viable abalone farm. Through careful, enriched feeding and controlled light and temperature conditions, he hopes that maricultured abalones will put on their desired weight twice as fast as the ten years they would normally take in the wild. Lockwood also sells small abalones to the Cali- fornia Department of Fish and Game, which plants them in the ocean.

More prosaically, Fish and Game patrols set up abalone fishing areas to enforce the strict regulations enacted to protect already established natural beds. Sport divers are permitted a maximum of four abalones a day, and these cannot legally be stockpiled in the refrigerator since it is against the law to possess more than four at a time. There are also rules about minimum permissible length. Red abalones, the largest species, have to be at least seven inches; pinks and greens, six inches. Tougher, less desirable blacks, which cling to rocks in the surf, are legal at five inches.

Divers measure their take underwater with the irons they use to pry their prey loose from the rocks. These long flat blades are marked off at five, six, and seven inches, and by law, they must not be thinner than an eighth of an inch so that they don't cut the abalone. Since abalones have no clotting agent in their blood, a cut means certain death, making it futile for divers to put back those that are too small.

Despite all these apparently stultifying regulations and what may sound like a tedious amount of time spent checking length, catching an abalone is still mostly a matter of stealth and speed. Give the gastropod warning that you are there and it tightens its grip on the rock, tightens it so that its potentially delectable foot exerts a force of 400 pounds per square inch. In practice, once this happens, the game is up: the hapless diver cannot pry the abalone loose. Good abalone hunters slip the blade swiftly under the foot and pull immediately. Hesitation lets the animal seize the blade, and once that happens, hard prying can do little more than bend and break the metal.

"The new diver has a difficult time," says Bert Kobayashi, a Ph.D. in marine biology from the Scripps Institute of Oceanography at La Jolla, who supervises the physical education program at the University of California, San Diego. Kobayashi also teaches scuba classes and is the guiding light of the UCSD diving club, known as the Sea Deucers.

Recently I went with Kobayashi and the Sea Deucers out beyond the famous surf that pounds into Black's Beach in La Jolla. With the town's sheer sandstone cliffs behind us, we pitched and rolled out into the chilly, fifty-degree Pacific in an inflated boat, until we came to a field of kelp. The water was about sixty feet deep where we dropped anchor.

"Right down the anchor line," said Kobayashi in his bass announcer's voice. "Let's do it." Several wet-suited bodies with breathing apparatus flipped backward into the ocean and disappeared except for the constant stream of bubbles they sent up to the surface.

Feeling queasy from the movement of the boat while I sat waiting, I tried to relieve the nausea by staring at distant points on the shore. We had come quite far out to sea, I thought. As Kobayashi had told me, "It has gotten harder and harder to find abalones. There are still areas that appear to be virgin, but even there the average size has decreased."

A pod of curious sea lions swam around the boat, distracting me periodically from the cliffs, which are really the visible portion of an immense undersea canyon whose walls cause La Jolla's splendid surf. Surfers, little black dots much farther in, were out in force riding the big waves.

After a few minutes, Kobayashi emerged with a bag of red abalones, the world's largest *Haliotis*. Some of the other divers had found them too, but the dive had been particularly hard because the surge of the waves had reached down abnormally deep and roiled the bottom, sweeping the Sea Deucers along at a speed that disrupted the intricate search and surgical lunge of abalone fishing. Even so, they had pried loose enough abalones to make a meal for all of us.

After red abalones have been shelled, cleaned, and cut into several thin slices, two of these big univalves will generally feed three people. But getting to the cooking stage with abalones is quite a job and, among other things, requires a grasp of abalone anatomy and physiology.

On the outside of the elliptical shell, near one of the long outer edges, is a line of holes. The animal's gills are behind the holes, which are outlets for water expelled from the gills. There is a lip on the inner rim of the shell on the side with the holes. The opposite side has no lip, giving easier access to the abalone iron.

You set the abalone on a table upside down (with the foot up) and insert the iron between the flesh and the shell, pushing down as far as it will go and then pulling it back and forth while exerting some pressure upward, until the muscle pops loose from the shell. Done properly, this maneuver will remove the abalone in one piece from the shell, which has a beautifully iridescent interior, really a muscle scar where the foot was once attached. Sometimes a tiny, dark shrimp, *Betaeus harfordi*, drops out of the shell. It is a commensal organism, sharing shelter and meals with the abalone.

Along with the muscular, edible foot comes a large blob of gonads—green in females, cream-colored in males. Discard these and cut away the black skin and the leathery outer layer of the foot. What remains is a thick wedge of hard abalone muscle. It has to be sliced as thin as possible, which can be done in a trice with a professional meat slicing machine, the kind used in delicatessens. The Sea Deucers had improvised special boards with two metal rods set in them (or in one case, two thin strips of wood). Kobayashi showed me how to set a large, very sharp knife flat on the supports and use them as a guide. With the abalone placed between the knife supports it was possible to slice through the bottom of the muscle, making a transverse cut about an eighth of an inch thick. He removed one slice and then kept on slicing in this manner until the entire muscle had been reduced to several scaloppine, which should be chilled for three hours to relax the muscle. Then you pound them with the same kind of toothed mallet that is sold for flattening veal scaloppine.

This is not an optional step. An abalone cannot be eaten until each slice has been thoroughly pounded into flaccidity. At first, when you pound, the slices curl up as if alive. You turn them over and pound some more until finally you have a docile, extremely thin piece of meat, but you must not pound so energetically that you turn the abalone to mush or cut it to fragments.

Kobayashi soaks pounded abalone slices in milk or beer. Then he dredges them in seasoned cracker meal. Bread crumbs or cornmeal would also work well. Once you have done this, it is at last time to sauté the abalone in hot oil. When they are golden brown, you eat them, saying a little prayer so that conservation and mariculture will prevent the extinction of this very fine gift from the sea.

☞ SEAFOOD SIMMER

(Adapted from The Northwest Cookbook, *by Lila Gault, Quick Fox, Inc., New York)*

4 tablespoons butter	2 large abalones, sliced, pounded, and cut into strips
¼ cup dry white wine	
1 tablespoon shallots, peeled and finely chopped	2 large scallops, cut into pieces
1 tablespoon parsley, finely chopped	

(1) Melt butter in a medium skillet over medium high heat. When bubbling subsides, add wine and boil for a minute or so.

(2) Add shallots and parsley and cook over medium heat for 2 minutes.

(3) Add shellfish. Cook for 5 minutes, stirring occasionally.

Y I E L D : 3 to 4 servings.

BREAKFAST
AT SHUNGOPAVI:
HOPI COOKING

They don't sell tickets to the Niman dance. There are no posters for it slapped on the walls of the pueblo villages, and not even the weekly paper, *Qua 'Toqti, The Eagle's Cry*, "serving the Hopi Nation," mentions when Niman—the last and most important kachina ceremony of the season, celebrating the gathering-in of the first ears of corn from the parched fields—will occur at Shungopavi and Bakabi. The only way to find out about this ritual is to ask a Hopi, and even that is no simple matter. The handful of telephone lines that connect the remote, high Hopi mesas in northeastern Arizona with the outside world are almost always busy. But word gets out. On the eve of Niman, the Hopi Cultural Center's motel, a modern version of traditional Hopi village architecture on Second Mesa, is booked solid with Indian buffs, transcendental meditators, and European tourists doing the grand tour of *le Far West*.

To protect their ancestral culture from twentieth-century, high-tech rubbernecking, the Hopis forbid photography, sketching, and recording in their villages. You can buy a kachina doll, carved from cottonwood root and originally intended to help Hopi children learn about the elaborately masked and feathered, sashed and buskined supernatural beings who are impersonated by members of the Kachina Society at the various dances. But the dolls are meager preparation for the real kachinas.

Without warning, they file into the plaza at Shungopavi, moving slowly and with the precision of Rockettes, chanting, consecrating the ground of the plaza with cornmeal, while an eagle chained on a nearby rooftop flaps its wings. Around the edge of the plaza and on the flat roofs that overlook it, Hopi and non-Hopi spectators sit in rapt absorption. The mysterious force of the Niman holds everyone. For a few moments, after the kachinas file out and disappear into the underground houses called kivas, it is impossible not to feel the power of a ritual that has been practiced since before Columbus, when Hopis built what is now the oldest continuously inhabited town in the United States at Oraibi.

Then the tension breaks. Hopi children scamper through the plaza, holding ears of corn, one of the special food gifts of the day. Another edible present is piki—a brittle, thin toasted bread made from cornmeal. Piki is the highest expression of Hopi cuisine and the most intricate symbol of the intertwining of traditional Hopi life with corn.

There is nothing quite like it. Hopis compare piki to corn flakes; it tastes as corn flakes would if they were unsugared and unsalted. But piki is cooked in big papery sheets, then rolled up tightly into eight-inch-long cylinders about two inches thick. Also, and crucially, piki is blue.

Sometimes, it is true, piki is baked from white cornmeal

and then dyed red and yellow. But standard piki is slate blue, the glory of a prescientific culture whose caprice was to glorify a genetically freakish corn with kernels the color of the sky.

Indian corn comes in most of the colors of the rainbow because of pigmentation in the pericarp and aleurone layers of the kernel. Paul Mangelsdorf, the dean of American corn scholars, once wrote that the multicolored corns of our Southwest were part of a lineage that could be traced back to Peru and had been cultivated for centuries throughout Indian America. The original strain is called *kculli*. Prehistoric remnants of it have been found in former Inca territory, and it still grows in the high Andes. In its pure blue form, this corn is still widely cultivated in the American Southwest and milled commercially for Indian consumption in Arizona and New Mexico. Blue tortillas and other blue breads appear in Navaho and Pueblo cooking, perhaps as part of some general fascination with the blue of heaven. An outsider, wondering about the importance of blue to the Indians of the desert, will find ample impetus for symbolic interpretation in the omnipresent turquoise jewelry and blue-dyed clothing.

The truth, it seems, is simpler. "It's pretty," one Hopi told me. Others supported him. Blue is an attractive color. Symbolic explanations do not appeal.

Because of this aesthetic bias and the paramount significance of maize, foods made from blue corn, and piki, in particular, are as important to Hopi culture as the kachina ceremonies, the communal architecture of the mesa villages, and the Hopi language. All of these tribal peculiarities mark off the 8,000 ethnic Hopis from the rest of the world and give them an identity that has allowed them to survive in modern America as a distinct people entirely surrounded by unfriendly and more numerous Navahos.

"They say no man will marry a girl unless she can make

piki," wrote Helen Sekaquaptewa in her autobiography, *Me and Mine*. At eighty-one, she is the grande dame of Hopi women, mother of the tribal chairman and a revered spokesperson for Hopi tradition, despite her modern education and broad experience off the reservation. Her life exemplifies the conflict between tradition and assimilation in recent Hopi history. Her parents were "traditionals" and hid her so that she would not have to go to the *bahana* ("white man's") school. Eventually, the truant officer found her and dragged her off to a schoolhouse in Keams Canyon at the edge of Hopiland, where they deloused her, dressed her in *bahana* clothes, and taught her English. Helen Sekaquaptewa turned out to like school, but in 1910, she came back to Oraibi for a year at home and learned "the things a Hopi girl should know." Piki was one of the main lessons.

First, she learned to make the stone piki griddle, starting with a granite slab and polishing it smooth, by hand, with pebbles. She also ground corn into flour, working it between two stones, one held in the hand, until she produced a very fine blue flour, much finer than the meal one sees today in Indian supermarkets. "We have electric mills now," she says. "It was hard work in my time, with stones, but good exercise. No one had a big stomach."

The old technique of hand grinding is still passed down from mother to daughter. Young women have to grind flour in the traditional way as part of the preparation for marriage. But stone grinding is no longer a part of normal life. In a recent editorial in *Qua 'Toqti*, Mrs. Sekaquaptewa's son Wayne, the paper's editor-publisher, fulminated against milling machines, the "iron daughters-in-law" that were, he said, sapping Hopi culture of its vigor.

The Hopi ritual calendar, however, has helped to keep traditional piki making alive. Before the Niman dance, women are busy in special piki rooms, building fires under piki stones. They sit in front of the red-hot stones, rubbing melon seeds over them until the oil comes out and greases the stone. When the stone has cooled to a moderate temperature, the women make piki batter from blue corn flour, water, and an infusion of ashes from greasewood (*Sarcobatus vermiculatus*), a shrub that accentuates the batter's blueness and gives it a characteristic flavor. Before actual cooking begins, the stone is lightly greased once more with a piece of cooked sheep's spinal cord. Then the women spread batter thinly on the stone, a little at a time until the stone is covered. As it cooks, the sheet begins to peel away from the stone, like a crepe, and can be pulled off by hand. The first sheet is discarded. As subsequent sheets cook, they are covered with a finished sheet of piki. The steam from the raw sheet underneath softens the top sheet enough so that it can be quickly rolled up and set aside on a mat.

The process is similar to the one used to make Chinese spring roll skins and the Moroccan leaf pastry called *warka*, but piki is even more intricate and sophisticated in method, while at the same time more primitive. The steaming and rolling stage is unique in its culinary refinement. The hand spreading of batter on a hot stone harks back to a stage of cultural development before metal was known. All in all, it is hard to think of a recipe that demands more skill from a cook or that displays more ingenuity with simple materials.

Precisely because of its complexity, piki is the epitome of a food that cannot be made without a steady flow of cultural apprenticeship from one generation to another. In this respect it is the opposite of steak and hamburger, dishes that can be taught in minutes and which can infiltrate foreign cuisines with the ease of a virus invading a bacterium. Hopi blue corn cookery, however, is so full of tricky culinary maneuvers that a *bahana* cook will have trouble duplicating a dish, even with a recipe and plenty of blue cornmeal on hand.

Mrs. Sekaquaptewa demonstrated to me an "easy" Hopi breakfast dish called *pö-vö-pi-ki,* or blue marbles (see recipe). She made a straightforward dough and then rolled it into small blue orbs, which she then poached. To get the texture right is a matter of exquisite judgment. No recipe can give exact quantities.

She went on to make an elegant poached corn bread called *tsu-ku-vi-ki,* V-shaped packages of blue dough wrapped in moistened corn husks that held the dough together until it had cooked. After cooling, the breads solidified into their boomerang shape. Tying the raw dough up in the corn-husk packages, so that they hold together and look right, is a knack not easily learned at one sitting. It took Helen Sekaquaptewa a week when she was a girl. Today's Hopi girls may learn these tricky techniques when they marry, but they rarely use them in daily life. Consequently, older Hopis like to drop in for a visit at Helen Sekaquaptewa's house, because they know they will find traditional food there that their younger family members don't make for them. Mrs. Sekaquaptewa says: "We still eat the old food when we are hungry for it. My son Abbott [the tribal chairman] travels all over the country eating *bahana* food. He gets hungry for this and I make it for him."

While Mrs. Sekaquaptewa cooked and talked and remembered, in the modern kitchen of Abbott's ranch house in New Oraibi, her granddaughter Allison helped her at the stove. Allison, in corduroy jeans and Adidas sneakers, had obviously never cooked blue marbles or *tsu-ku-vi-ki* before. Will she learn how to make either, or piki, in the course of her ritual education? In theory, she will. But the television in her living room is teaching her other, easier lessons. Convenience foods fill the supermarket in New Oraibi. Disco evenings compete with the kachina dances. No doubt, the Hopis can survive without their religion or their piki but, as an old kachina-doll carver in Shungopavi asked me, "Will they still be Hopis?"

Note: Blue cornmeal is available in supermarkets throughout the Southwest. It can be ordered by mail from Casados Farms, P.O. Box 852, San Juan Pueblo, New Mexico 87566. Anyone with access to an electric grain mill should grind commercial blue cornmeal to the fineness of flour before making these recipes.

☞ BLUE MARBLES (PÖ-VÖ-PI-KI)

1½ cups blue cornmeal or ½ pound, approximately	2 tablespoons wheat flour
2 tablespoons ashes from burned bean leaves or sagebrush, or substitute 1 teaspoon baking powder	

(1) Bring 2½ quarts of water to a boil in a large pot.

(2) In a large mixing bowl, divide the blue cornmeal into two separate mounds, one about 1¼ cups, the other ¼ cup.

(3) Scald the larger mound of cornmeal with about ½ cup of boiling water or just enough to moisten it throughout. Stir the moistened flour as you add the water.

(4) In a small bowl, stir the ashes together with 1 cup boiling water. Push the mixture through a fine strainer, then add gradually to the cornmeal along with the wheat flour. If

you are using baking powder, simply mix it into the cornmeal in step three and then moisten the cornmeal with about 1 cup boiling water. Let cool until you can handle it comfortably.

(5) Add additional dry cornmeal from the smaller mound to the dough as you work it. Use only enough to produce a smooth, workable dough. The end product should be gray blue and elastic. (Reserve any unused dry flour for future use.)

(6) Break off a piece of dough and roll it into a long coil about 1 inch in cross section. Break off small pieces from this coil and roll them into balls the size of cherry tomatoes. With practice you will be able to roll two at a time between your hands. (If the dough is too sticky to work, add more cornmeal.) Continue until you have used up all the dough.

(7) Spoon the blue marbles into the pot of boiling water. When they are all in, pour off any excess water, leaving just enough to cover them.

(8) Simmer slowly, uncovered, for 8 to 10 minutes. Remove from water with a slotted spoon. Cool.

(9) Serve the blue marbles in their cooking liquid for breakfast. Accompany them with stewed fruit, hard-boiled eggs, and raw onion, or fried (dried) chilis.

Y I E L D: 3 to 4 servings.

Recipes adapted from *Hopi Cookery,* by Juanita Tiger Kavena, University of Arizona Press:

☞ CORN TORTILLAS

2 cups blue cornmeal

(1) Mix cornmeal and 1¼ cups water until dough is pliable and moist (but not sticky or wet).

(2) Shape dough into 12 balls.

(3) Flatten balls by patting out with hands or rolling between two sheets of greased wax paper.

(4) Cook on lightly greased griddle over medium heat about 4 minutes on each side, or until brown.

YIELD: 12 tortillas.

In the past, Hopis either had to mine their own rock salt near Zuni or the Grand Canyon, or had to trade for it, and it was so difficult to obtain that it was almost a delicacy. Salt gathering, therefore, is a very special ceremony. Consequently, many early recipes, such as this one, didn't call for salt. Actually, the flavor of blue corn is so delicate that some cooks don't like to interfere with it by adding salt.

BLUE TORTILLAS

1 cup crushed piki
½ cup finely ground, packed blue corn flour

⅛ teaspoon salt (more if desired)

(1) Combine ingredients in a mixing bowl.

(2) Gradually stir in 1 cup boiling water and knead dough until smooth.

(3) Divide dough into 4 2-inch balls.

(4) Flatten balls by hand to ¼-inch thickness. Work cracks with a wet finger to smooth and seal.

(5) Cook on a lightly greased griddle approximately 4 minutes on each side. Continue to smooth tortillas with wet fingers as they are cooking.

YIELD: 4 3½-inch tortillas.

☞ JOSEPHINE JAMES'S HOPI OMELET

1 dozen fresh eggs, warmed to room temperature	Seasonings, as desired
⅜ cup finely ground blue cornmeal	4 tablespoons shortening or drippings

(1) Preheat oven to 400 degrees.

(2) Beat 10 eggs until light and frothy.

(3) Gradually add blue cornmeal to eggs, while continuing to beat. Add seasonings.

(4) Slightly stir 2 remaining eggs and fold into mixture.

(5) Heat shortening in heavy skillet or pan with deep sides, coating it thoroughly.

(6) Pour egg mixture into hot pan and bake for 10 minutes. Reduce heat to 350 degrees and continue baking until eggs are firm but still fluffy (15 to 20 minutes).

YIELD: 4 servings.

☞ HOPI HUSH PUPPIES

2 cups blue cornmeal	2 beaten eggs
1 teaspoon salt	1 small onion, chopped fine
2 teaspoons baking powder	Shortening
1¼ cups milk	

(1) Measure cornmeal, salt, and baking powder into a mixing bowl.

(2) Stir milk into beaten eggs and gradually add to cornmeal mixture.

(3) Add chopped onion to cornmeal and mix well.

(4) Drop by teaspoonful into 1½ inches of very hot shortening.

(5) Fry hush puppies until golden brown, turning to brown all sides.

Y I E L D: 6 servings.

Note: Hush puppies are served with stews or beans instead of bread. Although made of corn, they are corn in a different form and add variety to meals. Yellow cornmeal can be substituted for blue, but does not have as delicate a flavor.

☞ HOPI MILK DRINK

1 cup powdered milk   Sugar or salt
1 cup finely ground blue
  cornmeal

(1) Put powdered milk in a saucepan and add ¾ cup of warm water, stirring until milk is smooth.

(2) Add 5 cups warm water and place saucepan in a double boiler or over low heat.

(3) Cook slowly for 10 minutes, stirring to prevent scorching.

(4) In a small bowl, mix the cornmeal with ¾ cup of cool water, stirring to remove lumps.

(5) Add cornmeal mixture to the simmering milk, stirring until well mixed.

(6) Continue to cook for 5 more minutes, stirring often.

(7) Add sugar or a dash of salt to taste.

Y I E L D: About 2 quarts.

Note: This is a tasty drink that has little or no sugar, according to taste, and a lot of vitamins and minerals. It is adapted from an old recipe and is used frequently by modern Hopis, especially as a bedtime drink or instead of cocoa.

☞ PARCHED BEANS

White tepary beans   Salt

(1) Heat clean, fine sand in a cast-iron pot until it becomes dark brown and hot. Test sand by dropping in a bean; if it browns quickly, the sand is hot enough. Or drop a little water on the sand; if it sputters, the sand is hot.

(2) Wash and sort several cups of white tepary beans or other small, white beans. Older beans from last year work best.

(3) Pour beans into sand and stir briskly to keep them from burning.

(4) When beans have browned lightly, remove them from the sand with a sieve and pour them into a bowl.

(5) Sprinkle beans with salt water (1 tablespoon salt dissolved in 1 cup of water), and stir well.

Note: This recipe comes from the western part of the reservation and was often served at Christmastime. I am told that parched beans are often the first salty food to be served to Hopis who are ending a fast.

OLYMPIA OYSTERS

"A loaf of bread," the Walrus said,
"Is what we chiefly need:
Pepper and vinegar besides
Are very good indeed—
Now, if you're ready, Oysters dear,
We can begin to feed."
But answer came there none—
And this was scarcely odd because
They'd eaten every one.
—Lewis Carroll, *Through the Looking Glass*

Oysters naturally just stay put, lying in their salty beds, waiting for people to eat them. As Saki put it, "There's nothing in Christianity or Buddhism that quite matches the sympathetic unselfishness of an oyster." Taking advantage of such com-

plaisance has been a human habit since prehistoric times. And
in each place where people have found abundant colonies of
oysters, they have attacked them wholesale, downing dozen
after dozen, until what had begun as a cheap snack for Every-
man was so depleted that only the wealthy could continue to
feast with traditional abandon.

In Britain today, Colchester oysters are now a luxury, but
in Dickens's *Pickwick Papers* (1837), Sam Weller observes:
"Poverty and oysters always seems to go together." The same
process occurred in this country: early settlers on the Atlantic
coast considered oysters poor people's food, while contemporary
New Yorkers pay a premium price for increasingly scarce
specimens of *Crassostrea virginica.* On our Pacific coast, the
situation is far worse.

The native Olympia oyster, *Ostrea lurida,* is so rare that
it is almost never seen, even in the state of Washington, where
it was once an important feature of the local economy. The
tiny, 1½-inch-long bivalve, with its distinctive violet-tinged
inner shell walls and intense marine taste, was a unique and
toothsome part of pioneer days in the Pacific Northwest.
Delicate "Olys" were the favored sweetmeat of Gold Rush San
Francisco. In our ill-favored era, you cannot even buy one at an
oyster bar in Seattle. Instead, you find insipid Pacifics (*Crassostrea gigas*) grown locally from Japanese seed. They are huge,
attaining a length of ten inches, and they grow fast. Young
ones, eaten directly from the shell, do have a certain tang to
them. But full-size Pacifics, shucked industrially and assid-
uously washed—the normal practice on the West Coast—are
as flat in flavor as a hunk of wet foam rubber. Meanwhile, the
elegant little Oly has all but vanished into the folklore of Puget
Sound and the Northwest Coast.

James G. Swan, an early settler in the Washington
Territory—and a pioneer Indian ethnographer, inveterate

diarist, debauchee, and opportunist—worked in the oyster
business in its infancy during three years (1852 to 1855) he
spent at Shoalwater Bay. Swan, who took a precise interest
in what he ate, wrote of the "strong, coppery taste" of the
Shoalwater Bay oysters, which he attributed to the mud flats
where they grew. "What is called a coppery taste," he went
on, "is simply a strong, fishy, saltwater flavor, which, however is driven off by cooking."

Taste changes over time, and the coppery, "fishy" taste
Swan boiled or fried away is probably the taste modern oyster
lovers seek. Still, it is risky to rely on descriptions of flavor
from the past. After all, in his memoir of Shoalwater Bay,
Oysterville, Willard R. Espy states that "the Puget Sound oyster,
known as the Olympia, had a copper taste offensive to refined
San Francisco palates. But the same gourmets who rejected
the Olympia oysters sang hosannas" to the oysters of Shoalwater Bay.

Presumably, all those Northwest Pacific oysters in the
middle nineteenth century were examples of *Ostrea lurida*,
what we would call Olympias. Their coppery taste, or lack of
it, will probably remain a subject of gastronomic confusion.
There is no doubt, however, that literally tons of oysters were
consumed after gold was struck in California. San Francisco
Bay was stripped bare first. And so the devastation went, on up
the coast. Puget Sound was the most remote source and held
out longest.

At the turn of the century, whole communities of oyster
folk lived and worked on float houses in the tidal inlets of
southern Puget Sound near Olympia. Steamers came daily to
Mud Bay, Oyster Bay, and Little Skookum to pick up sacks
of Olympias. To fill those sacks, oystermen and their families
worked through the night, when the tide was usually out and
the oysters could be raked from the mud flats.

Cora G. Chase spent part of her childhood, from 1898 to 1914, on a float house in Oyster Bay. In a memoir, written as a research paper at the University of Washington in 1944, she interviewed one of the pioneer oystermen, Dick Helser, an old neighbor at Oyster Bay:

He worked his own bed in the early days, getting up at night according to the tides, raking oysters in windrows around a float that had been staked out when the tide was in, then forked them up into the float by lantern light. In the gray of cold winter mornings the loaded float was "poled" to the culling house anchored some distance from shore. There the oysters were forked into a sink float, an upside-down float holding two feet of water to keep the oysters fresh.

From the sinkfloat they were forked into a wheelbarrow, rolled into the culling house, up a plank and dumped onto the culling table. All day long the cullers sorted out the larger oysters, knocking off barnacles, smaller oysters and debris with a culling iron (a thin piece of metal easily grasped) and dropping the marketable oysters into a five-gallon kerosene can, then raking the cullings down the hopper at the edge of the table.

Cheap child and nonwhite labor kept the barnacles and oyster shells flying and filled the sacks with precious mature Olympias. Many hands, chilly from long days and nights of dull work in the damp and cold, made rapid work of the depletion of Washington's natural oyster beds. By the nineties, it was necessary to construct artificial beds, diked so that water would shelter the seeded oysters from extremes of heat and cold. Chinese did the work for ten cents an hour. Today, it costs $12,000 to construct an acre of oyster beds, according to Vivian Ellison Bower of Ellison's Oyster Company outside Olympia. At that price, no one is building new beds for

Olympias anymore. In fact, almost no one is even seeding the old beds anymore. "Everyone's given up," says Mrs. Bower. "It's all hand labor and takes four years."

Olympias mature slowly and never get very large. Inevitably, they have lost out to the larger Pacific oysters. The decline has gone so far that it is virtually impossible to taste an Oly without going to Olympia itself, and even there the line of supply is very thin.

The only restaurant in town that makes a practice of serving Olympias is the historic Olympia Oyster House. On one of the walls is a framed menu from 1921 listing an Olympia oyster stew for thirty cents. Today the restaurant's menu still lists Olympias but gives no price. Instead, in parentheses, it warns that "market" will determine the cost of the oysters, "when available."

"We used to ship them fresh anywhere," the manager told me. "Now we buy a gallon or two at a time."

For a plate of crisply fried, breaded Olympias, I paid $16.95, which was fair enough for so rare an item. But all that breading and cooking had effectively removed too much of the oysters' essential flavor for me to get a true impression of their taste. I wanted freshly opened Olympias on the half shell, but the Olympia Oyster House bought them already shucked from a supplier.

Of the several oyster companies in the Olympia area, only two process Olympias. The Olympia Oyster Company opens only three to four bushels a week and didn't happen to have any in stock when I passed through. But the Skookum Bay Oyster Company, a family operation located on a small bay in the hinterland of Shelton, Washington, at the end of a dirt road, is in its gray way a landmark of contemporary American gastronomy. It processes Olympias with regularity.

Outside the company's weathered building, you notice a

derelict boat and big piles of oyster shells. Some of those piles are made of tiny, irregular, purple-tinted shells, which thousands of Olympias once lived in.

Inside, John Blanton supervises his little factory. In the first work area one comes to, a woman jabs at humongous Pacifics, flipping them out of their shells like great pale tongues. In back, Blanton's grown daughter Donna works more delicately, with a scaled-down oyster knife especially modified for Olys. Donna can open roughly 4,000 of them on an average day, about two gallons of shucked Olys altogether. Her brother culls the day's load of mud- and shell-filled pickings from the family's Olympia beds. He passes a small number of harvestable oysters on to his sister.

The scene is not quite as romantic as the floating world of Oyster Bay that Cora Chase describes. But the Blantons are certainly in the same tradition.

Donna let me fumble with her knife until I got an oyster open. Straightaway, I sucked the thumbnail-sized mollusk out of its shell.

The taste was sharply marine but also refined, and in no way did it remind me of copper. I confirmed this judgment some hours later at the place where Dungeness Spit arcs out in a thin ray of sand for miles into the Strait of Juan de Fuca. Sitting on driftwood in the perpetual drizzle, I devoured thirty or more shucked Olys, feeling favored but wondering why tradition-crazed Westerners and the Northwest Coast's rabid environmentalists haven't put their money as well as their mouths behind the preservation and encouragement of a unique, vanishing, and most toothsome native bivalve. If we are finally ready as a nation for the small car, why not also insist on our right to the small oyster?

☞ DOANE'S PAN ROAST

(Courtesy of Olympia Oyster House)

1 pint shucked oysters	Pepper
2 tablespoons butter	Toasted bread
3 to 4 tablespoons catsup	

(1) Wash oysters well.

(2) Put in a pan and let come to a simmer. Immediately add butter, ketchup, and pepper. Stir gently and serve on toasted bread as soon as butter melts.

Y I E L D: 2 servings.

☞ LILA GAULT'S NORTHWEST OYSTER STEW

(Adapted from **The Northwest Cookbook,** *Quick Fox, Inc., New York)*

1 pint shucked oysters	1 tablespoon Worcestershire
1 cup heavy cream	sauce
3 cups milk	Cayenne
1 teaspoon salt	2 tablespoons butter
	Chopped parsley

(1) In a large Dutch oven, simmer oysters in their liquor over low heat for about 3 minutes or until the edges begin to curl. Add cream and milk, and heat until bubbles form around edge of pot, but not until boiling.

(2) Add salt, Worcestershire sauce, and cayenne in small amounts to taste.

(3) Remove from heat and add butter. Garnish with chopped parsley.

Y I E L D : 4 servings.

PACIFIC SALMON

The best fish story I know revolves around a Finnish-American woman called Vanessa and an extremely large salmon. Some years ago, Vanessa was spending a weekend with a friend in Cooperstown, New York. The salmon arrived the same weekend, brought from Alaska by a neighboring plutocrat. Vanessa's host heard about the majestic fish and knew that it was languishing in the refrigerator of its owner, whose culinary ineptitude was local legend. Vanessa, a cook of skill and daring, resolved to liberate the noble salmon and give it fitting gastronomic treatment. Seizing a moment when the plutocrat and his family were busy at tennis, she crept into the house, purloined the *Oncorhynchus,* and poached it to a turn in her host's kitchen. She boned and glazed the fish and returned it to the owner's refrigerator.

In fact, Vanessa only returned half the salmon and kept

the other half for the delectation of herself and her friends. It seemed only fair, in light of the service rendered. And when the rightful owner saw the beautifully decorated, flaky, pink *chaud-froid* salmon, he was delighted.

Not all the salmon stories have such happy endings. The Pacific Northwest, once a salmon paradise, is today a region made glum and angry by the salmon's decline. As an outsider, I want to speak with caution about Pacific salmon. It is a most complicated subject. Ask almost anyone in Washington State about salmon and the usual reply is a shake of the head, because the salmon question has as many sides as a sockeye has scales.

Consumers blame industrial polluters. Environmentalists lambaste the power companies that built the dams that block the rivers and impede salmon from making their way upstream to spawn. Non-Indian fishermen bristle over the federal court ruling that compels them to share the shrinking salmon catch with Indian fishermen on a strictly equal basis. But the Indians, prospering materially because of this judicial interpretation of their treaty rights, will still probably never regain the salmon-centered way of life they led before the coming of the white man.

Northwest Coast Indians had some 9,000 years in which to perfect an intricate salmon-catching technology, a salmon cuisine, and various rituals celebrating the importance of salmon in their culture. Hilary Stewart's exhaustive *Indian Fishing: Early Methods on the Northwest Coast* (University of Washington Press) is a fascinating encyclopedia of salmon lore that shows, for example, exactly how to make bentwood hooks and how the Nootka tribe trolled for salmon in open water just before the run. Stone sinkers, bone barbs, spruce-root lashings, leaders of human hair or doeskin or cedar-bark twine—all these natural materials were combined laboriously, baited with fish caught in small stone dams, and run out on a long line. The fisherman fastened the line to his paddle handle so that he could locomote and make his baited hook move at the same time.

Other fishermen used harpoons or gaff hooks carved from antlers and elaborate nets made of willow-bark twine or home-spun nettle fiber. In rivers, they could intercept running salmon with traps and weirs.

Indian salmon cookery was also a sophisticated business. Watertight boxes and baskets were filled with water; then hot stones from a campfire were added by means of tongs. After the stones made the water boil, in went pieces of salmon in an openwork basket.

Lacking metal ovens, the Indians dug steam pits in the ground or cooked split salmon over heated rocks, methods very close to the East Coast clambake.

The simplest and most famous method of salmon cookery in the Pacific Northwest was to roast the fish over a wood fire. Split salmon were held flat on roasting tongs or skewered on crossed sticks. The tongs and sticks had sharp ends so that they could be stuck in the ground at the edge of the fire. The whole apparatus was tilted slightly and the salmon were extended over the heat. First one side of the fish was roasted, then the other.

Traditional Indian salmon roasting continues to be practiced widely in Washington. The alderwood typically used in the process imparts a superb flavor to the fish, as I can attest, having tasted some that had been cooked over alder chips on a not-so-picturesque but effective metal grill at an open-air take-out counter in Seattle.

Roast salmon was, however, much more than a gourmet treat for Northwest Coast Indians in the old days. Rivers clogged with salmon were a guarantee of survival all through the year.

Without refrigerator-freezers, Indians built large smokehouses and drying racks and perfected the arts of drying and smoking salmon to a high level. Some fish were half smoked, for immediate eating. That way the flesh was still soft. Other fish were fully dehydrated by longer smoking so that they would keep through the winter.

On a recent visit to Lummi Island, a settlement in the north part of Puget Sound accessible by ferry, I bought some of this hard-smoked salmon, which had been prepared by Lummi Indians. It resembled beef jerky in its tough, brittle texture and salty taste. During the drive back south to Seattle, which was frequently whited out by a freak fall blizzard, I understood graphically how earlier generations of Lummis and their coastal neighbors had found this preserved fish a handsome and convenient protein source in cold weather.

Necessity taught the Indians to eat every part of the salmon—from cheeks to spine. Even salmon roe were hung in strips and dried or smoked. Some Indians put roe in bags made from deer stomachs and hung the bags in their smokehouses. Each day they would knead the bag until the moisture evaporated and the eggs turned into a kind of cheese. Another route to the same result involved burying the roe in a three-foot pit lined thickly with maple leaves. Holes poked in the leaves at the bottom of the pit allowed oil to drain away. After two months, the eggs turned to cheese and could be eaten plain or boiled with water for soup. Some Indians preserved salmon roe by leaving it to cure in saltwater.

None of this salmon-based economy could have evolved without the seemingly supernatural, superabundant annual return of the fish from saltwater to freshwater. Each year, grateful and awe-struck Indians greeted the arrival of the first salmon with joyful celebration and a variety of ritual observances.

When a Kwakiutl troller caught his first nine salmon, he clubbed them only once, stunning but not killing them. Then he strung them on a twisted cedar withe, tied it in a hoop, put the hoop around his neck, and prayed: "I do not wish to club to death your souls so that you may go home to the place you came from, Supernatural Ones . . ."

After eating the first salmon of the season, the family wiped their hands on cedar bark but did not wash them. Any bones and leftovers were thrown into the sea, along with the new mats used as a table, to insure a repetition of the run the following year.

These days, no one practices these rituals, but the Indians of our Northwest Coast have found new ways to foster and control the life cycle of the salmon. The Lummis, for example, manage a modern program of aquaculture. And like other Indians in the area, they have benefited from a federal court decision handed down by Judge George H. Boldt in 1974. Boldt ruled that treaties between Indians and the federal government signed in 1854, which guaranteed Indians the right to fish "in common" with non-Indian fishermen, had in fact reserved 50 percent of the catch for the tribal signatories.

Overnight, the relatively small tribal fishing fleet, which before the decision had only been able to catch 10 percent of the commercial salmon in the area, now had a positive right to half. Higher courts have upheld Boldt and today salmon fishing in Puget Sound is so strictly regulated that every salmon caught must be officially tagged as Indian or non-Indian. Since there are fewer Indian fishermen than white, the season for Indians is substantially longer. To maintain as fair a balance as possible, careful records of the progress of the catch are stored in a computer at the University of Washington. The Boldt decision also secured Indians an equal role in the administration of the new regulations, and at the fishery school on Lummi Island,

Lummis are learning to run computer terminals that have access to the salmon records at the University. They are also learning other dry-land skills that will help them play a complete role in the brave new world of equal salmon opportunity. But even Indians suddenly in full enjoyment of their treaty rights must face the fundamental problem of exploiting a fragile and diminished fish population with intelligence. Even if they approach each year's run with the traditional reverence and spirituality of their tribes, they can never restore the balance of supply and demand that once obtained on the precolonial, sparsely populated shores of Puget Sound.

Three recipes from *The Market Notebook,* a collection of recipes from the Pike Place Market in Seattle, compiled by Pamela Sovold, Margaret Wherrette, and Eilisha Dermont, Madrona Publishers, Seattle:

☞ BAKED SALMON WITH VEGETABLES

The fish is covered with a thick layer of vegetables and baked in tightly closed foil (really steamed). Good straight from the oven, it is even better the next day, served cold.

Buy a whole fish and have your fishmonger book-fillet it,

leaving in the backbone. To "book-fillet" means to cut the fish in such a way that the fish opens like a book on both sides of the spine. In this recipe the combination of the backbone and the wine makes an amber gelatin that sets when refrigerated and tastes sensational. Serve the fish and gelatin with fresh mayonnaise. Superb.

To prepare, mix together chopped celery tops, chopped onion, minced garlic, chopped green and red peppers, parsley, and jalapeño pepper. How much you use of each ingredient depends on the size of your fish; you want to put a ½-inch covering on it. Lay your fish on a large piece of foil in a baking pan. Cover with the chopped vegetables. Squeeze the juice of one lemon over the top and sprinkle with a tablespoon each of dillweed and sweet basil. Top with ½ cup of white wine. Seal the foil tightly. Bake at 375 degrees.

☞ GEFILTE FISH WITH SALMON

1 cup matzo meal	2 pounds raw salmon (save
5 eggs	head and bones), ground
4 teaspoons salt	1½ pounds raw white fish
1½ teaspoons pepper	(save head and bones),
1½ quarts water	ground
2 onions, sliced	Salt and pepper to taste
4 carrots, sliced	3 large onions, ground

(1) Mix together the matzo meal, eggs, salt, and pepper; let stand at room temperature 1 to 2 hours.

(2) Put into a large roasting pan or stockpot the water (pot should be about one-third full), sliced onions, carrots, fish

heads and bones, and a few teaspoons each of salt and pepper. Bring to a boil while you prepare the fish balls.

(3) In a large bowl, mix together the ground onions and fish. Add the matzo mixture and more water and salt, if necessary (mixture must be moist enough to hold together). When water has come to a boil, wet your hands and form the fish mixture into balls, about 2 inches in diameter. Drop the fish balls into the water and let them cook for 2½ hours.

(4) Remove from heat and cool in the pan for 1 hour. Remove fish balls and strain the liquid. To save some for later use, freeze the fish balls on cookie sheets; when they are solid, transfer them to plastic freezer bags. Freeze the liquid separately. To use frozen gefilte fish, thaw broth and bring it to a boil; add thawed fish balls and simmer 30 minutes. Gefilte fish is usually served cold.

YIELD: 8 servings.

☞ FISH WITH RHUBARB SAUCE

2 cups rhubarb cut in small pieces	2 teaspoons sugar
	½ cup water
½ cup tomato sauce	Salt
3 tablespoons olive oil	1 pound salmon, cut in pieces

(1) Wash rhubarb well. Peel off hard skin, if any.

(2) Cook all ingredients (except fish) together for about 30 minutes.

(3) When rhubarb is cooked thoroughly, add cut up pieces of fish and simmer until fish is done.

YIELD: 3 to 4 servings.

Three recipes adapted from *The Northwest Cookbook* by Lila Gault, Quick Fox, Inc., New York:

☞ GRAVLAX

1 2-pound salmon fillet, skin intact	⅓ cup salt
⅔ cup sugar	2 tablespoons dill seed
	1 bunch fresh dill

(1) Cut fillet crosswise into two large pieces.

(2) Mix sugar and salt together, and rub completely into fish. Place one piece, skin side down, in enameled dish and sprinkle with 1 tablespoon dill seed and cover with several sprigs of dill. Cover with other piece of fillet, skin side up, and sprinkle with remaining dill seed and sprigs. Place heavy plate or weight on top of fish and leave in refrigerator for 3 days. Turn twice a day and baste with liquid that forms around fish.

YIELD: 6 servings.

☞ BAKED SALMON

1 5-pound fresh salmon	½ cup olive oil
3 large onions, thinly sliced	2 large garlic cloves, mashed
2 lemons, thinly sliced	

(1) Preheat oven to 400 degrees.

(2) Wash salmon thoroughly and pat dry. Line baking sheet with aluminum foil and place ¾ of onions and lemons on top.

(3) Stuff cavity of fish with remainder of onions and lemons and place fish on foil. Mix olive oil and garlic and

brush over fish. Fold edges of foil over top and ends of fish and seal. Bake 15 minutes per pound or until flesh flakes when touched with fork.

YIELD: 4 to 5 servings.

☞ STEAMED SALMON

Salmon can be steamed by wrapping the fish as for poaching and placing it on a rack above a pot filled with boiling water. The pot should be covered tightly and the fish allowed to steam for 12 to 15 minutes per pound. This method works well for steaks and fillets and guarantees that the flesh will remain moist.

INDEX

(INDEX OF RECIPES FOLLOWS)

abalones, 8, 223–8
  assault on, and scarcity of,
    223–4, 226
  catching of, 225–6
  divers for, 8, 223–6
  farm for, 224
  pink, green, and black, 224
  preparation of, for cooking, 226–8
  protection of, 224
  recipe for, 229–30
  red, 224, 226
acorn, of Jupiter, 174
Agricultural Statistics, and geese, 59
All Maine Cooking, 154
Allen's Neck Clambake, 138–41
  menu for, 142–3
  see also clambake, New England
Allen's Neck Friends Cook Book,
    142, 143
America, and black walnuts, 173,
    175
  food habits of Jews in, 158–9
  and gooseberries, 181–2
  regional food events of, *see* food
    and chili
American Sheep Producers Council,
    and lamb recipes, 192
Americans, Native, *see* Indians
Ancelet, Barry Jean, 126–8, 130
Anderson, Beth, 44
Anderson, Ernie and Cindy, and
    rice processing, 39
Annual World Championship Chili
    Cookoff, 203–4, 207
  see also Fourteenth Annual
Anser anser, see goose
Appalachia, and black walnuts, 175
  and white lightning, 92

apple pie, 13–14, 17
  contest, 15
  recipe for, 20–2
apples, Crèvecoeur and, 14
Assyria, and *boudin*, 129–30
Atencio, Jim, shepherd, 192–5
Atz, James W., fish handlist of, 162
Audubon, John James, and Key
    West, 83

Bailey, Mary Ellen, and blueberries,
    149
Bakabi, Niman dance at, 230
Baker, Vaughan Burdin, 128
Bar H-L Road, sheep on, 189, 194,
    197
Barrens, and blueberries, 149, 151
Barton, Elizabeth W., 156
Bates, Bud, and mushroom contest,
    47
Battle of Beecher Island, 158
Bay City, Oregon, country store in,
    219
beans, and chili, 206, 208
Bear Wallow Books, persimmon
    cookbook of, 28–9
Beard, James, and Tillamook cheese,
    218
Bearss lime, 84
beef *vs.* lamb, 191–2, 197
Benjamin, Jacques, and *boudin*,
    131–2
benne, 110–11
Berry Hill Farm, and ham, 103, 106
Betaeus harfordi, and abalone, 227
Big Sandy Lake, harvesting wild
    rice on, 37–8
black currant, and fungus, 182

black walnuts, 173–7
  "butter" from, 174
  colonists and, 173, 175
  cracking of, 9, 173–4, 176–7
  cultivation and improved varieties
    of, 175–6
  danger to, 174, 176
  Indians and, 174–5
  recipes for, 177–9
  suggestions for planting, and
    description of, 176–7
  use and value of, 175, 177
Blanton, Donna, and Olympia
  oysters, 247
Blanton, John, and oysters, 247
blood pudding, 8, 129–30
blue, Indians and, 232
blue marbles, 235
  recipe for, 236–7
"Blueberries," 152
blueberries, highbush, 9, 147–8
  baking with, 149
  picking of, 148
  yield of, 149
blueberries, lowbush, 8–10, 148–52
  baking with, 149
  clones of, 151–2
  future of, 152
  pests of, 150
  picking of, 147–8, 150–2
  propagation and growth of, 149–50
  rake for, 148, 150–2
  recipes for, 153–7
  yield of, 149
blueberries, rabbiteye, 148
Blueberry Hill Environmental Farm,
  151–2
Boldt, Judge George H., and Indians
  and salmon, 254
boucherie, 126, 128
boudin blanc, 126–31
  etymology of, 129
  recipe for, 131–3
boudin rouge, 8, 130–1

bourbon, 93–4
  aging of, 94
  recipes for, 99–100
Bower, Vivian Ellison, and oyster
  beds, 245–6
*Bowl of Red, A: The Natural History
  of Chili with Recipes*, 204
Boyne City, Mich., mushroom hunt-
  ing in, 46–50
Boyne River Inn, 47
Brother Willie and Sister Lilly's
  Salvation Chili, 205–6
Broussard, La., and sausage (*boudin
  blanc*), 125–6
Brown County Sorghum Mill, 23–4
Brown County State Park, persimmons and, 28
Brown, Kathleen, and gooseberries,
  181–2, 184–5
Brunswick County, Va., 75–7
Brunswick stew, 9, 75–8
  origin of, 75
  recipes for, 76, 82
Buchanan (Iowa) County Fair,
  15–16, 20
  4-H and, 18–19
  Porkettes and, 19
burgoo, 78–9
  history of, 78–9
  Looney's recipe for, 79
  mutton, 8, 79–80
  recipes for, 79, 81
Burgoo King, 79

C & W Markette, and cheddar, 219
Cajuns, culture and background of,
  126–9
  food of, 126–8
  and French language, 126–8
  music of, 128
  and sausage (*boudin*), 8, 125–7,
    129–30
  see also boudin blanc
California, and abalones, 8, 223–4
  and mussels, 224

California Department of Fish and
	Game, and abalones, 224
California Nursery Company, and
	persimmon trees, 28
Canada, wild rice from, 37
Canopy à la Lorenzo, 112
Carroll, Lewis, quote from, 242
Carvalho, Solomon, 158
Carya illinoensis, 174
Cass Lake, Minnesota, jigged rice
	from, 39
Castanea sativa, 174
Catalina Island, abalone shells on,
	223
Cate, Carol, 220
challah, meaning of, 165
Champion, Joe, and Tillamook,
	215, 219
Charleston, S.C., culinary tradition
	in, 112–13
	Southern foods in supermarkets
	of, 112
Charleston Receipts, 113, 116
Chase, Cora G., and oysters, 245, 247
Chasen, Dave, and chili contest, 204
Chaucer, Geoffrey, and pasties, 66
cheddar, 216–19
	first U.S. factory for, 216
	old, 219
	origin of, 216
	recipes for, 220–1
	see also cheese
cheese, Tillamook, 4–5, 216–19
	manufacturing of, 217–18
	marketing of cheese by, 217
	and milk, 215–16
	plant of, 217–19
	see also cheddar
cherries, Traverse City, 45
chestnut, European, 174
Chiang Jung-feng, and geese, 56
chickens *vs* geese, 56, 59–60
Chili Appreciation Society
	International, 203–7
	rules of, 206–7

chili con carne, 203–8
	CASI rules for, 206–7
	origin of, 207
	recipes for, 208–14
	song about, 205
chili heads, 8, 208
China, and geese, 56
Christmas, choice of main dish for,
	55
	goose and, 55–6, 58–9
Christmas Carol, A, and goose, 56
Citrus aurantifolia, see Key limes
Clam Dishes and Rock Fishes, 220
clambake, New England, 4, 111,
	137–42
	distortion of, 139
	eating of, 141–2
	as national feast, 139
	process of, 139–41
	recipe for, 142–3
	utensils for, 137–8
Clements, Bill, and chili, 206
Colchester oysters, 243
colonists, and black walnuts, 173,
	175
	and gooseberries, 182
Colorado, sheep and, 190–7
Compleat Blueberry Cookbook, The,
	156
Conch Cooking, 89
Conchs, and Key limes, 85–6
Congress, and liquor excise tax,
	92–3
corn, blue, 232
	Hopis and, 231–2
corn bread, poached, 235
corn liquor, *see* whiskey
Cornish, and pasties, 65–8
Costner, Susan, 88
Cousin Jacks, 66–7
Cousin Jennies, 66
Coville, Frederick V., and blue-
	berries, 148
cow peas, 113–14
coyotes, and sheep, 195–6

crab, oyster or pea, 111–12
Craig, Rev. Elijah, and bourbon, 93
Crassostrea gigas, 243
Crassostrea virginica, 243
Creeks, and Juglandaceae, 174
Crèvecoeur, Michel Guillaume Jean
    de, 13–14
Criswell, Howard, and moonshiners,
    92
Cronartium ribicola, 182
Crow, James, and bourbon, 93–4
currant, black, and fungus, 182
Cutler Cookery, 153

Dashiell, Nancy Warner, and curing
    of ham, 103–4
    and hog slaughtering, 106
David, Elizabeth, 186
Davidson, Alan, 111–12
Department of the Interior, Bureau
    of Land Management of, and
    grazing rights, 194
Dermont, Eilisha, 255
desert cuisine, Hopis and, 9
de Soto, Fernando, and persimmons,
    26
Dickens, Charles, 56, 243
Diospyros kaki, *see* persimmons,
    Oriental
Diospyros virginiana, *see* persim-
    mons, native
Drisko, Clarence, and blueberry
    rake, 151
Dud Breaux's, and *boudin*, 126

Eberly, Carole, 70
Egyptians, and geese, 57
Ellison's Oyster Company, 245
England, black walnut trees in, 175
    and goose for Christmas, 56
    and gooseberries, 180, 183
    and turkey, 56
English walnut, 173–4
environmentalists, and Olympia
    oysters, 247

and salmon, 251
and sheep, 195–6
Erickson, Karl, and clambake, 139–
    41
Espy, Willard R., 244
Europe, and gooseberries, 182
    Christian, geese and, 57

fat, as basis for cuisine, 110
field peas, 113
Finland, *see* Finns
Finlandia, Marquette, Mich., 65
Finnish Cookbook, The, 66
Finns, and pasties, 65–8
    and Upper Peninsula, 65, 68
Fishman, Larry, and shell collec-
    tion, 223
Fleming, Marjorie, and gooseberries,
    180
Florida Keys, 83
    Conchs and, 85–6
    and Key limes, 84–7
Flying Colors, 208
folle avoine, *see* wild rice
food, and American regional events,
    204
    authenticity of, 204, 206–8
    kosher and nonkosher, 158–63
    Tex-Mex, 207
Food of France, The, 110
Ford, Gerald, and Michigan cuisine,
    45
Forest Service, and sheep, 194
4-H program, 18–19
Fourteenth Annual Wick Fowler
    Memorial World Championship
    Chili Cookoff, 204–6
Fowler, Wick, and chili, 203–4
Foxfire Book, The, 95
France, and *boudin blanc*, 129–30
Franklin County, Va., and moonshine,
    96–7
Franklin County Steamer, 97
Franklin *News-Post*, and moonshine,
    96–7

Fredericks, Devon S., 88
Freetown, Va., and persimmon beer, 29
Frémont, John Charles, 158
Frost, Robert, and blueberries, 152

Gault, Lila, 228, 258
Gaylord, Mich., restaurant in, 46
Gerardi Nursery, and persimmon trees, 28
Germans, and geese, 57
Girouard, Elmer, 125–6
Gnaw Bone, Indiana, 23–4, 29
Godwin, Davis Lee, and curing of ham, 104–5
goose (geese), advantages of, 56–8
    for Christmas, 55–6, 58–9
    cost of, 60
    depinning of, 60
    Lorenz and, 58
    plucking regulations for, 9
    production of, 58–60
    raising of, 58–60
    recipe for, 62–3
    superstitions about, 57
    various peoples and, 56–8
Goose Day, 57–8
gooseberries, 180–5
    color and range of, 184
    cultivation, hybridization, and propagation of, 182, 184
    etymology of, 183
    fresh, rareness of, and difficulty of raising in America, 181–2
    and fungus, 9, 182–3
    prepared products of, 181
    production and popularity of, 183
    recipes for, 185–6
Gower, John, and pasties, 66
Greene, Bert, 221
Griffin, Mrs. Dewitt, and hog slaughtering, 106
Griffin, Parke, and ham, 101–3, 107–8
Guercino, 190

Guide to Kashrus, 162–3
Gwaltney, packing house, 106–7

Halandras, Christine, cooking of, 192–3
    recipes of, 192
    and sheep, 191
Halandras, Gus, and coyotes and lost lambs, 195–6
    and environmentalists, 195
    and grazing rights and federal regulation, 194–5
    and sheep, 190–6
    sheep camp of, 192–3
Halandras, Regas, 196–7
Haliotis, see abalones
Hampton, Emma Stark, collection of, 222
hams, country, 9–10, 101–8
    curing, smoking, and aging of, 101–5
    effect of mass production on, 107
    as endangered species, 107
    official regulations and, 102, 106
    recipe for, 108
    taste of, 105
Hardman's, Owensboro, and mutton burgoo, 80
Haskins, Dr. A. B., and Brunswick stew, 76
Haskins, Dr. Creed, 75–6
Haskins, Meade, and Brunswick stew, 76
Hebert, Dudley, 126–7
Helser, Dick, oysterman, 245
Hemingway, Ernest, and Boyne Valley, 46–47
Hemingway Mansion, 83
Hesse, Zora Getmansky, 211
Hibbits, Jim, and chili contest, 206
Hill, Bertha, background and cooking of, 67–8
    pasties of, 67–9

Hitler, Adolf, 159
hogs, slaughtering of, 106–7, 125–6, 128
Hoosiers, and persimmons, 4–5
Hopi Cookery, 237
Hopi Cultural Center, motel of, 230
Hopis, 230–5
    breakfast dish of, 235
    and corn and piki, 231–5
    culture and traditions of, 231–3, 235
    and desert cuisine, 9
    and Niman dance, 230–1
    recipes of, 236–41
    and rock salt, 238
Hoppin' John, 113–14
Houghton, Abel, Jr., and gooseberries, 182
Howland, Skipper, and clambake, 141–2
Hughes, Phyllis, 213
Humboldt County, Calif., champion black walnut tree in, 175
Hunter, Archibald, and Goose Day, 57–8

Illinois, and burgoo, 78
Independence, Iowa, annual fair in, 15–16
Indian Fishing: Early Methods on the Northwest Coast, 251
Indiana, southern, and burgoo, 78
    see also Hoosiers *and places in*
Indians, and abalone and mussels, 223–4
    and black walnuts, 174
    and blue, 232
    and blueberry picking, 151
    corn of, 231–2
    and desert cuisine, 9
    and salmon, 9–10, 251–5
    at Tillamook, 215
    and wild rice, 36–9
    see also names of tribes

Iowa, Buchanan County Fair in, 15–16
Ireland, and geese, 57
Islamorada, and Key limes, 85–6
Ismail, Dr. Amr, and blueberries, 151–2
Ivanovich, Betty, 51

Jamestown, colonists of, and black walnuts, 173
Jensen, M. Wayne, Jr., and Tillamook cheese, 218
Jews, and kosher food, 9, 158–63
Jovis glans, 174
Juglandaceae, source of name, 174
Juglans nigra, 173–4
    see also black walnut
Juglans regia, 173–4
    see also English walnut
Junior League of Charleston, 113, 116
    of Lafayette, 128
Jupiter, acorn of, 174

kachinas, 231
kalakukko, 67
Karelia, Finland, and pasties, 66
kashrus, *see* kosher
Kavasch, Barrie, 174
Kavena, Juanita Tiger, 237
kculli, 232
Keegan, Marcia, 212
Kentucky, and burgoo, 8, 78–80
    legal and illegal distilleries in, 93
    see also places in
Key limes, 8, 10, 84–7
    description of, 84–5
    juice and peel of, 85
    origin of, 86
    pie, 8, 83–5, 87–8
    recipes for, 88–91
Key West, attractions of, 83
    limes and, 8, 10, 85–6
Kitchen Bouquets, 221

Kobayashi, Bert, and abalone, 225–8
Kosbau, Harold, and wild rice, 41
kosher butchers, 162
    and nonkosher food and principles,
        158–63
    recipes for, 164–72
    supervision of, 161–2
Kuz'n Jax, Marquette, Mich., 67
Kwakiutl troller, and salmon, 254

La Jolla, Calif., and abalones,
    225–6
Lake Superior, whitefish of, 45
lamb, 191–7
    American consumption of, 191–2
    as endangered species, 191
    loss of, from predation, 195–6
    preparation of testicles of, 192
    recipes for, 198–202
    see also sheep
Lamme, Louise, 90
Larousse Gastronomique, 129
Larry's Lunch, Lawrenceville, Va.,
    and Brunswick stew, 77
Le Bouef's, and blood pudding,
    130–1
Leibowitz, Zelda and Irving, and
    kosher laws, 159–63
Lesher, Harry, and black walnuts,
    177
Lewis, Edna, and persimmon beer,
    29
Libertus, Ron, and paddy rice, 41
lightning, white, *see* white lightning
limes, *see names of various kinds*
liquor, corn, *see* whiskey
literature, and pasties, 66
    shepherds in, 190
Livy, and geese, 57
Lloyd Papers, 60
Loaves and Fishes Cookbook, The,
    88
Lockwood, George S., and abalones,
    224

Longfellow, Henry Wadsworth, 36–7,
    42, 127
Looney, James T., and burgoo, 78–9
Lorenz, Konrad, and geese, 58
Louise's Florida Cookbook, 90
Louisiana, sausage makers of, 8
    see also Cajuns *and places in*
Louisiana Boudin Festival, 126,
    129
Louisville Courier-Journal, and
    burgoo recipe, 79, 81
Low Country, of South Carolina,
    cooking traditions of, 112–14
    and oyster roast, 111
    plantations of, as nature
        conservances, 114
    recipes from, 115–25
    and rice culture, 109
Lubavitcher Women's Organization,
    160, 163, 164
Lummi Indians, and salmon, 253–5
Lummi Island, smoked salmon of,
    253

McClellanville oysters, 111
McIntosh, Peter, and cheddar, 216,
    219
Macomber, Ralph, and clambake, 141
Madelyne's, and pasties, 64–5
Magaño, Tomás, shepherd, 192–5
mahnomen, 39
Maine, blueberries of, 8–10, 147–52
    geese in, 58
Mangelsdorf, Paul, and corn, 232
Manny and Issa's Restaurant, and
    Key limes, 86
marbles, blue, 235
    recipe for, 236–7
Market Notebook, The, 255
Marryat, Frederick, and burgoo, 78
Maryland, and persimmon brandy,
    29
Maryland Historical Society, Lloyd
    Papers at, 60

Maryland's Way: The Hammond-Harewood House Cook Book, 60–1
Matthews, Uncle Jimmy, 75–6
Me and Mine, 233
meat, kosher and nonkosher, 161
Meighan, Clement W., and abalone shells, 223–4
Menominees, 39
Merry Wives of Windsor, The, and pasties, 66
Mexican lime, 84, 87
Michaelmas, and geese, 57
Michigan, blueberries of, 9, 148–9
  cuisine of, 45
  and morels, 10, 45–6
  wild rice from, 36
  see also places in
Michigan Cooking . . . and other things, 70
Micmac Indians, and blueberries, 151
Midwest, county fair of, 15
  morels of, 4–5
milk, Tillamook and, 215–16
Minnehahas, and wild rice, 36
Minnesota, and wild rice, 36–8, 40–2
  see also places in
Minnesota Mahnomen Recipes, 39
moonshine, *see* white lightning
Moore, Suzanne, 155
Morchella, 48–9
Morchella semilibera, 49
Morel Mushroom Cookbook, 51
morels, 4–5, 10, 45–50
  appearance and safety of, 48–9
  preservation of, 49–50
  recipes, 51–4
Morning Star, 216–17
  II, 218
Morrison, Wilfred, and clambake, 137–8, 141
Morristown, N.J., Jewish conference in, 160

Mr. Bordley's Christmas Pie, 60–1
Mrs. Chiang's Szechwan Cookbook, 56
mushrooms, toxic and inedible varieties, 48–9
  see also morels
mussels, Indians and, 224
mutton burgoo, 8, 79–80
  see also burgoo
Mytilus, see mussels

Nashville, Indiana, 23–4
National Goose Council, and sale of geese, 60
National Mushroom Hunting Championship, 46–50
Native Harvests, 174
Navahos, and Hopis, 232
Neale, Gay, 82
New England, blueberries of, 148
  and cheddar, 216
  clambake, *see* clambake *and* Allen's Neck Clambake
  see also Maine
New York Times, The, and Franklin County raid, 97
Niman dance, 230–1, 233
Nixon, Richard M., and poison, 195
Nootka Indians, and salmon, 251–2
Norbert, John, 127
North America, *see* America
North Atlantic Seafood, 111
Northern Lakes Wild Rice Company, processing by, 39
Northwest Coast Indians, and salmon, 9–10, 251–4
Northwest Cookbook, The, 228, 248, 258

oil, discovery of, in Jennings, La., 127
Ojakangas, Beatrice, 66
Ojibways, and commercial rice processors, 39

harvesting wild rice by, 37–8
processing wild rice by, 38–9
Oliphant, Sandy, and garden contest,
    19
Olympia Oyster Company, 246
Olympia Oyster House, 246, 248
Olympia oysters, 9–10, 243–7
    artificial beds for, 245–6
    oystermen and, 244–5
    vs. Pacifics, 246
    rarity and depletion of, 243–6
    taste of, 244, 246–7
Olys, see Olympia oysters
Oncorhynchus, see salmon
Oraibi, Hopi town at, 231
Oregon, see Tillamook and other
    places in
Ostrea lurida, 243–4
Overton, W. Q., 97
Owensboro International Barbecue
    Festival, 79–80
Owensboro, Ky., and barbecue
    mutton, 79–80
Oyster Bay, Calif., oystermen and,
    244–5, 247
oyster crab, 111–12
oysters, 242–7
    brown stew, 110–11
    depletion and scarcity of, 243
    recipes for, 248
    roast, in Low Country, 111
    see also Olympia and other kinds
Oysterville, 244

Pacific Northwest, and oysters, 243–4
    and salmon, 251
    see also Northwest Coast
Pacifics (oysters), 9, 243, 247
    vs. Olympias, 246
Pale of Settlement, Russia, 159
pasty, of Upper Peninsula, 64–9
    controversy about, 68
    recipes for, 69–71
    sources of, 65–6
pea crab, 111–12

peas, cow, 113–14
    field, 113
pecans, 174
Pennsylvania, and Goose Day, 57–8
    and persimmon wine, 29
Persian lime, 84
    walnut, 173
persimmon, 4–5, 24–9
    cookbook devoted to, 28–9
    fudge, 24, 29
    oriental, 5, 25, 28–9
    pudding, 24
    recipes for, 30–5
    trees, nurseries for and planting
        of, 28
    wine, brandy, and beer, 29
Peter Simple, and burgoo, 78
Pickwick Papers, Sam Weller and
    oysters in, 243
pie, Buchanan Fair contest and,
    19–20
    see also apple and Key limes
Pietrus Foods, and goose production,
    59–60
piirakkaa, see pasty
Pike Place Market, Seattle, recipes
    from, 255
piki, blue, 232
    griddle for, grinding and preparing
        of, 233–5
    Hopis and, 231–3
Pilgrims, and clambakes, 4
    and persimmons, 26
pine, white vs. gooseberries, 182–3
Pinnotheres ostreum, 111–12
Pioneer Museum, Tillamook, 217–18
pirog, see pasty
Pontius, Andrew, tenant farmer of,
    57–8
pork, salt-cured, as cooking fat, 110
Poussin, Nicolas, 190
pö-vö-pi-ki, 235
Priebe family, farm of, 16–18
prosciutto, Italian, curing of, 103–4
pudding, 129–30

Pueblo Indian Cookbook, 213
Pueblo and Navajo Cookery, 212
Puget Sound, oysters of, *see* Olympia
    oysters
    regulation of salmon fishing in,
    254

Qua 'Toqti, The Eagle's Cry, 230
    editorial in, 233

Ramble, Wilbur, and raising geese,
    59
Reid, Rachelle, scrapbook of, 19
Restaurant de la Pyramide, Vienne,
    46
Reynolds, Joshua, 190
Ribes grossularia, 180, 182
Ribes hirtellum, 182
rice, and *boudin blanc*, 129
    demise of production of, 109–10,
    112
    South Carolina plantation for,
    109–10
    South Carolina predilection for,
    112
    see also wild rice
Rice Recipes, 115
Roadfood, 24
Roberts, Nancy, 23–4, 29
Rockland County, N.Y., morels in,
    46
Rocky Mountain oysters, 192
Romans, and geese, 57
Romney, George, and pasties, 69
Root, Waverley, 110
Rush, Tom, and blueberries, 152
Russells Mills, Mass., clambake
    at, 137–8
Rutledge, Caroline P., 124

Saint Michael's Day, and geese, 57
Saki, and oysters, 242
salmon, 250–5
    cooking of, 252
    decline and scarcity of, 251, 255

drying and smoking of, 253
Indians and, 9–10, 251–5
methods of fishing for, 251–2
recipes for, 255–9
regulations for fishing of, 251, 254
roe of, 253
Vanessa and, 250–1
salt, rock, Hopis and, 238
saltpeter, and health, 103
Salyer, Kermit W., and moonshine,
    97
Sarcobatus vermiculatus, and piki,
    234
sausage, 8
    stuffing and preparation of, 125–6,
    130–1
    *see also boudin blanc and boudin
    rouge*
Scheffel, R. L., and black walnuts,
    177
Schlesinger, Sigmund, 158
Schrecker, Ellen, 56
Sea Deucers, 225–7
sea otters, and abalones, 223
seafood, kosher and nonkosher, 162
Seattle, Pacifics (oysters) in, 243
    see also Pacifics
Sekaquaptewa, Abbott, 235
Sekaquaptewa, Allison, and Hopi
    tradition, 235
Sekaquaptewa, Helen, 233, 235
Sekaquaptewa, Wayne, editorial of,
    233
Seneca, 129
sesame, *see* benne
Shakespeare, William, and pasties,
    66
Shaler, Dana, and mushroom
    contest, 47, 50
sheep, camps, 192–3
    of Colorado, 190–7
    environmentalists and, 195–6
    open-range grazing of, 9, 191,
    195–7
    pasturing of, 194

weakness of producers of, 196
see also lamb
Shelter Island, gooseberries on, 181
shepherds, and immigration laws,
195
and literature, 190
Shibles, Loana, 154
Shoalwater Bay oysters, 244
shrimp, and abalone, 227
Shungopavi, Niman dance at, 230–1
Skookum Bay Oyster Company, 246–7
Sleepy Eye, Minn., production of
geese in, 59
Smith, H. Allen, and chili contest,
204
Smith, J. T., and clambake, 140
Smith, John, and persimmons, 26
Smith, Margaret Chase, 154
Smithfield ham, *see* ham, country
Smithfield Inn, ham at, 105
Smithfield, Va., ham packing houses
in, 102, 106–7
as peanut capital, 106
Song of Hiawatha, The, 36–7
South, food and wine of, 112
see also places in
South Carolina, and rice culture, 109
see also Low Country *and places
in*
Southeast, blueberries of, 148
and Brunswick stew, 76
and moonshine, 95–6
Southwest, blue cornmeal in, 236
corn of, 232
and variations of chili, 207
Southwestern Indian Recipe Book,
211
Sovold, Pamela, 255
*Spice and Spirit of Kosher-Jewish
Cooking, The*, 164–5
Spivey, Tip, and curing of ham, 104
squirrel, and Brunswick stew, 9,
75–8
and burgoo, 78–80
Stern, Jane and Michael, 24

Stewart, A. L. and Sons, and
blueberries, 151–2
Stewart, Hilary, 251
Suffolk, Va., and peanuts, 106
sugar, and moonshine, 93, 95–6
Sugar Bowl Restaurant, morels and,
46
Summer Cooking, 186
Suomi College, 65
Swan, James G., and oysters, 243–4
Syfert, Homer, and mushrooms, 48–9

Tabbutt, Abijah, and blueberry rake,
150–1
Tahiti lime, 84–5, 87
description of, 84, 87
origin of, 86–7
Talk About Good, 128
Tara, foods grown on and cooked at,
112–13
lunch at, 114
oyster roast at, 111, 114
rice plantation at, 109–10
Taste of Country Cooking, The, and
persimmon beer, 29
Taylor, Elizabeth, and chili contest,
204
Taylor Grazing Act of 1934, 194
Tendler, Rabbi M. D., and kashrus
supervision, 162–3
Terlingua, Tex., and chili contest,
203–8
Tex-Mex foods, 207
Texas, *see* Terlingua
Theocritus, 190
Three-Alarm Chili, 203
Through the Looking Glass, quote
from, 242
Tigua Indian Reservation, and chili,
207
Tillamook, 215–19
museums at, 217
see also cheese
Tillamook County Creamery
Association, 217

timber industry, and gooseberries
and black currants, 9, 182–3
Tolbert, Frank X., and chili contest,
204
Tradescant, John, and black walnuts,
175
Traverse City, cherries of, 45
Tree Nuts, 175
trees, black walnut, see black walnuts
tsu-ku-vi-ki, 235
Tucker, Harriet, 143
turkey, England and, 56
raising and production of, 59
200 Years of Charleston Cooking, 122

Ulster County, N.Y., and apples,
13–14
Union of Orthodox Jewish Congrega-
tions of America, fish handlist of,
162
United Methodist Church, 153
United States, and Goose Day, 57–8
United States Treasury, Bureau of
Alcohol, Tobacco, and Firearms
of, 92
propaganda campaign of, 95
raid by, 97
University of Southwestern Louisiana,
and Cajuns, 127, 129
Upper Peninsula, Mich., 64–9
Upper Peninsula Sunday Times, and
pasty controversy, 68
Ute Indians, 194

Vaccinium angustifolium, 148, 152
see also blueberries, lowbush
Vaccinium ashei, 148
see also blueberries, rabbiteye
Vaccinium corymbosum, 147
see also blueberries, highbush
Vanessa, and salmon, 250–1
Virginia, home-cured hams of, 9–10
and persimmon brandy, 29
restaurants of, and Brunswick
stew, 9, 77

see also ham, country, and places
in
Virginia Department of Alcoholic
Beverage Control, raid by, 97

Wakefield Virginia Diner, ham at, 105
Walker, Wayland, and chili contest,
206
Wall Street Journal, The, 152
walnuts, black, see black walnuts
English, or Persian, 173
family of, 174
Walz, Frank, and cheddar, 219
Washington County, Maine, and
blueberries, 147, 151–2
see also under Maine
Washington State, Olympia oysters
of, 9–10, see also Olympia
oysters
and salmon, 251
see also places in
Waynesboro Nurseries, and persimmon trees, 28
West Indian lime, 84
West's Supermarket, and hams, 107
Wherrette, Margaret, 255
Whipple, Paul, and mushrooms,
48–50
whiskey, 93–4
see also bourbon and white lightning
Whiskey Rebellion, 93
white lightning, 9–10, 92–8
demise of, 92
flourishing and decline of
industry of, 94–6
legends and jargon of, 95
recipe for, 100
sugar and, 93, 95–6
taste of, 98
see also whiskey
white pine vs. gooseberries, 182–3
whitefish, Lake Superior, 45
Wiggin, Ruth, 154

Wild Mushroom Recipes, 53
wild rice, 36–7
  domesticating of, 39–41
  harvesting of, 37–8, 40–1
  paddy *vs.* lake, 40–2
  processing of, 38–9
  recipes for, 43–4
  yield and cost of, 38–41
Wild Rice for All Seasons Cookbook,
  44
Williams, Arthur ("Bad Eye"), 96

Williams, Jesse, and cheddar, 216
Wisconsin, wild rice from, 36
Woodroof, Jasper, and black walnuts,
  175
World War I, and Cajuns, 127
Wyman, Jasper, and blueberries, 151

Yankee clambakes, *see* clambakes,
  New England

Zizania aquatica, see wild rice

INDEX OF RECIPES

Abalones, Seafood Shimmer, 228
Apple Pie, Wilma Priebe's, 20–2
Artichoke Pickle: Chopped, Harriet
  Maybank Royall's, 121; Whole,
  Josephine Walker's Great-
  Grandmother's, 120–1
"Awendaw," Mrs. Ralph Izard's, 116

Baked Beans, Cape Cod, 144–5
Baked Salmon, 258–9; with Vege-
  tables, 255–6
Beans: Baked, Cape Cod, 144–5;
  Parched, 241
Bear Paws, Roast, 71–2
Bear Wallow Persimmon Pudding, 30
Beef, Morel, Oriental Style, 53;
  see also Chili
Bertha Hill's Pasties, 69–70
Beth and Millie Gardner's Baked
  Blueberry Pudding, 153
Big Challah, 166–7
Biscuits: Ham, 108; Persimmon, 32
Black Walnut: Cake, Mrs. Viola
  Bricker's, 178–9; Ice Cream, 177
Blackberry Wine, Ruth Walker
  Gasden's, 118
Blue Cornmeal: availability of, 236;
  recipes with, 236–41
Blue Marbles, 236–7
Blue Tortillas, 238

Blueberry: Cottage Cheese Cake,
  Susan's, 154; Melt-In-Your-
  Mouth Cake, 155–6; Muffins, 154;
  Pudding, Baked, Beth and Millie
  Gardner's, 153
Boudin Blanc, Cajun, 131–3
Bourbon Balls, 100
Bread: Challah, 165–72; Persimmon
  Yeast, 33; Spicy Persimmon, 33;
  Walt's Fruit-Nut, 156
Brown County Persimmon Fudge, 31
Brunswick Stew, 76; Authentic, 76;
  1975, 82
Burgoo, Cissy's, 81; for 5,000 people,
  79

Cajun *Boudin Blanc*, 131–3
Cake: Black Walnut, Mrs. Viola
  Bricker's, 178–9; Blueberry
  Cottage Cheese, 154; Blueberry
  Melt-In-Your-Mouth, 155
Calapash, 123–4; II, 124
Cape Cod Baked Beans, 144–5
Caroline Darden Hurt's Smithfield-
  Ham Stuffed Chicken Breasts,
  119–20
Challah: Big, 166; Classic, 167–8;
  Famous, 165–7; Practice for
  shaping of, 168–9; Raisin, 168;
  Six-braided, 171–2; Three-
  braided, 169

Cheese: and Fish Casserole, Oregon, 220; Welsh Rarebit, 221

Chicken Breasts, Smithfield-Ham Stuffed, Caroline Darden Hurt's, 119–20

Chili con Carne, 210; with Beans, 211; Frank X. Tolbert's "Simplified Texas," 208–9; Green Stew, 212; Juniper Lamb Stew, 214; Pueblo Green Stew, 211–12; Stew with Corn Dumplings, 213; with Tomatoes, 210

Chinese Greens with Pork and Morels, 53

Chopped Liver, 164–5

Chops, Lamb, 198

Cissy's Burgoo, 81–2

Clambake, Menu for, 142–3

Classic Challah, 167–8

Conch Salad, Raw, 89–90

Corn: Dumplings, 213; Pudding, 144; Tortillas, 238–9

Cornmeal, Blue, availability of, 236; Recipes with, 236–41

Cottage Cheese Blueberry Cake, Susan's, 154

Crawfish Salad, 90

Doane's Pan Roast, 248

Dolly Ward Batten's Vegetable Ham Bone Soup, 120

Dumplings, Corn, 213

Egg Lime Soup, 90–1

Eggs, Josephine James's Hopi Omelet, 239

Esther Gregorie Gray's Iced Green Tomato Pickles, 122

Famous Challah, 165–7

Fish: and Cheese Casserole, Oregon, 220; Gefilte, with Salmon, 256; with Rhubarb Sauce, 257

Fondue, Morel, 52

Fool: Gooseberry, 185–6; Mary Peacock and Amanda Stinchecum's Illinois, 185–6

Frank X. Tolbert's "Simplified Texas Chili," 208–9

Frederick A. Traut's Rice Wine, 118

Fruit-Nut Bread, Walt's, 156–7

Fudge, Brown County Persimmon, 31

Gefilte Fish with Salmon, 256

Goose, Roast, with Potato and Sausage Stuffing, 62–3

Gooseberry Fool, 185–6; Mary Peacock and Amanda Stinchecum's Illinois, 185–6

Graham-Cracker Pie Crust, 89

Gravlax, 258

Green Chili Stew, 212

Green Peppers, Stuffed, 201

Green Tomato Pickles, Iced, Esther Gregorie Gray's, 122

Ham: Biscuits, 108; Smithfield, Stuffed Chicken Breasts, Caroline Darden Hurt's, 119–20

Harriet Maybank Royall's Chopped Artichoke Pickle, 121–2

Hopi Hush Puppies, 239–40; Milk Drink, 240–1; Omelet, Josephine James's, 239

Hoppin' John with Hog Jowl, 115

Hubbard Squash, Stewed, à la Nantucket, 143–4

Hush Puppies, Hopi, 239–40

Ice Cream, Persimmon, Jeffrey Steingarten's, 31

Jeffrey Steingarten's Persimmon Ice Cream, 31

Joe Robertson's Calapash, 123–4

Josephine James's Hopi Omelet, 239

Josephine Walker's Great-Grand-
mother's Whole Artichoke
Pickle, 120–1
Juniper Lamb Stew, 214

Keftethes, 200
Key Lime Pie, Gene Barnes's, 88–9

Lamb: Avgolemono, 199; Chili Stew
with Corn Dumplings, 213;
Chops, 200; Green Chili Stew,
212; Juniper Stew, 214; Keftethes
(Meatballs), 200; Liver in Salsa,
201; Pueblo Green Chili Stew,
211–12; Shanks Kapama, 198–9;
Stuffed Tomatoes, 200–1
Lila Gault's Northwest Oyster Stew,
248–9
Lime Egg Soup, 90–1
Liver, Chopped, 164–5; Lamb, in
Salsa, 201
Lobster Stew, 145–6
Lone Star Texas Chili with Beans,
209
Louisa Stoney's Brown Oyster Stew
with Benne Seed, 116–17

Margaret Walker's Scuppernong
Wine, 119
Meatballs, 200
Melt-In-Your-Mouth Blueberry Cake,
155–6
Milk Drink, Hopi, 240–1
Mint Julep, 99
Morels: Beef, Oriental Style, 53;
Chinese Greens with Pork and,
53; Fondue, 52; Pickled, 52;
Soufflé, 51–2
Mrs. Ralph Izard's "Awendaw," 116
Mrs. Viola Bricker's Black Walnut
Cake, 178–9
Muffins: Blueberry, 154; Wild Rice,
44

Old Sour, 89
Omelet, Josephine James's Hopi, 239
Oregon Fish and Cheese Casserole,
220
Oysters: Doane's Pan Roast, 248;
Lila Gault's Northwest Stew,
248–9; Roast, 111; Stew, Brown,
Louisa Stoney's, 116–17

Parched Beans, 241
Pasties, 69–71; Bertha Hill's, 69–70;
Upper Peninsula, 70–1
Persimmon: Biscuits, 32; Bread,
Spicy, 33; Bread, Yeast, 33;
Christmas Date, 34–5; Fudge,
Brown County, 31; Ice Cream,
Jeffrey Steingarten's, 31;
Pudding, Bear Wallow, 30; Spicy,
Rich, 34; Tea Loaf, 32
Pickle, Artichoke: Whole, Josephine
Walker's Great-Grandmother's,
120–1; Chopped Artichoke,
Harriet Maybank Royall's, 121–
2; Iced Green Tomato, Esther
Gregorie Gray's, 122; Morels, 52
Pie: Apple, Wilma Priebe's, 20–2;
Crust, Graham-Cracker, 89; Key
Lime, Gene Barnes's, 88–9
Pilau, Shrimp, 123
Plantation Special, 100
Pork and Chinese Greens with
Morels, 53
Pö-Vö-Pi-Ki, 236–7
Pudding: Baked Blueberry, Beth and
Millie Gardner's, 153; Bear
Wallow Persimmon, 30;
Christmas Persimmon-Date,
34–5; Corn, 144; Gooseberry
Fool, 185–6; Spicy Rich Persim-
mon, 34
Pueblo Green Chili Stew, 211–12

Raisin Challah, 168
Rice Wine, Frederick A. Traut's, 118

Roast Bear Paws, 71–2
Roast Oysters, 111
Ruth Walker Gasden's Blackberry
    Wine, 118

Salad, Crawfish, 90; Raw Conch,
    89–90
Salmon: Baked, 258; Baked, with
    Vegetables, 255–6; Gefilte Fish
    with, 236–7; Gravlax, 258; with
    Rhubarb Sauce, 257; Steamed,
    259
Scuppernong Wine, Margaret
    Walker's, 119
Seafood Shimmer, 228–9
Shrimp Pilau, 123
Smithfield-Ham Stuffed Chicken
    Breasts, Caroline Darden Hurt's,
    119–20
Soufflé, Morel, 51–2
Soup: Egg Lime, 90–1; Turtle, 117;
    Vegetable Ham Bone, Dolly
    Ward Batten's, 120
Squash, Stewed, à la Nantucket,
    143–4
Steamed Salmon, 259
Stew: Brown Oyster, Louisa Stoney's,
    116–17; Brunswick, authentic,
    76; 1975, 82; Chili, with Corn
    Dumplings, 213; Green Chili,
    212; Juniper Lamb, 214; Lila

Gault's Northwest Oyster, 248–9;
    Lobster, 145–6; Pueblo Green
    Chili, 211–12
Stewed Squash à la Nantucket,
    143–4
Stuffed Green Peppers, 200–1
Stuffed Tomatoes, 200–1
Susan's Blueberry Cottage Cheese
    Cake, 154

Tea Loaf, Persimmon, 32
Terrapin in the Back, 123–4
Tomatoes, Stuffed, 200–1
Tortillas: Blue, 238; Corn, 237–8
Turtle Soup, 117

Upper Peninsula Pastry, 71

Vegetable Ham Bone Soup, Dolly
    Ward Batten's, 120

Walt's Fruit-Nut Bread, 156–7
Welsh Rarebit, 221
Wild Rice: Basic Recipe, 43; Muffins,
    44
Wilma Priebe's Grand Champion
    Apple Pie, 20–2
Wine: Blackberry, Ruth Walker
    Gasden's, 118; Rice, Frederick
    A. Traut's, 118; Scuppernong,
    Margaret Walker's, 119